Stars of 21st Century
Dance Pop and EDM

ALSO BY JAMES ARENA
AND FROM McFARLAND

Stars of '90s Dance Pop: 29 Hitmakers Discuss Their Careers (2017)

Europe's Stars of '80s Dance Pop: 32 International Music Legends Discuss Their Careers (2017)

Legends of Disco: Forty Stars Discuss Their Careers (2016)

First Ladies of Disco: 32 Stars Discuss the Era and Their Singing Careers (2013)

Fright Night on Channel 9: Saturday Night Horror Films on New York's WOR-TV, 1973–1987 (2012)

Stars of 21st Century Dance Pop and EDM

33 DJs, Producers and Singers Discuss Their Careers

JAMES ARENA

Foreword by Moto Blanco's Danny Harrison
Afterword by Martha Wash

McFarland & Company, Inc., Publishers
Jefferson, North Carolina

LIBRARY OF CONGRESS CATALOGUING-IN-PUBLICATION DATA

Names: Arena, James, 1960– interviewer.
Title: Stars of 21st century dance pop and EDM : 33 DJs, producers and singers discuss their careers / [interviews by] James Arena ; foreword by Moto Blanco's Danny Harrison ; afterword by Martha Wash.
Description: Jefferson, North Carolina : McFarland & Company, [2017] | Includes index.
Identifiers: LCCN 2017017679 | ISBN 9781476670225 (softcover : acid free paper) ∞
Subjects: LCSH: Singers—Interviews. | Sound recording executives and producers—Interviews. | Popular music—2001–2010—History and criticism. | Popular music—2011–2020—History and criticism.
Classification: LCC ML3470 .S753 2017 | DDC 781.648092/2—dc23
LC record available at https://lccn.loc.gov/2017017679

BRITISH LIBRARY CATALOGUING DATA ARE AVAILABLE

ISBN (print) 978-1-4766-7022-5
ISBN (ebook) 978-1-4766-2894-3

© 2017 James Arena. All rights reserved

No part of this book may be reproduced or transmitted in any form or by any means, electronic or mechanical, including photocopying or recording, or by any information storage and retrieval system, without permission in writing from the publisher.

Front cover design by the author

Printed in the United States of America

McFarland & Company, Inc., Publishers
Box 611, Jefferson, North Carolina 28640
www.mcfarlandpub.com

For my loving parents.
And for all the singers, songwriters, producers and DJs
across every generation who made
(and continue to make) dance music an art form.

Table of Contents

Acknowledgments	ix
Foreword by Moto Blanco's Danny Harrison (DJ, producer, remixer)	1
Preface	7

THE ARTISTS

Alcazar—Andreas Lundstedt (vocalist)	13
Dave Audé (DJ, producer, remixer)	22
Terri B!—Terri Bjerre (vocalist, songwriter, DJ)	31
Bart & Baker—Bart Sampson, Jo Baker (DJs, producers, remixers)	39
Bimbo Jones—Lee Dagger, Marc JB (DJs, producers, remixers)	49
Ferry Corsten (DJ, producer, remixer)	60
Chris Cox (DJ, producer, remixer)	67
Darude—Ville Virtanen (DJ, producer, remixer)	77
Inaya Day (vocalist, songwriter)	87
Deepend—Bob van Ratingen, Falco van den Aker (DJs, producers, remixers)	95
Dirtydisco—Lajos (Louis) Polgár (DJ, producer, remixer)	104
D.O.N.S. / Warp Brothers—Oliver Goedicke (DJ, producer, remixer)	109
Freemasons—James Wiltshire, Russell Small (DJs, producers, remixers)	119
Xenia Ghali (DJ, producer, songwriter)	128
Groove Coverage—DJ Novus (Markus Schaffarzyk), Singer Mell (Melanie Münch)	137
Gryffin—Dan Griffith (DJ, producer, remixer)	150
Harrison—Harrison Shaw (DJ, producer, remixer, vocalist)	157
In-Grid—Ingrid Alberini (vocalist, songwriter)	165
Kimberley Locke (vocalist, songwriter)	173

Milk & Sugar—Michael K (Mike Milk), Steven Harding (Steven Sugar) (DJs, producers, remixers)	181
Sak Noel—Isaac Noell (DJ, producer, remixer)	190
Paul Oakenfold (DJ, producer, remixer)	197
Suzanne Palmer (vocalist)	202
Ralphi Rosario (DJ, producer, remixer)	209
Richard Vission (DJ, producer, remixer)	218
Afterword by Martha Wash	227
The Digital Dancefloor: Other Noteworthy Artists and Tracks	233
Index	241

Acknowledgments

This chronicle of the first 17 years of the 21st century in dance music was only possible because, once again, a small village helped me complete it. I'd like to express my gratitude to the many people who stood by me, gave me support and offered truly invaluable assistance.

I wish to thank all the artists featured in this book, who kindly and generously granted me the extraordinary privilege of sharing their stories and viewpoints.

I am extremely grateful to Nick Bunning, who spent many hours helping me edit this project. He is a great friend, and his contribution to this and previous books in my dance music series has been immeasurable.

My great thanks to a brilliant artist and awesome person—Moto Blanco's Danny Harrison. He kindly and enthusiastically contributed his valuable commentary to the opening pages of this project, and I am greatly honored by his presence here.

A very special thank you to the one and only Miss Martha Wash—for everything, really. Your voice and legacy are unparalleled.

I'd like to acknowledge the following kind individuals for their invaluable assistance: Ewa Maszkowska, Maria Olanders, Tamar Juda, Scott Enright, Jeff Dorta, Zoltan Foldes, Amanda Charney Harris, Nick Groff, Shelli Andranigian, Danielle Natte, Galina Galkina, Rodney Hill, Selina Dagger and Letizia Pignagnoli at Energy Productions, Italy.

I am very thankful for the help and cooperation of Vass Lauricella at Urban Rebel PR (a great supporter of this project) and to Alister Jamieson for going way, way beyond the call of duty.

Special thanks to James Washington for his guidance, friendship and belief in me. "Bitch, it is 9:30!"

Thanks to Robert and Maureen Arena, Taco Ockerse, Elvis Bramble, Larry Flick and all the dance music fans and media worldwide who have supported this book series.

Thanks to the late Andrea True for a lifetime of inspiration with "More, More, More."

McFarland & Company—thank you for giving many of my books a stable home and the distribution needed to send their messages around the world.

I'd like to make note that *Billboard*, Discogs™ (discogs.com), Joel Whitburn's *Billboard's Hot Dance/Disco 1974–2003* (2004, Record Research, Inc.) and my collection of *Music & Media* charts were most helpful as data verification resources.

There were many others who took an interest in this project and offered their encouragement and assistance. If I have neglected to mention you, please forgive the oversight and know that I am deeply grateful for your contribution.

Foreword
by Moto Blanco's Danny Harrison
(DJ, producer, remixer)

South London's Danny Harrison, an accomplished dance music production wizard in his own right during the late '80s and throughout the '90s, teamed up with musical partner Arthur Smith to officially form the red hot remix and production team Moto Blanco in the early 2000s. The pair was later joined by musician Jon Cohen. Together, they transformed the songs of countless artists into masterpieces of dancefloor soul and energy, creating the definitive versions of numerous dance and pop chart hits of the period. Among their achievements were remixes of Adele's "Set Fire to the Rain" (2011), "Paparazzi" (2009) by Lady Gaga, Pussycat Dolls' "I Hate This Part" (2008), Annie Lennox's "Sing" (2007) and Mary J. Blige's "Just Fine" (2008) and "Be Without You" (2005), the later productions both Grammy nominated. Under Harrison's direction today, Moto Blanco continues to be an influential force in dance music, and his work can be found on the latest releases by Kristine W. ("Out There"), Amy Grant ("Every Heartbeat (Remix)"), Tony Moran featuring Jason Walker ("So Happy"), The Ritchie Family's 2016 comeback single "Ice" and many more.

I grew up in a very musical family—not that anyone played instruments or were in the profession—but my mum and dad loved music. Jazz, swing—that kind of sound. I had an older brother who loved playing soul, funk and disco. It was that disco sound that really turned me on. I didn't know why, but I loved it. I can remember listening to Michael Zager Band's "Let's All Chant" and wanting to do all the moves—and being terrible at them, obviously. But I still felt it in my core! Dance music stayed with me as I grew up, but I didn't realize I would have anything to do with it on a professional level. It was a natural, eventual progression for me. I started working in record shops and then eventually wanted to try my hand at making tunes. Increasingly, I became immersed in it.

Initially, I was working at a regular job (delivering all the hot labels' records of the time to the shops—imports were a big business in the UK). I started off back in 1988, also making lots of music on my own, under many different names, working with a variety of friends. (Truth be told, I'd build the names up over a few years, then kill them off. I think I've had a longer career because of this!) Working with Jude Hudson during the rave days of 1990, we took a piano track, put some drums under it and fucked about with it. We recorded it in about a day in a friend's studio, called it "Manifestation" by D-Magnify,

Danny Harrison of Moto Blanco (photograph by joel-ryder.com).

pressed some white label copies of it, and, to our great surprise, someone at the Tam Tam label offered us £5,000 for the song! Eagerly, we signed the track over, publishing and all—we didn't know what we were doing. We were like, "Take it, fuck it, yeah!" Then we did another similar track that received more interest. It dawned on us that we could, in fact, make money from this. It didn't have to be just for the fun of it. Pretty soon it became clear there was no way I could continue to pursue my regular job and this creative one.

That was when I took the leap and began making dance music my professional focus. In the late '90s, I met Arthur Smith, who had a studio above one of the record shops in Croydon called Big Apple Records (which was the birthplace of dub-step). We had similar tastes in music, a similar sense of humor and really got on well. We had a real meeting of the minds when we first met. We began working under the names Bobby Blanco and Miki Moto. Roughly around 2002, we became known as Moto Blanco. We never planned to have any success and never took it seriously.

Whatever our mindsets may have been at the beginning, Arthur and I enjoyed some really great success with our remixes in the twenty-first century. The key for us was to analyze the records we were given to re-imagine, dissect them, and find a way to alter the chord structure and progression to transform them into viable dance tracks. I have to say, this got us into some trouble over the years. Sometimes we changed the original vocals to fit our chords, and artists would say, "What the fuck are you doing? I didn't sing that note there!" We did our mixes the way *we* thought the tracks would work best. We never had a standard formula. We had a third member join us—an amazing man named Jon Cohen. He was classically trained and could score for orchestras—he could do anything. Arthur and I could get by, but I have to say Jon's magic really took some of our mixes to another level. I think we all collectively felt that Chic-like inspiration (bass, piano, guitar, strings—don't need anything else but that). Chic used that pattern on every record they ever did, and it was amazing. We tried to keep that kind of vibe. I guess that was our point, wasn't it? We wanted to make modern disco. Sometimes that style was in favor, sometimes it wasn't—we couldn't win them all, but we won a lot.

I recall one story from those early days that still makes me shake my head and laugh. Moto Blanco was offered the opportunity to remix Leona Lewis' "Bleeding Love." I sensed she was going to be massive, and this song was a real heart-wrenching ballad. We added some nice chords and made it all happy, hands in the air—that's what we were paid to do. It went back to the label, which was headed by Simon Cowell of *American Idol* fame. His reaction (which we viewed in an email) was something like—"This is shit! What have they done? They've ruined an amazing record!" Well, we were hired to make a happy club track. He basically told us to fuck off. We leaked our version to a few people, and within a week or two it was on Radio One and KISS FM. We got paid, but it was never officially released as a single in the UK, despite being a huge hit. Yet it was, at the time, one of our biggest mixes. Ultimately, the label had to add it as a bonus track on some CDs or whatever. It was such a mad thing—paying us to make a dance mix and then being angry that we—*made a dance mix!*

Over the years, we got a tremendous amount of work, but I must admit we did fuck up at times. There were periods where everyone wanted the sound we had, and we did it for *everyone*. Obviously, you risk an eventual backlash. When that happened, we tried to change our sound a bit, but it wasn't always quite as successful. In dance music, you can get caught in a spiral. For us, any given record company wanted us to do exactly what we did for Mary J. Blige ("Be Without You" in 2005, and then nearly three years later, "Just Fine"—both Grammy nominated mixes, although we didn't win). So, we did what they asked, and then you'd see snide remarks on YouTube from critics who said we were doing the same thing every time. Moto Blanco, and many other remixers, often find themselves in a difficult position in this business—having to satisfy an A&R man and an artist who are asking you to create the "Mary J. Blige thing" over and over, and fans who want something else. That's what you're up against.

Moto Blanco has been fortunate to have worked with some of the best and most popular artists in the business over the years. The Mary J. Blige records were, of course, a major highlight, and it's amazing what a Grammy nomination can do for you. People still ask me to play Mary's records. Those years early in this century were a great time in music—we had that classic R&B sound that was very popular, and it translated so well to our style. Leona Lewis' "Bleeding Love" and Jennifer Hudson's "Spotlight," for example—they were such beautiful songs to work on and their vocals were amazing. As that sound died out, we began to shift more towards working with pop bands and rock tracks. We had some big successes, but it was challenging for us at times because we were trying to make that type of music sound more emotional and soulful.

Pop and rock being converted into dance music has been the order of the day for the past few years. Don't get me wrong—I think dance music today *is* in a really healthy state. The commercial side of it has maybe fucked things up a bit, but there are hot sounds emerging from the genre that are creating great energy. There's a lot of really good things going on with it. I just think it's time for a new sound, like the way punk or acid house suddenly exploded—something to turn dance music on its head. Dance music needs an injection, doesn't it? Music just needs to keep evolving, always.

However, I think the bigger problem for dance artists and the dance music industry, the whole music industry in fact, rests in how the music is sold—the business model. During the course of this century, the Internet has made the world so small and, in the process, the currency of music has been severely devalued. I can rip anything by anybody and never pay a dime. Even DJs in clubs are doing it, despite the fact that many MP3 rips sound terrible. Someone spent a lot of time and effort to create a track in the studio (one hopes), but it sounds like shit coming out of a massive sound system. The whole thing is fucked up. Can we as dance artists survive this? Well, maybe, if one has the ability to perform live and can get the bookings.

I can tell you I wish I had DJed a bit more back in the day and built up that platform, because it is now an important part of my profession. There used be 10 dance music festivals in the UK a year, now it's 10 every month. For someone like me, who has perhaps been in this business a bit longer than others and—dare I say it—is even a little bit jaded, it does concern me that live performance has eclipsed the actual creation of music. It concerns me that more artists must take directions that represent jobs rather than artistic growth. For remixers, you may be faced with a terrible song and a terrible singer—do you feed the kids this month or do you tell the artist they shouldn't be making music? Again, I am guilty of having been in this position and having chosen to pay the bills.

Creating original dance music is something I still enjoy tremendously. However, times have changed in this area as well. There was a time when I could make a track, and it would be signed by a label by the end of the week. As the industry realized they were making less and less money (remember that back in the '90s, some singles were bought by labels for as much as £150,000, until recouping this expense became harder and harder), advances disappeared and you ended up sharing what money comes in at the very end of the line. If I was young, didn't have a family and a house, I could manage such hurdles a good deal easier. I'm not saying my heart isn't in creating this music—I simply could *not* go without dance music—but reality has a way of creeping into circumstances. I often think about James Brown sitting in a room with a bunch of musicians and them coming up with an amazing new song. I think about the path those records once took—I've come to appreciate that a lot more today.

As this century rushes forward, I think the dance industry will also have to adjust to the speed at which it moves. London is still great for creating new sounds and hybrids of music, but it is clear these emerging trends get jumped on by major labels immediately. Before, it might take a sound a year or two to grow and develop. Now, within a month or so, an artist is signed and promoted with that sound. The underground roots of dance music seem to have gotten very shallow. I should not be saying this—it goes back to jumping on trends—but, yes, I've told labels I can give them this or that type of sound as the buzz hits. It's all coming up so fast, and it sometimes doesn't deserve to be moving at that speed.

This, in turn, has fed the "superstar DJ" fever. Being a DJ myself, I've been very blessed by the phenomenon and have flown to some amazing places to play. Still, I can't help but think that something's wrong when a DJ comes out of nowhere, throws his hands up in the air and earns a monster salary. I'm sorry—it feels wrong somehow. There are, naturally, many talented DJs out there who are also producing progressive, quality music. At the same time, however, it seems like *everyone* is a DJ now—you don't need to be that talented to get by. I cringe when they are out of tune or out of key and seem to be unaware of the basics. Or you have good DJs who realize they must be producers today and just aren't very good in that role. Or producers who feel they must be DJs and don't have the right kind of personality. There's a lot of pressure and a lot of misdirected energy in our business.

God, I hope I don't sound bitter. It's just that I do see a real mix of positive and negative elements at play in the dance music scene today. Part of it may be that perhaps I am overly sentimental. I see us losing some of the great dance artists from the past—Prince, Bowie, Michael—and they were gods. Do we have the stars that can follow them? The artists who can write brilliant songs and set real, genuine trends? Will the songs from the twenty-first century be given the high marks and respect that classics from the past have had bestowed upon them? The truth is, the love people have for twenty-first century dance music will have a lot to do with what they were experiencing in their lives at the time, just as it has for past generations. We all think the music of our youth is the best. (Note: I pulled out an old dance record the other day that I loved back in the day—I hate to admit it, but it didn't sound as good as I remembered it!)

I can tell you, though, I am *very* happy and honored to be a part of the long line of artists who have tried to move dance music forward over the past 50 years or so—although I never think of myself in a league with these great people and their amazing works. I was just a guy who loved the music and did the best he could. Like I said earlier, I think of the best session musicians in the world from past decades getting together to create the brilliant dance music that formed its history—and I think my accomplishments may be a bit laughable in comparison. But I am still proud to be a part of the story.

In addition to reflecting on the subject of this book by James Arena, twenty-first century dance music and its stars, I have been tasked in this piece to describe to you what I think makes the genre so special—and it's a difficult process to come up with an answer. But I think I've got it: Dance music *can* be very underground, forbidden and a very dangerous experience. That's what I *loved* about it! It wasn't something your mum and dad would be listening to—it was *your* shit, for sure, and you came together with other like-minded souls, like a tribe on a dancefloor, who knew how special, how unique this music was. The goal was to have fun. It's one of the reasons I so admired and envied the gay culture for many years—they set all the trends, and they were on the very pulse of this music.

The mainstream has taken over dance music today. While the benefit of that is the masses can enjoy this genre, I privately long for those days to return when dance music rises from the underground, and its secret power can be appreciated as something very rare, incredibly beautiful and irresistibly compelling.

Preface

This is one kick-ass century for dance music! It is the pop music of Generation Z, and over the past 17 years it's been twisting and turning, morphing and evolving at a speed I don't think even the most progressive and forward-thinking DJ could have ever imagined. Modern dance music is truly the product of a spectacular revolution in rhythm, freedom and movement that caught fire in the mid–'70s, and is still burning today—with a startling ferocity.

Between unparalleled, head-spinning advancements in technology and a new world dynamic that mixes infinitely shorter human attention spans (we are, I'm told, on a par with goldfish today) with a plethora of entertainment distractions, dance music has been forced to innovate this century as never before. As it transforms, it assimilates new arrangements, rhythms and sounds into its make-up in its bid to stay relevant and exciting. While stars from its glorious past must often break a sweat to remain in the game, the genre has given rise to new artists almost daily, young people who must be savvy enough to unhesitatingly handle the pressures of business management, production/app know-how, social media and hip performance appeal with cutting edge and competitive skill. They must do so while coming up with a song that's got the two irresistible elements essential in dance music—an easy-access hook and a body-rocking beat. As these requirements become ever more daunting for its artists, somehow dance music has managed to stay on top as today's most popular form of pop music worldwide, evidenced by the vast majority of songs that comprise *Billboard*'s Top 40 (and other world charts), whose mandatory dance remixes are the versions that most often become the hits.

I am nearly out of breath after putting this collection of interviews together.

As I write this preface, I'm inspired to take a few moments to reflect upon the personal journey that helped pave the way for this book. It was a quest I embarked upon nearly six years ago to document the memories and observations of what has amounted to nearly 200 singers, songwriters, producers, DJs and industry professionals from over a dozen countries, all of whom helped define dance music over the past five decades. I attempted this not so much as a journalist or historian, but more as a fan—someone who loves this music intensely. The diverse thoughts of these individuals, who range from some of the most widely popular artists of their time to those who fell a bit shy of becoming household names, have (hopefully) been effectively preserved in my series of books: *First Ladies of Disco, Legends of Disco, Europe's Stars of '80s Dance Pop, Stars of '90s Dance Pop* and the volume you now hold, *Stars of 21st Century Dance Pop and EDM*.

The artists featured in each of these tomes have shared three things in common, regardless of the level of fame they achieved, the period in which they were most active, or where they come from:

—An unstoppable passion for music.
—A burning desire to make people feel good.
—A music résumé that significantly helped move the dance genre forward in profoundly creative and entertaining ways.

It has been my tremendous honor to have spent time with these gifted people, to have earned their trust and support and to have had the privilege of learning so much about them as they shared their observations and recollections. In my mind and heart, they did something extraordinary—they made people feel good on a global scale—in a world where that's often a nearly impossible task. They are the ultimate ambassadors of all that is good about dance music, and they have made people's lives better (including my own) because of their talents.

If you'll indulge me, I'd like to acknowledge each of these people once again. My motivation to list these great names is, of course, to reiterate my gratitude for their interviews and participation in past book projects, but also to revel in the extraordinary range of skill and talent this list represents. Clearly, the scope of their artistry is staggering. I think you'll agree, this roll call also reveals a phenomenal time-line of some of the world's most powerful and uplifting songs.

Martha Wash ("It's Raining Men"), Gloria Gaynor ("I Will Survive"), The Ritchie Family (I) w/Cassandra Wooten, Cheryl Mason-Dorman, Gwendolyn Wesley ("Best Disco in Town"), Claudja Barry ("Boogie Woogie Dancin' Shoes"), Pattie Brooks ("After Dark"), Miquel Brown ("So Many Men, So Little Time"), Linda Clifford ("If My Friends Could See Me Now"), Carol Douglas ("Doctor's Orders"), The Ritchie Family (II) w/Dodie Draher ("Put Your Feet to the Beat"), Yvonne Elliman ("If I Can't Have You"), Rochelle Fleming of First Choice ("Dr. Love"), Debbie Jacobs ("Don't You Want My Love"), Madleen Kane ("You Can"), Evelyn "Champagne" King ("Shame"), Suzi Lane ("Harmony"), Cynthia Manley (of Boys Town Gang) ("Remember Me/Ain't No Mountain High Enough"), Kelly Marie ("Feels Like I'm in Love"), Maxine Nightingale ("Right Back Where We Started From"), Scherrie Payne ("I'm Not in Love"), Wardell Piper ("Super Sweet"), Barbara Roy of Ecstasy, Passion & Pain ("Touch & Go"), Pamala Stanley ("Coming Out of Hiding"), Evelyn Thomas ("High Energy"), Jeanie Tracy ("Time Bomb"), Anita Ward ("Ring My Bell"), Carol Williams "(More"), Jessica Williams ("Queen of Fools"), Norma Jean Wright ("Saturday"), Harry Wayne Casey (KC & The Sunshine Band) ("Get Down Tonight"), remixer Tom Moulton (Andrea True's "More, More, More"), Village People's Felipe Rose ("In the Navy"), Michael Zager ("Let's All Chant"), James "Tip" Wirrick (songwriter, Sylvester's "You Make Me Feel [Mighty Real]"), the late Henry Stone, founder of T.K. Records, producer Rick Gianatos, Alfa Anderson, formerly of Chic ("Le Freak"), William "Bubba" Anderson, LA Blacksmith, Tyrone Cox, Mark Lipetz, Phil "Flip" Thomas and the late James "Ajax" Baynard, of Crown Heights Affair ("Dreaming a Dream"), Clare Bathé, formerly of Machine ("There but for the Grace of God Go I"), Anthony Brooks of Harold Melvin's Blue Notes ("Bad Luck"), Ed Cermanski and Robert Upchurch of the Trammps ("Disco Inferno"), Sarah Dash ("Sinner Man"), producer John Davis (The Monster Orchestra's "Ain't That Enough for You"), Leonard "Butch" Davis and Joe Harris of Double Exposure ("Ten Percent"), Venus Dodson ("Night Rider"), Joy Dorris of Lime ("Your Love"), songwriter Bob Esty (Donna Summer's "Last Dance"), Jimmie Bo Horne ("Spank"), Geraldine Hunt ("Can't Fake the Feeling"),

Carol Jiani ("Hit'n Run Lover"), Janice Marie Johnson, formerly of A Taste of Honey ("Boogie Oogie Oogie"), France Joli ("Come to Me"), Randy Jones, formerly of Village People ("Y.M.C.A."), Shirley Jones, formerly of the Jones Girls ("You Gonna Make Me Love Somebody Else"), Denis LePage/Nini Nobless, formerly of Lime ("Babe, We're Gonna Love Tonite"), Studio 54 DJ Robbie Leslie, producer W. Michael Lewis (El Coco's "Cocomotion"), George McCrae ("Rock Your Baby"), Denise Montana ("#1 Dee Jay"), producer Eddie O'Loughlin (Carol Douglas' "Doctor's Orders"), Rob Parissi, formerly of Wild Cherry ("Play That Funky Music"), Bonnie Pointer ("Heaven Must Have Sent You"), producer Warren Schatz (Vicki Sue Robinson's "Turn the Beat Around"), Debbie, Joni and Kim Sledge of Sister Sledge ("We Are Family"), Arthur "Pooch" Tavares of Tavares ("Heaven Must Be Missing an Angel"), Richie Weeks, Trudy Miller & Lynná Davis, formerly of Weeks & Co. ("Rock Your World"), James "D-Train" Williams ("You're the One for Me"), producer Patrick Adams (Musique's "In the Bush"), Teri DeSario ("Ain't Nothing Gonna Keep Me from You"), Eruption's Precious Wilson ("I Can't Stand the Rain"), Luci Martin, formerly of Chic ("I Want Your Love"), Tom Hayden of TSR Records, Amii Stewart ("Knock on Wood"), Audrey Landers ("Manuel Goodbye"), Big Fun's Phil Creswick ("Blame It on the Boogie"), Boney M.'s Liz Mitchell ("Rivers of Babylon"), Carlos Pérez ("Poco a Poco"), Carmelo La Bionda, producer, composer (La Bionda's "One for You, One for Me"), Caroline Loeb ("C'est la ouate"), Christian de Walden, producer, composer (Bonnie Bianco's "Miss You So"), Dead Or Alive's Pete Burns ("You Spin Me Round Like a Record"), Debut De Soiree's Sacha Goëller ("La Vie la nuit"), Claudie Fritsch (aka Desireless) ("Voyage Voyage"), Engelbert Humperdinck ("The Spanish Night Is Over"), Ric Tess Teiges (aka Fancy) ("Slice Me Nice"), Five Star's Stedman Pearson ("System Addict"), Paul Mazzolini (aka Gazebo) ("I Like Chopin"), Gold's Alain Llorca ("Capitaine abandonné"), Hazell Dean ("Who's Leaving Who"), Hubert Kah's Klaus Hirschburger ("Limousine"), Imagination's Leee John ("Just an Illusion"), Jack Robinson, songwriter (Stéphanie's "Irresistible"), Jaki Graham ("Round & Around"), Jennifer Rush ("The Power of Love"), Joy's Andy Schweitzer ("Touch by Touch"), Junior Giscombe (aka Junior) ("Mama Used to Say"), Kristian Conde ("Dolce Vita"), Les Avions' Jean-Pierre Morgand ("Nuit sauvage"), Lian Ross ("Fantasy"), Linda Jo Rizzo ("You're My First, You're My Last"), Lino Nicolosi, producer, composer (Valerie Dore's "The Night"), Luv's José Hoebee ("You're the Greatest Lover"), MaiTai's Harriette Weels ("History"), artist photographer Manfred Esser, Milli Vanilli's Fab Morvan ("Girl You Know It's True"), Modern Talking's Thomas Anders ("You're My Heart, You're My Soul"), Opus' Kurt René Plisnier ("Live Is Life"), Pedro Marín ("Que No"), Phil Harding, PWL Mixmaster (Divine's "You Think You're a Man"), Pierluigi Giombini, producer, composer (Gazebo's "I Like Chopin"), Romano Musumarra, producer, composer (Jeanne Mas' "En rouge et noir"), Rondò Veneziano's Maestro Gian Piero Reverberi ("La Serenissima"), Fabio Roscioli (aka Ryan Paris) ("Dolce Vita"), Sabrina Salerno (aka Sabrina) ("Boys"), Roberto Zanetti (aka Savage) ("Don't Cry Tonight"), Silent Circle's Jürgen CC Behrens and Martin Tychsen ("Touch in the Night"), Ivana Spagna (aka Spagna) ("Call Me"), Taco Ockerse (aka Taco) ("Putting on the Ritz"), Technotronic's Jo Bogaert ("Pump Up the Jam"), The Twins' Ronny Schreinzer ("Ballet Dancer"), Tom Hooker ("Looking for Love"), Tony Esposito ("Kalimba De Luna"), Yasmin Evans (aka Yazz) ("The Only Way Is Up"), Mel Brooks ("To Be or Not to Be—The Hitler Rap"), Thomas M. Stein (former CEO, Bertelsmann Music Group, Europe), Christa Mikulski (General Director of ZYX Records, Germany), Thea Austin (formerly of Snap!) ("Rhythm Is a Dancer"),

Angie Brown (formerly of Bizarre, Inc.) ("I'm Gonna Get You"), Sannie Carlson (aka Whigfield) ("Saturday Night"), No Mercy's Marty Cintron ("Where Do You Go?"), Nance Coolen (formerly of Twenty 4 Seven) ("I Can't Stand It"), Right Said Fred's Fred and Richard Fairbrass ("I'm Too Sexy"), Nicki French ("Total Eclipse of the Heart"), Nestor Haddaway (aka Haddaway) ("What Is Love"), Sten Hallström (aka StoneBridge), DJ, producer, remixer, (Robin S' "Show Me Love"), composer, lyricist Nosie Katzman (Culture Beat's "Mr. Vain"), Sybil Lynch (aka Sybil) ("Don't Make Me Over") Robin Jackson Maynard (aka Robin S) ("Show Me Love"), La Bouche's Lane McCray ("Be My Lover"), Rozalla Miller (aka Rozalla) ("Everybody's Free"), DJ, producer, remixer Tony Moran ("HIStory"), Ultra Naté ("Free"), Alban Nawapa (aka Dr. Alban) ("It's My Life"), CeCe Peniston ("Finally"), Frank Peterson (formerly of Enigma, producer) ("Sadeness, Pt. I"), Alfredo "Larry" Pignagnoli, producer (Spagna's "Call Me"), Paul Spencer (aka Dario G) ("Sunchyme"), Rafael "Dose" Vargas (formerly of 2 in a Room) ("Wiggle It"), Kristine Weitz (aka Kristine W) ("One More Try") and DJ Susan Morabito.

This book series opened the door for me to participate in several electrifying dance music events over the past few years, including numerous concerts and television and radio interviews (with many of the stars I interviewed right beside me). These episodes were, quite frankly, very stirring moments in my personal timeline. Among the most rewarding surprises spurred by these books was the formation of the group and show First Ladies of Disco (primarily featuring heritage artists Martha Wash, Evelyn "Champagne" King and Linda Clifford), inspired to come together by my book of the same name and produced by Ms. Wash's recording label, Purple Rose Records, under the direction of James Washington. Their first single, "Show Some Love," became a Top 10 *Billboard* dance chart hit in 2015, and I had the honor of introducing these amazing women at a number of brilliantly executed events. These are just a few of the truly extraordinary milestones of this journey I hope time will never erase from my memory.

Back to the present.

To be quite honest, I never envisioned myself covering the dance music of the twenty-first century and its artists. But the world of popular dance music did not stop on December 31, 1999, and I eventually felt this series would be incomplete if I did not attempt to explore the modern era (in which we are now nearly two decades deep). With the arrival of the twenty-first century, however, a whole ocean of dance sub-genres (and, in turn, stars) have become part of the scene, branching out in directions far beyond the styles with which I was so comfortable. I was unfamiliar with many of them, which meant endless hours of *Billboard*, Soundcloud, Beatport, Spotify and YouTube research to enlighten myself about this new generation of sounds and artists, broadly classified as dance pop and contemporary EDM—electronic dance music.

During the course of this century, the very nature of dance music artists has changed. The performer, songwriter, producer and DJ are no longer necessarily separate entities. And the record labels now range from the still familiar major institutions to the operations of thousands of indies and individuals working out of home enterprises. There are new forces affecting dance music that I would need to address in this project as well. The business model of selling music has completely changed, affecting everything from how money is made, to who actually makes it, to the public's perceived value of that product. How and where we experience dance music in this century is also remarkably different, with clubs giving way to enormous festivals. Our planet has become smaller and more vulnerable over the past 17 years, too. Perhaps the most sobering change of all has been the once unimaginable influx of violence that has made its way into the very environments where humanity once found euphoric sanctuary amidst the beats.

As a result of all these developments, you'll find that the dialogue in this book is often very different from the other volumes in the series. The participants themselves are part of a unique generation, people who are facing very different challenges from the past and who speak quite frankly about them. Yet I've discovered that some aspects of their personalities, life experiences and careers are exactly the same as those who came before. I can tell you that all of the individuals featured in this book recognize (and are firmly dedicated to) the irresistible power and beauty of dance music.

I sought to interview artists and professionals who were accessible, were drawn to the purpose of this book and who express themselves primarily through the art of dance music, as opposed to those who utilize a dance mix to satisfy a requirement to expand their audience (not that there's anything wrong with dipping a toe in the lake to boost one's presence in the Top 40). I am honored that these 33 focused dance music artists from around the world saw merit in this project and were kind enough to grant me interviews or provide commentary:

Alcazar's Andreas Lundstedt, DJ Dave Audé, Terri B!—Terri Bjerre, Bart & Baker's Bart Sampson and Jo Baker, Bimbo Jones' Lee Dagger and Marc JB, Chris Cox, Darude—Ville Virtanen, Inaya Day, Deepend's Bob van Ratingen and Falco van den Aker, Dirtydisco's Lajos (Louis) Polgár, Freemasons' James Wiltshire and Russell Small, D.O.N.S./Warp Brothers' Oliver Goedicke, Xenia Ghali, Groove Coverage's DJ Novus (Markus Schaffarzyk) and Mell (Melanie Münch), Gryffin—Dan Griffith, Harrison—Harrison Shaw, In-Grid—Ingrid Alberini, Kimberley Locke, Milk & Sugar's Michael K (Mike Milk) and Steven Harding (Steven Sugar), Sak Noel—Isaac Noell, Paul Oakenfold, Suzanne Palmer, Ralphi Rosario, and Richard Vission. I am thrilled to be able to also include the unique perspectives of Moto Blanco's Danny Harrison and two-time Grammy nominee and heritage star Martha Wash. All of these artists effectively bridge where we have been in dance music with where we are going.

In the course of researching and developing this book, I observed media criticism sometimes levied against twenty-first century dance music that bears mentioning. It alleges that modern era dance music can be impersonal, mechanical and unmemorable. This observation is noted and addressed by several artists in this volume. There is a notion that dance music created by people using apps somehow lacks the soul of the beat-fused hits of the past, which were more often created with traditional instruments, live musicians and by artists who we now increasingly consider to be legends. With the possible exception of some pop star hits (and remixes), some say that today's dance music lacks the once powerful connection with the magnetism and performance appeal of the vocalist (who used to bask in most of the glory of a hit song). And it's not uncommon to hear charges that song structure and melody have been lost in favor of a quick turnaround for a hands-in-the-air anthem. These criticisms are perhaps, at times and to varying degrees, true—but let's not forget that a healthy chunk of twentieth century dance music was deemed just as vapid and disposable. Today we label many of those so-called frivolous songs as classics.

It wouldn't be fair to dismiss all of today's dance music, as there is an astonishing amount of beauty, complexity and positivity to be found in it—no matter how it has been created. If it is the music of your time and it moves you, it is important, and the Generation Z crowd has an intimate connection with today's dance music. In the process of learning about many of the talented artists who are making it, I have been no less impressed by the depth of their passion and dedication than I was by their predecessors. Twenty-first century artists are carrying on a grand tradition. Make no mistake—they are creating joy, harmony, unity and movement on a colossal scale that the dance genre has never seen before. I believe these artists are earning their right to be respected as an integral part of this magnificent evolution and history, and they are doing so in the face of some truly formidable contemporary challenges.

I love dance music, and I am profoundly grateful to the singers, songwriters, producers, DJs and industry professionals whose inspired efforts have lifted my soul and spirit for nearly 40 years. Yes, it's great to be young and jumping around to dance music. It's also wonderful to grow into maturity with it and to let it keep you feeling young. I hope this music will always touch me as powerfully as it has up to this very moment. And I hope these books I have created to celebrate these artists and this music will help preserve wonderful memories of the inspired human feeling that dance music generates—the communion for which this art form and its creators are so uniquely responsible. Perhaps the most important reason why this genre is so special is because of its dual nature. Dance music isn't just heard—it's also felt as a physical experience—universally, around the world.

Above all, I hope dance music will continue to be embraced as a panacea for so many of our formidable ills and that future generations will feel and appreciate the joy and unifying healing power it so miraculously delivers.

THE ARTISTS

Alcazar

Andreas Lundstedt (vocalist)

"Crying at the Discoteque" (2001)

"The girls and I have been through some shit, and it has made us better artists—better at communicating the 'art of disco'... We bring conviction to disco, which is what this music is all about."—Andreas Lundstedt

The Swedish group Alcazar released a well-received album in 2009 called *Disco Defenders*. Few can argue that the trio, which originally featured members Andreas Lundstedt, Tess Merkel and Annikafiore Kjaergaard, are, indeed, one of disco music's most prolific and successful supporters. Formed in 1998, the group failed to initially find a sizable audience with their debut single release, "Shine On," distributed by BMG Sweden. But the game changed with the turn of the century, when their track "Crying at the Discoteque" (from the album *Casino*) broke in Finland and caused a chain reaction across Europe. By 2001, the hook-laden dance song, meticulously produced by Alexander Bard (of Army of Lovers/"Crucified" fame), Anders Hansson and Johan S. (Strandqvist), was a global smash, selling reportedly over two and a half million copies. The track reached U.S. clubs in 2002, making an impression on Billboard's *dance chart*, along with the follow-up single, a cover of Human League's "Don't You Want Me."

"Crying at the Discoteque" cleverly incorporated a sample of Nile Rodgers' melody and guitar licks from the 1979 Sheila and B. Devotion hit "Spacer." Rodgers' sound would be incorporated into more of the group's hits, including "Sexual Guarantee" (2001) and "This Is the World We Live In" (2004), the latter borrowing from the Diana Ross evergreen, "Upside Down." The group expanded to four members when singer Magnus Carlsson joined the ensemble, with Alcazar then resembling a modern day Abba. The quartet went on hiatus in 2005, but returned as a trio in 2007 (with the departure of Magnus and singer Lina Hedlund replacing Annikafiore). Alcazar

Lead vocalist Andreas Lundstedt of the Swedish group Alcazar, one of disco's most prolific and successful supporters.

released the single "Young Guns (Go for It)" in 2015 and are currently at work developing a new album.

While visiting New York City, Lundstedt, handsome, fit and decidedly upbeat (not to mention a self-professed "disco nerd"), enthusiastically discusses his experience in Alcazar and his happy connection with dance music.

What brings you to New York, Andreas?

I am making a TV show for Sweden, which features a total of 14 artists, and it's about gospel music. We are going to perform at the Apollo Theater later this month, and we're going to sing our hits with a gospel choir on that stage. I'll be doing "Crying at the Discoteque," and, you know, they are filming the whole process. Singing at the Apollo is something I never dared to dream about when I lived here in New York on the Upper West Side from 1993 to 1995. It's mind-blowing. Swedish singers at the Apollo! Imagine that! I am a big gospel music fan—I listen to Kirk Franklin and his gospel choir all the time. So they are filming some side stories with me, and I'm having a great time.

I didn't realize you used to live here.

Yes, and I worked at the Equinox gym and taught dance aerobics. I started out at Crunch [gym] on Amsterdam and 83rd. I met some friends from those days while visiting here, and it's been amazing. New York is my number one place to visit. It's been an emotional trip for me. I got kicked out of the U.S. in '95. I had been working "under the table," as you say, going back and forth to Sweden, and when I renewed my tourist visa here, they grew suspicious. My life ended in New York just like that [*Andreas snaps his fingers*], and they shipped me out on the next plane. I had an apartment and a boyfriend—everything just ended. I lost almost all my friends (we weren't good at connecting long distance, the way you had to in those days), and I never got to grieve or to work through what happened.

I guess the universe had a different plan for me, and I wasn't going to be an aerobics instructor anymore. I went home to Sweden and started my music career. A month after I got home, I would meet the producer of Alcazar. Now, over 20 years later, I'm doing a show that is kind of retracing my footsteps here. I met a friend I haven't had any contact with in over two decades, and I really feel that—it actually makes me emotional. But there's a reason for everything. When we reunited, it was like no time had gone by. I'm just so happy and seeing everything so much sharper now. I really see how fast life goes by.

Let me ask you to go back a bit further to give me an idea of what life was like for you as a child.

Both my mother and father want to take credit for influencing me to become a singer. My father played the guitar when I was young, and my mother was always dancing. She actually taught dance in our town, but just on an amateur level. The first song I remember really well was Village People's "Y.M.C.A."—I hate it today. I can't stand it—I'm sorry. I know they were great back in the day, and when everyone talks about disco they mention that song. But there was so much more to disco than just Village People. It's funny—my father loved that song because he thought it was so macho, with the cop, the Native American, the soldier. [*Andreas laughs.*] Who knew? I did love the song at the time. My mother listened to a lot of Baccara ("Yes Sir, I Can Boogie" and "The Devil Sent You to Loredo"). I must have been four or five when I heard all this music. So disco was there from my beginning.

I don't think there was ever a doubt in my mind that I would sing. My parents were very encouraging about that. They never said things like, "What are you *really* going to do with your life?" I did my first talent show when I was five, and I think my parents saw some flair for entertainment in me, so they didn't have to say at some point—how do you say it—get a real job. I think to have success as a singer, or any profession, you can never doubt yourself. I never thought, "I want to be a singer, but I probably can't." I never had that "maybe" feeling—even with setbacks I experienced. Life goes up and down, but music and singing were so natural, so clear for me.

Did the country of Sweden provide a nurturing environment for young artists?

Sweden is definitely a good place for artists, musicians and producers. I think that comes from school, where you are introduced to choir at an early age. People develop an interest in using their voices and harmonies early on. Abba, of course, was a big inspiration for us Swedes, being that we are a small country (just nine million people), and yet they made it so big. So [I thought] if ABBA can make it, maybe I can, too. So many great artists have come from here—Roxette, Ace of Base, Robyn. It's really cool that we've often been at the forefront of contemporary music, and that makes us very proud.

How did you become connected with the Alcazar project?

As I mentioned, after I got booted out of the U.S., I started working with a great producer named Alexander Bard, who, of course, is known for Army of Lovers. I worked with him on a song entry for *Melodifestivalen*, Sweden's music competition event. The winner of this event represents Sweden at *Eurovision*. I have done the competition solo four times, and the first time was in 1996. I came in second place. Alexander wanted to try with me again the following year. I competed again, and I came in second to *last*. It didn't work out the way he or I planned. That was my first career setback.

My relationship with Alexander has always been very, very good. We respected each other. He's very, very intelligent—almost overly intelligent. I don't remember a bad day ever working with him. I have a lot of respect for him. We are still connected, though much more casually today. I did recently introduce him to a concept that would incorporate two blonde gentlemen called Nordic Sonar, who I feel are amazing singers. He's offered to listen to them, see how he feels about them and will see if he can help. So, Alexander and I are cool with each other. Of course, we've had fights, but nothing serious. He's not a small talk kind of guy—he's very to-the-point. Cut and dry. He doesn't show his feelings a lot—he keeps a kind of aloof persona.

Getting back to Alcazar, about two years after the *Melodifestivalen* setback, Alexander told me he'd written a song with Anders Hansson called "Crying at the Discoteque," and he asked me if I wanted to try it. I agreed, but I told him I didn't want to do it alone. I wanted to try it as part of a group. He was okay with that idea, suggesting a boy band concept. I told him I didn't work as well with guys as I do with girls. So I asked him to meet two friends of mine, Annika (Kjaergaard) and Tess (Merkel). He fell in love with us as a group and felt we should be something like an Army of Lovers (but we would sing for *real*). I think we recorded the song in 1998 or '99.

I understand "Crying at the Discoteque" was not an instant hit and took a bit of time to catch on.

That's right. The record company gave it to Swedish radio something like five times. They wouldn't play it because they just didn't like it. We were like, "What the fuck—this is a good song!" We believed in it, and so did the record company, but nothing happened. Then, all of a sudden, it started to get some play in Finland and Italy. It slowly became a European hit. Then it didn't matter that Sweden wasn't interested in the song. I remember we really started to become big in Italy, and it just took off from there. We ended up working that song for the next two years.

The song is famous for its sampling of the Sheila and B. Devotion 1979 disco hit "Spacer" and that vintage Nile Rodgers/Bernard Edwards melody and guitar lick sound. It's an important song that boldly bridged a retro-disco sound with the modern pop feel of the new century. Do recall anything about the creation of the song?

What you hear on that song—it's really what we delivered in the recording session. It wasn't created from a demo or done in a half-assed way. There wasn't the need to do a lot of work on it after we recorded it. That's actually Nile Rodgers playing in the song sample. They tried to do a cover of his sound, but they weren't able to capture his groove, his feeling and essence—Nile was just too good. They tried a number of guitarists, but nobody could duplicate that sound. And that's why Nile gets all the money from the song. [*Andreas laughs.*]

I'm curious; did you ever get feedback from Nile himself about the song?

I don't remember, and I'll be honest with you—back then I didn't really know who he was. I wasn't quite as disco nerdy as I have become over the years. But I can tell you Richard Gere heard the song not long ago in England. (There's a lyric in the song about wearing a tie like Richard Gere). I was told he thought it was really funny that he was mentioned in it. The most amusing thing about that lyric is that so many people think we are singing, "You're old and tired like Richard Gere."

That's very funny. The album *Casino*, released in a variety of editions between 2000 and 2002, was a massive worldwide hit as well, spawning two more hits, "Don't You Want Me" (a remake of the Human League classic) and "Sexual Guarantee" (which samples Chic's "My Forbidden Lover"). How did Alcazar's building momentum change your lives?

It's funny because we initially never thought of international success. We were only focused on Sweden, and, as I said, "Crying" just took forever to get off the ground. One of the biggest things that changed was that time began moving so fast. We were traveling so much that we referred to our airport in Stockholm, Arlanda Airport, as our breakfast hangout.

It was a crazy schedule. It hurts me to say this, but we never had the chance to really enjoy it. I know people say "stay present" and "be in the moment"—I say it, too, to young artists—but it's really difficult. The pace is just so incredibly fast. I think it took Tess and me about five or six years to start actually talking about our success. We were so tied up in it that we never talked much about it and kept our feelings to ourselves. Swedes are very modest, so we don't brag about things. There also wasn't really social media back when we were breaking. It's really only now that we as artists are able to see the video clips, etc., and begin to appreciate all the things we went through and the great things that happened.

How valuable has your connection to gay audiences been for Alcazar?

This connection came so naturally. *They got us.* That's why we didn't work so well in Sweden at the time; they tend to be a more modest people. (It's better today, but back in the day the country was more conservative.) But the gay community got our style and extravagance. Our music was kind of campy, with a wink in our eye, and that appealed to this audience. Our songs weren't overly serious—some might even call them shallow. (I don't.) You know, our first big audience in Sweden was for Stockholm Pride—and while the rest of the country didn't get us yet, [the gay community] always wanted us to perform.

If you speak to a gay person in New York—is that what I should call such a person here? Well, maybe not the very youngest, but many gay men will know the name Alcazar.

Were you out at the time Alcazar started to hit it big? Did you feel any pressure as an artist to represent or be a champion for the gay community?

Yes, I was out. But I did not feel I had to represent the community. I never thought about that. I never pulled the gay card. Even when we performed at straight clubs, it wasn't like I'd come on stage and it would be like "and now here's the gay guy." I was just a guy—not too feminine and not overly masculine. Not too threatening, I guess.

I believe you made it public in 2008 that you are HIV positive, and you wrote a book, *My Positive Life*, about your experience. How big an impact did this diagnosis have on your life at the time, and how did it affect your career in pop music?

In the beginning, I kept it a secret from my colleagues, family and friends. The only one who knew was my boyfriend at the time. Today, I wonder why I waited so long to be so open about it. I was young and afraid that I would be left with no work. My dream was to be an artist, and I saw getting the virus as a death sentence. I thought, okay, my career and life aren't going to be what I wanted them to be now. I feared experiencing a lot of prejudice, and so I said nothing. I always looked fresh and tanned and made sure nobody would ever notice. That plan worked for a while, but then I started to feel like I was bringing the virus with me on stage. By that I mean I'd come home from shows feeling like I was faking it. After a while, I was feeling so fucked up from trying to project that I was this person who *didn't* have the virus.

For a short while, I experimented with drugs. One day I was invited to try some stuff, and it was suddenly like, oh yeah, here's the solution. Now I could escape from all the things I was feeling. I finally realized I had to choose what I wanted to do with my life. My levels weren't good because of the drug use, and they were affecting my immune system. It was all a wake-up call—life or death, roughly speaking. Beginning in 2007, I realized I had to come clean with myself and with all the people in my life. I thought to myself, "who wants an HIV guy standing there singing disco?" I thought I would lose my career for sure. But so be it—I couldn't live the way I was existing.

I was so nervous when I came out with all this publicly. I stayed with my mother in Spain for two weeks and didn't look at social media, email—nothing. It was in all the papers and on the news—everywhere. They never came to me for comments, so the media just kind of did their own viewpoint of the story.

But to my surprise, everything turned for the better after that. The love I received and the work I got was crazy. I am so thankful that I came out about all of it and that I may have inspired or helped others in some way. My life has never been better. You build up all this negativity in your head, and you're so certain all these bad things will happen. Then it's completely different. Not all people are evil (though I admit some are). And people don't see me as the HIV positive singer.

After about six months of talking a lot about it, I eased up and went back to talking about the music with Alcazar. I don't get many questions about it anymore. It says something that I was able to get some of the stigma off the subject. I still do lectures, but it's just not my focus anywhere near as much.

I know it may sound strange, but I must say the virus has been my enemy and my best friend. I wouldn't be the person I am today without it.

Do you feel more responsible for your happiness today than in your past? Do you feel more independent than you did before?

Wow, what a tough question. I like it. I love that I make people happy and that I spread some good energy. I think I am kind of in charge of my own destiny and happiness now. I am very self-sufficient and independent. But I'll admit to you, I've been a sucker for love. In the past, when one relationship ended, I'd often start a new one immediately or overlap them, before I processed the previous one. Today, I know that's not a great idea.

I've been single now for a year and a half, and it's the best ever. I was never single before—and sometimes seeking love doesn't always create happiness. I think maybe in the past I needed too much validation from [a partner]. I think it's also easy to point a finger at another person and say they aren't a nice person. And yet I wasn't a nice guy at times, either. I guess it's all about being needy, and I don't feel I'm that way anymore.

In the world of pop stardom, how difficult is it to read other people, to gauge the intentions and motivations behind how others act with you?

Maybe I am naive, but I always wanted to see the good in people or think good of everyone I encountered. But over time I did realize in my relationships with some people that maybe they wanted to be with me or whatever because *they* really liked the spotlight themselves. But I thought their actions were love or friendship. Now when I look back or speak with close friends, it's more like, "Girl, he wanted to be a star himself." Sometimes people want to live on your stardom. So, yes, it can happen. I like to spend time in New York or Barcelona—outside of Sweden—because people may not know me as much, my life or career. I don't like when people gush over my career or whatever. But that's part of the game I guess. I'm not regretting that I have enjoyed celebrity. It's helped me with everything. It's a weird business. It's a challenge to live a normal life in such a fucked up business.

The truth is, I'm really kind of normal and boring. I love to do nothing. I'm not a big party guy—not anymore. Sundays—I love to lie on my sofa, no phone, eating chips and watching TV.

There's a challenging business side to being a music performer and the monetization of your craft continues to evolve. The music is changing—the way you earn income from it—and the club scene itself (which appears to possibly be retracting). What are your observations about all of this?

It's very difficult now. There's no money in the traditional record business, whether it be dance music or any other genre. Even the big companies are dying. It's concerts, live performance gigs, that are the best way to keep moving today. Alcazar is so fortunate that we are a live act. We do sometimes sing to tracks, but we never do playback or lip-synching.

We always sing live. We try to show we aren't just a product. We continue to tour and book engagements at, for example, the same venue, doing five shows a week—things like that. It's been fantastic. We are very blessed that there is demand for our show. Especially in Sweden—where they finally know, 20 years later, what Alcazar is all about. It took a while. Alcazar means disco, party and energy. In Sweden, it's kind of like we've come to own disco. No one can touch us right now! I've even seen reviews of other artists where they are described as "Alcazar-style disco." It's very cool. We have our own genre.

Music for the clubs is changing. The number of clubs may be dropping. I think that may have to do with the increase in phone apps. Not as many people feel the need to go to a club. I don't know—I loved going to a club for dancing and hearing the amazing music and DJs—fuck the flirting. Losing that experience will mean not as many people will hear those big, really great songs that are part of dance music. Commercial radio is horrible, so that won't help.

Alcazar appears at events all over the world, attracting large crowds. Does the climate of fear and acts of terrorism that are affecting the world at present weigh on your decisions to play live events?

You know what? A little bit—yes, it does. Not long ago, there was a suspected terrorist in Stockholm where we were performing our shows every night. I remember that we were concerned that events like ours might be a potential target. We have up to 600 people at these shows. Just the fact that we were actually talking about it—right after the 2015 attacks in Paris—it's very scary. But what can we do? What choice is there? We're not going to stop working because of fear—nobody can. You have to try not to be afraid, not to show fear or to be [intimidated].

What's next for Alcazar? Will you return to the studio?

Yes. We have three songs in preparation at the moment. One is called "Clap Your Hands"—a great disco track. We also want to release a Christmas song that is more guitar-based; a different kind of sound for us. And, of course, we plan to keep doing our live show all over the world.

Alcazar helped define the sound of twenty-first century dance music, and it looks like you will continue to in the future. Do you think the dance music produced since the beginning of this century will be remembered years from now—the way disco from the '70s is currently embraced some 40 years later?

Wow—I don't know. Maybe the music of this generation is still too new to be sure. Ask me again in 10 years. I certainly hope so. That's a very quick answer, I know. But to be honest, I really don't feel sure what the answer will be.

You mentioned a moment ago how great it was to just hear a fantastic dance song booming in a club. What do you think makes the art form of disco, of creating energized dance songs, so appealing?

A lyric, a melody and a beat combine in a dance song in just an amazing way. Take "I Will Survive." I've heard it a million times, but when you hear it blasting through club speakers, you can't help but feel, "That's a damn good song!" There are so many songs like this. I think we get caught up in the drama of them, the campiness and the energy of the whole experience.

I know many people think of disco and dance music as a happy sound, but it's also reflected many dark, melancholy things, whether in its lyrics or in the clubs themselves, with drugs and such. I'm not sure if I'm saying this quite correctly to you—but dance music is like life itself, the good and the bad about it. I can tell you, I would not be able to be in Alcazar, singing and dancing in the glitter, unless I experienced the opposite in my life. Do you know what I mean? The girls and I have been through some shit, and it has made us

Alcazar (currently represented by Lina Hedlund, left, lead vocalist Andreas Lundstedt, center, and Tess Merkel, right) rocked the world with the Chic-inspired hit "Crying At the Discoteque."

better artists—better at communicating the "art of disco," as you said. We bring conviction to disco, which is what this music is all about.

I believe [my Alcazar colleague] Lina said that if you look at the disco ball, the mirror ball, when the lights are on—it's so flashy and glamorous. But when the lights aren't reflecting on it, it is gray and lifeless. If you look closely, there are always a few pieces of glass on it that are cracked. The disco ball is like life—colorful and beautiful, but like life, it has cracks and a dark side. There's a powerful statement that is made by the disco ball and dance music.

Lightning Round with Andreas

A dance song you never get tired of hearing.
"Blame It on the Boogie"

Is that The Jacksons' version or Big Fun's from the UK?
The Jacksons. Oh wow, you mean Big Fun from the '80s? They just came back to me! God, I haven't thought of them in a long time. That's so crazy!

Most satisfying recent discovery?
Yoga. It's amazing.

Craziest thing you ever saw take place on a dancefloor?
Oh, gosh. I have to tell you—I'm near-sighted. And I don't see as well in the dark. So the truth is, I couldn't see much of anything!

Favorite thing to eat after a night in the clubs?
Pizza. But if I even look at carbs, I get fat. So I can't eat stuff like that very often.

In your performances with Alcazar, what's the funniest thing that ever happened on stage?
In our current Alcazar show, I do a few solo numbers, and I was singing "Don't Leave Me This Way" (the Thelma Houston classic). In the middle of the song, I move out onto a little satellite stage into the crowd. The ladies, to this day, start screaming like crazy. They know I'm gay, but I move my hips, and they go insane. I improvise a lot, and one time I did like an Elvis squat and had no idea that, in doing so, I ripped my pants—the whole crack of my ass was visible! (I was wearing a dance belt—so it looks like I'm naked.) Now, every time I do that number, I always discretely feel my butt a little as I sing—just to make sure everything's okay!

If you weren't a singer today, what would you be doing?
Not breathing! I wouldn't be alive. There's not a day that goes by without music—work or pleasure. I can't even think of anything else I would be doing. *I would not be alive!*

Dave Audé
(DJ, producer, remixer)
"Uptown Funk" (Dave Audé Remix)—
Mark Ronson ft. Bruno Mars (2015)

"I think people are hitting the clubs for three reasons. Number three is to hear music. Number two is to drink and just party. And number one is to be seen, hook up or socialize. In the past, I think going to the club to hear great music was higher on the list."—Dave Audé

Dave Audé speaks with a gentle, relaxed tone that almost seems at odds with the explosive energy found in many of his best remixes and original productions. He is, it quickly becomes clear, at ease with his craft, his flair for house, dance pop and tech, and his standing as one of the twenty-first century's top remixers, producers and DJs. For years, Audé has been a widely revered master architect of dance-floor excitement. His vast repertoire of powerhouse club and radio mixes include standouts such as Madonna's "Music," Britney Spears' "I'm A Slave 4 U," Beyoncé's "Upgrade U," Coldplay's "Talk," "Hello" by Adele, "Til It Happens to You" by Lady Gaga, Mylène Farmer & Sting's " Stolen Car" and "True Original" featuring Andy Bell. Audé's work has reached the top of the Billboard dance chart well over a dozen times, and in 2016 he earned a Grammy for his remix of the megahit "Uptown Funk" by Mark Ronson featuring Bruno Mars. Though appreciative of his success and the accolades he regularly receives, the artist seems more focused on the art of dance music and his drive to contribute a very personalized brand of creativity to this century's pop culture scene.

In 2016, Dave Audé won a Grammy for his remix of Mark Ronson featuring Bruno Mars' "Uptown Funk" (photograph by Micah Smith).

Dave, please tell me what it was like for you growing up and how you first connected with dance music.

I grew up in the San Fernando Valley, aka "The Valley," a northern suburb of LA. I still live here today and have spent most of my life in this area. I grew up listening to a lot of rock, and I always thought I was going to be a keyboard player in a rock band. I never really knew about club or house music when I was young, just pop and rock—the stuff I heard on the radio. When I was in my early 20s and was finally able to go to clubs and hear house music for the first time, it changed my life. I fell in love with it, and I've been making it ever since.

I always think it's interesting when an artist initially connects with rock music, since traditionally dance music and rock have been viewed (perhaps mistakenly) as polar opposites.

Well, look, in those days I was really connected to the radio, and they focused on pop rock—stuff like Journey and Foreigner. A little later on I fell in love with Erasure, which surely wasn't rock but rather pop. Erasure became my favorite band of all time. But I never really saw myself in those days as someday [who would be] a DJ or remixer. I saw myself being part of a band, thinking how cool it would be to be in Erasure or Depeche Mode.

How did your professional career in dance music actually get off the ground?

I was in an underground rave/dance club, and I overheard someone say they were looking for a keyboard player. The band that I formed was Lunatic Fringe, and the label Moonshine Music was born to distribute the band's music. Moonshine Music was the first label in the U.S. to champion DJ culture and DJ mixes. Some of the first DJs signed to the label were Carl Cox and Paul Oakenfold and guys like that who were big in that era. I broke my cherry, so to speak, working for Moonshine for many years in the studio, handling manufacturing in the daytime and writing and producing in the studio in the evening. Doing that got my name out there. Producing and remixing really kind of blew up at the time my career was getting started, and my first major remix was for the band Barenaked Ladies—a song called "One Week" (on Reprise Records). That was my first work for a major label. It was a time when big beat was popular, and I chose to do the song in that style. It was the same time when The Crystal Method and Norman Cook (aka Fatboy Slim) were hot.

Would you give me an idea of how your remix process worked back then vs. now?

Well, the technology today is much different from when I first started. Today you can almost do anything—you can stretch vocals, you can manipulate pitch, and because of how fast technology allows you to do this, it gives you pretty much endless options. But when I started my career, you kind of had to stay in a certain range close to where the original song was. That probably had a lot to do with why that first remix for Barenaked Ladies was a big beat mix, since the tempo wouldn't allow me to do a 130 or 135 bpm [beats per minute] remix, which was a popular tempo at the time. I think I spent a week or two on remix work for just one song back then, whereas today I'm working on four or five remixes every day.

As your talent came to the attention of more top level artists, did you ever experience any anxiety? Did you ever feel pressure to make sure your mixes lived up to the dance-floor reputation and past work of artists such as Rihanna, Katy Perry and Jennifer Lopez?

You know, it's funny you ask that because for some reason I never really think about the artist actually listening to my mix. For the most part, it's usually the label and the artist's management that I have to appeal to and make happy. I guess that's just the way the business is—I don't know if it's a good thing or a bad thing. Probably a bad thing. The way I've been taught or molded over the years—man, it's so crazy that you ask that because I forget about the artist. My head is just focused at wanting to do the best job I can, and they kind of trust that I've done this a few times and I should sort of know what I'm doing. But what a great point you brought up. To be truthful, I don't always know if an artist is even aware of what I'm doing, which is unfortunate.

Even somebody like Madonna? I would imagine she'd be very hands on.

Yeah, I would say for sure she's hands on, but she may be the exception to the rule. I think she's had over 45 number ones on the dance chart alone, and no one will ever catch her as an artist, at least as far as I'm concerned. She's given more to dance music that any other artist out there, especially as far as remixes go and the culture as a whole.

Let me say this: if you start thinking about the pressure of living up to an artist's legacy or reputation, you're never gonna make it. You'll be second guessing yourself forever. I'll be the first one to tell you that I don't hit the ball out of the park every time I create a remix. I certainly try. Sometimes I have to re-do a remix—like this morning I woke up and realized I wasn't happy with the new remix I am working on for Enrique Iglesias. So I'm completely redoing it from the ground up. That's just my thing, but I'm not doing it because I was thinking about Enrique. It just wasn't what I wanted it to be. So like I said, I don't hit a home run every time, but I always put the work in and the extra time as needed, without regard to it being for an artist you never heard of or Madonna.

Take a song like Adele's "Hello" or Lady Gaga's "Til It Happens to You." How do you approach material like that when it's not so obviously compatible with a dancefloor?

Adele's song was just huge, so you could almost—*almost*—do no wrong because it is so popular. You'd really have to do a crappy remix to mess that one up. In regard to Lady Gaga's song, the message was pretty heavy. It is probably the heaviest message of any song I've ever worked on—I'm gonna say it was *the* heaviest. I kind of initially thought, man, is this something people will want to dance to? It's sort of the same way I don't dwell on whether the artist is going to like my work or not, I kind of just try to let it flow. Whatever comes out, comes out.

Every song that I do isn't necessarily just played in a club. A lot of my work is heard in people's cars, on the radio, the Internet. Two decades ago when I did remixes, they were literally going straight to vinyl for DJs to play in a club. That was the only place the mixes would be played. Today, there's so many different places my remixes get played.

Back to Lady Gaga—the song was much bigger than the clubs. It was really about getting the message out. It wasn't about celebrating the subject, but rather celebrating the *awareness* of the subject. So that's how I approached the song. In a weird way, it kind of worked.

You are also a recording artist in your own right, producing original material. Do you tap into your creativity in a different way when working on your own productions? Is there more freedom? How much chemistry should there be between you and a vocalist, such as Rokelle (who you went to number one with on the *Billboard* dance chart with "Take Me Away" not long ago)?

I think I look at everything—remix or original—the same. We all have things we wish we could do more. For me, I wish I had more time to spend on my own material, and I'm trying to do more of that. When I do, there definitely has to be chemistry with the people you are working with. Rokelle was great. She's since moved on, has gotten married and just had a baby. So she's in a different place, but she had a story that was cool and we became friends. I met her in Vegas and started working with her because she was somebody with a great voice, and she was at a bit of a crossroads in her life. That appealed to me, I liked her as a person, and we started recording. We had two or three records that ended up doing really well.

One of the reasons I ask about your chemistry with vocalists stems from awareness of the diminished billing of the singer as the DJ increasingly takes the spotlight.

Well, my take is that it's just where we sort of are musically and technologically. The DJ has sort of become this iconic figure now. The number one record a few weeks ago on the dance chart was by The Chainsmokers. I bet most people have no idea who is singing on it just because it's promoted as The Chainsmokers (featuring Daya in this case). A lot of people won't know who Daya is. But you have to look at the flip side, too. A lot of singers are hooking up with DJs because they know it's an avenue to keep their careers moving. I think the DJs are actually helping a lot of vocalists keep their careers going.

I have a lot of opinions on this subject, but look—I do think a lot of singers wait for other people to make their careers happen, and they don't take charge themselves. I'm in the studio every day, sometimes 14 hours a day or more, and that's what I choose to do. It can all end tomorrow, but I'm still going to work as hard as I can every day and, hopefully, have continued success. Any artist who wants to keep going has to put in this same effort.

How are you coping with the dramatic monetization and technology changes in the business of dance music, such as streaming and declining digital sales?

I wouldn't just say dance music; I'd say music in general. There are lots of new ways to build the business. There's a company called SoundExchange that came about in 2003 that pays public performance royalties to the artist and the owner of the master, as opposed to BMI and ASCAP, who pay the writers and composers. That money, I hope, is only going to get better and better with all the lobbying by organizations like the Grammys, for instance. It can only get better because we're still getting paid by laws that were passed in the '70s, when nobody had any idea there would be this whole digital income stream—where companies like YouTube are making all the money and the artists aren't.

You can still make money in this business, but it's not from selling the music. The money is in live performance. In dance music, there's no easier way (in many people's minds) than DJing—which is why so many people, including vocalists, are going in that direction. For instance, Ultra Naté DJs now, and my good friend and singer Luciana is doing it. Their thinking is that more people are willing to pay them to DJ for a few hours than sing a couple of songs.

You can make a living in music, but if you think you can do it selling music on iTunes, then you are 100 percent wrong about what's going on in the world. The days of downloading MP3s are numbered and streaming income is the future—Spotify and Apple Music. That's what's going to replace downloading. You have to embrace technology because if you fight it, you're done. More importantly, an artist needs to build a fanbase. Take my friends Erasure—they have a lot of fans. Regardless of what they do, their core fans will buy tickets to their shows and will buy their albums, t-shirts and whatever they are selling. I think artists need to concentrate on that approach, as opposed to how to sell songs on iTunes or Beatport.

As a music consumer, I really miss holding vinyl and reading liner notes and credits from a CD. It seems like a whole generation has missed out on the added visual and physical experience of a striking album cover and layout.

I agree with you 1,000 percent. A lot of that whole experience is gone. Forget about the format, CD or vinyl (which was great, but that's a whole other story), just the information and pictures while you are listening to the music is a unique experience that's lost now. I'm hoping the world can figure out how to bring that experience back to the fans.

Do you think the dance music of the past 17 years will be regarded as classics in the way legendary hits from the '70s, '80 and '90s are now embraced?

I don't know, man. It's something I think about a lot. It's really hard when you're making the music to know what's gonna happen. I'm in here trying to do something that's memorable and will stick around longer than a week, but, you know, the society we live in now is very fast moving. It's kind of killing the ability of songs to last more than a few weeks or an album to do anything. Thank God for people like Taylor Swift, who really is the biggest artist right now. She does have an album that people actually buy. But she's one in a million. I have no idea whether people will look back in 10 or 20 years and appreciate our music. What are they gonna say? I just hope I can leave something for my kids to listen to that will make them proud of me.

In 2016, you earned a Grammy for the remix of the Mark Ronson and Bruno Mars smash "Uptown Funk." What did receiving this award mean to you, and what is it about your mix that made it such a perfect fit for the dancefloor?

It means I spent a lot of time in the studio and somebody actually noticed. That's pretty cool. "Uptown Funk" was one of the biggest songs (if not *the* biggest) of 2015, so I think it was a no-brainer to win a Grammy for it—whether it was me or anyone else remixing it. I also think I've done a lot of records, and you combine them with my work on "Uptown Funk" and maybe that's the reason I won a Grammy. People are just showing me respect—I think. It's a great song. Half of my Grammy belongs to Mark Ronson. The other half is maybe a reflection of me and working on my craft over the past several years.

I actually busted that remix out really quickly—I think three days. The label was trying to get another week at number one. The record had been at number one for 15 weeks, and they were trying to beat out Mariah Carey and Boyz II Men's record at the top. Unbeknownst to them, Wiz Khalifa and Charlie Puth were coming out with the theme to the *Fast and Furious 7* movie ["See You Again"], so it didn't happen. But I had an opportunity to mix a huge record, and it actually worked out great!

How would you characterize the competition that exists between DJs in the business today?

There's certainly a lot of competition, and I think there's a lot of guys out there that would love to be in my shoes for a day or two. Competition doesn't bother me because I know my career didn't happen overnight. It's taken a lot longer to get a Grammy than I would have hoped. [*Dave laughs.*] I don't worry about the competition thing—I just try to do my thing every day. If you start dwelling on that stuff, I think it can ruin you.

There's been this Top DJ list around for years, and I have never been the guy running around saying, "vote for me." It's just music, and I was DJing before there even was a DJ list—and before it was even cool to be a DJ. I still DJ on weekends, about two or three days a month, and I actually play the stuff I'm working on during the week. So that's cool. I look at it as a way for me to get out of the studio, which I definitely need to do. PS, I also *love* DJing

What makes you decide to play a particular record during one of your sets? Are there criteria (other than pure subjectivity) for selecting what to play at a gig?

Absolutely. I don't really consider myself like a Calvin Harris or a David Guetta. David started his career as a DJ, but he's now a big artist. When you have as many songs on the radio as he or Calvin, you end up playing or performing mostly your own music. I could easily play hours of Dave Audé music or remixes, but I've never done that. I don't know if I ever will. I've been DJing for so long, and I don't consider DJing playing just your own music. It's about playing great music by a variety of artists for whoever is dancing in front of you at a venue.

When I play somewhere, I do consider where I'm going and what I'll play—whether it's for the gay or straight market. But believe it or not, I'm playing similar stuff in both markets right now. When the gay market hires me for a club or event, I think it's because they want to hear what's being produced in the straight market. And the straight market may want more vocals in songs, as opposed to just beats and tech. They want to hear something they can grab onto.

You bring up a great point. In the past, the gay clubs were the barometer for what would be a hit dance song (with crossover potential)—gay men and women were in many ways the tastemakers of the genre. Is that still true?

Absolutely not. It's unfortunate, but the gay clubs are not the barometer any more. I hate saying that because I wish it was true. Again, I think a lot of that has to do with technology. Years ago, records came out on vinyl, and it took a long time to hit radio. Maybe six months. The clubs helped build the momentum. These days, with technology, you can literally finish making a song, release it, and 10 minutes later it's on the radio. The gay market has also changed a lot. It isn't a barometer anymore because of the way music is delivered to the listener.

I love the gay community, the gay market. I have a lot of respect for them, and I've made many friends playing for the gay community. I love this part of the world, especially because it's one I never thought I'd be a part of. So when you do remixes for Madonna and Beyoncé and such—you know this community really appreciates them. When I played New York Gay Pride with Cher a few years ago, it was a big moment for me. It never occurred to me that something like this could happen. I'm proud to be a part of the community and the gay scene. I wish I could say they have that same influence on the music as in the past, but I don't see how it will get back to that. As I see it, the gay scene's connection to dance music today is still circuit-tribal—which has been around for a couple of decades. The music that works in these events is the same; it hasn't really progressed. Big records, be it Ariana Grande or Katy Perry, still work, but the type of mix hasn't progressed.

In the past, gay or straight, drugs have played a role in influencing the club scene and the music played. How is it different today?

I am sure people are still taking drugs, but I don't feel it's as much a part of the club culture as it once was. It's not the focus of the experience of going to a club. I think people are hitting the clubs for three reasons. Number three is to hear music. Number two is to drink and just party. And number one is to be seen, hook up or socialize. In the past, I think going to the club to hear great music was higher on the list.

Look, I worry that saying these types of things makes me sound too conservative or mature, but it's always about the music for me. I would love to see everything get back to the music. I think we need to take some of the emphasis away from the DJ, to be truthful, from the guy standing above the crowd with his hands in the air. Don't get me wrong. I'm glad DJ culture has blown up, and I think it's awesome for dance music. But I think it's gotta be mostly about the music. When I DJ, I always ask them to turn the lights *off* me. Give me a great sound system and I'm really happy. I don't need any lights on me—I just want to make people dance with really good music. I'm not putting on a show and (necessarily) jumping around, but there were a few tequila moments. [*Dave laughs.*]

Other entertainers, artists and DJs I have spoken with tell me about the importance of staying unbothered by aging in the business. Is that an issue at all for you?

Am I concerned? I guess so, in that it crosses my mind and I'm aware of it. But I have three little kids, and they keep me running all day long. That's been a big blessing in my life—having them a little later in life. A lot of the guys I started DJing with years ago are still DJing. That's a good thing, too. Again, it's about the music. It's gotta be—or else why are we all doing this?

I definitely think, believe it or not, it's easier to be older than it was a few decades ago. As crazy as that sounds, I do think you can have a career in music (whether as a producer or vocalist or DJ) and be older. Obviously, if you're trying to do pop music and be on the radio, well that's a whole different thing. There are many other factors involved in that. But maintaining a career is about making great music and finding your fan base. The goal is to make music you love and connect with people that love it too.

What's been your greatest achievement at this point in your career or life? What do you still want to accomplish?

My greatest achievement is my kids—for sure. I don't even have to think about that question. I would love to give you an answer like, "I wrote 'Stayin' Alive.'" Or "Uptown Funk." But even so, I think I'd still say my kids are the best thing I've ever done.

As far as a future accomplishment—I still want a number one record on the pop chart. I want to write and produce a big, big record (like John Lennon's "Imagine") that people remember and play for 50 or 100 years. I'm pretty sure everyone working in music has that same goal, I think. But for sure, that's mine. I want to write something that I'm really, really proud of. I haven't done it yet. That's one thing that gets me out of bed every day and into the studio.

My whole career has brought me to where I am now, and I really believe there's something I haven't done—and it's gonna happen. Hopefully soon, but who knows?

You sound quite grounded and level-headed. I imagine your family has helped keep you that was, but you sound so unaffected by the madness of the music industry.

Oh, no. Believe me, it reaches you. But you get kind of used to it. I'm used to the drama. Well, not drama—but maybe somebody doesn't like a mix I do—there's a lot of negativity in the business. But you just take it for what it is, and if you let some of this stuff get you down, you're not gonna make it. You let it bounce off of you and move on to the next thing.

When you think about great dance music and clubbing from a pop culture and historical perspective, what comes to mind? What do you think makes dance music and the whole experience so great, so valuable?

That's a pretty large, heavy question. I don't get super, super heavy when I think of dance music. I just love it and the challenge of taking somebody's song and giving it a different twist. It might be better than the original—that's the challenge I love. As far as what dance music has done for the world—for me I think going out to clubs is a big part of life. I think everybody should experience a time in their life when they are clubbing and are able to get away from the rest of the world. I think the music, the environment—it's like going on vacation in a sense for a couple of hours. You have drinks, you do stupid things and try to remember the next morning what you did. You hear great music and act like a fool on a dancefloor. One of the things I love is being in a DJ booth and looking at the people doing crazy things. I just know they aren't doing this in their regular lives, and it's a way for people to sort of escape. I look forward to experiencing that with the crowd. Dance music has given people a way to escape the regular world for a little while. The night, going out, listening to great songs and having fun—that's what it's all about.

Lightning Round with Dave

So, while we're on the subject, what is the craziest thing you ever saw take place on a dancefloor?

Man! I guess people having sex. Is that crazy? I think when I saw that happen, it was the craziest thing I'd ever seen. Full on penetration. By the way, this was *not* recently.

Is there a dance track that you never tire of and can add into a set at virtually any time?

That's easy—Donna Summer's "I Feel Love."

Your preference—Donna Summer or Beyoncé?

Oh, for sure Donna Summer.

What do you have no patience for?

When I get requests to play hip-hop. I have nothing against it, but that's not what I play.

I also don't have patience for people who carry large bags on a plane and can't even lift them into the overhead.

With his single "Yeah Yeah 2017" (featuring Luciana), Dave Audé scored a number one *Billboard* Dance Club Songs smash. This accomplishment currently ties him with Enrique Iglesias for the most number ones on the chart among solo males, according to the publication (photograph by Micah Smith).

If you could be eternally stuck in one year of your career to date, which would it be?

I'd pick 2009. EDM was coming out of the shoot (it wasn't even called EDM then), and every major label artist and every major label A&R person thought they needed a remix that year. It was cool, and dance music and remixes were exploding. It was a very good year!

A single piece of advice would you give to an aspiring DJ?

This advice can really apply to any facet of life. Just try and be kind to everybody because you never know where people will end up. You don't have to kiss everybody's ass, but it's important to be respectful.

If you weren't in entertainment, what do you think you'd be doing?

Great question. I think I'd either probably be selling houses or maybe the owner of a sushi restaurant.

Terri B!

Terri Bjerre (vocalist, songwriter, DJ)
"Blind Heart"—Cazzette featuring Terri B! (2014)

"... it is the singer who often makes a track authentic—when you remember the song, you think of the voice that was singing it."—Terri B!

Terri B!, also known as Terri Bjerre, has one of the most formidable résumés in dance music today. She's a singer, songwriter, DJ and MC who has shared stages with David Guetta, Tiësto, Thomas Gold, DJ Antoine and many more. Her professional career began explosively, serving as the lead vocalist of 2 Eivissa, whose smash "Oh La La La" was one of the most popular world dance pop hits of the late '90s. Since then, her vocal and songwriting talents have turned countless songs into unforgettable dance music anthems.

In 2015, she found herself at the very top of the Billboard *club chart, not once but twice—as a featured vocalist on Cazzette's "Blind Heart" (which received over 60 million streams on Spotify) and, working with DJ/producer D.O.N.S., as the voice of the club smash "Big Fun" (a remake of the 1988 Inner City classic). Indeed, this is a rare accomplishment for a female artist. She's well versed in the world of club music, both in the U.S. and abroad, and after over 20 years on the scene, she remains one of the genre's most savvy and in-demand artists.*

Terri, would you tell me about life growing up for you and how you first connected with music?

I was the child of military parents; both were in the U.S. Air Force. I went to about nine schools in 12 years. I was always traveling—the advantage of that being that I was always ready and open to meet new friends in a new environment. We lived all over the United States and in Europe, but Florida was always my base. When my father was away on a tour of duty, I stayed with my grandparents, and that's where I began to define my musical tastes. I started singing in talent shows, self-made with an audience of cousins (and too afraid to actually stand in front of a real crowd of strangers), but that would change a few decades later.

I was a Prince fan from his very first record and loved his eclectic musical style. My father was a guy who reminded me very much of Obama, and he loved to make sure you knew that racism was ridiculous and that it was a tool used by the powerful to control the less powerful. He taught me that I had to be bigger than racism. It was important for him that I understood and [absorbed] different genres of music. So, I listened to classical music, Bob Seger, Roger Whittaker, Sly & The Family Stone, Diana Ross and many other artists.

Then I made discoveries of my own—The Carpenters, Steely Dan and a lot of new wave and electronic stuff in the '80s.

I found my way into the gay clubs in Tallahassee, Florida, where I first heard electronic house music (from 1982 through about 1985). I loved The Communards, New Order, Depeche Mode, Limahl of Kajagoogoo and similar music, and I knew that many of my friends, the kids I grew up with, pretty much thought my tastes were very strange. I fell in love with that bouncing beat. I always loved artists who could morph from one genre to another (Whitney Houston would be a good example, as well as Prince)—those who were not always locked into one category. As it turned out, one of my greatest talents has been to mix genres together and to make interesting songs.

In 2015, Terri B! was reportedly the first person to top the *Billboard* club songs chart twice within three weeks.

Your career kicked into high gear with the release of a 1997 dance song called "Oh La La La" by 2 Eivissa, produced by Team 33.

Yes. When I got started in music professionally, I came into the business as a songwriter. I got an opportunity to work at Studio 33 in Hamburg, Germany, with producer/engineer Luis Rodriguez. It was an amazing place to be for me. That was where Modern Talking had been created and had sold millions of copies of their records. Dieter Bohlen (producer/creator of Modern Talking) was often there—I didn't realize who he was at first or how famous he really was, but I figured it out over time. He was a funny man.

In 1997, I laid down some vocals for a track called "Oh La La La." I wrote some ad-lib parts of the song, and the song became a huge hit. It went to number one in Spain—I was like "*whaaaat*?" I couldn't believe a dance song like that could get to the top of the charts. It spread to other countries and finally to America and the *Billboard* dance chart. As I began writing songs, I always said to myself that I wanted to make it onto a *Billboard* chart. One year later, I was there!

We started to gain momentum as a group, and they asked me if I wanted to stay on. I did want to stay with it, but I did *not* want to be exclusive in my deal. It was a tough decision, and I took less money than I might have otherwise gotten, but I was able to do other projects—like Future Breeze (led by Markus Boehme and Martin Hensing—"Keep The Fire Burnin,'" "Temple of Dreams," etc.). "Temple of Dreams" hit the Top 20 in the UK [on the pop chart], and it was amazing to be a part of the trance scene. We went on to do a series of successful trance records. I also worked with Avante Garde and DJ/producer Jerry Ropero, and we had a big hit with "Get Down" in 1999, which was another top *Billboard* dance chart success.

I eventually left Studio 33. During my time there, I came to learn how important sound was to a production, and I was determined to always work at that high level of sound quality. I did a lot of songwriting and singing for many producers, and in 2007 went on to work in Sweden, summoned by Luciano Ingrosso, the uncle of superstar DJ Sebastian Ingrosso [formerly of Swedish House Mafia]. [Luciano] asked me to do a song with an artist named Henrik B. called "Soulheaven." I had never heard of him, but I did the record anyway. It ended up being played everywhere, from Sydney to London. But by the time I realized what a huge impact that record was having, it was already on the way out. I wasn't on top of my business with that one, but it led to working and/or touring with names like David Guetta, Roger Sanchez, Avicii, Eddie Thoneick, Laidback Luke, DJ Antoine and some other great artists of that caliber.

Do you ever look at that amazing résumé you have and get overwhelmed by the scope of the work you've done in dance music over the years?

You know, I get more overwhelmed by thoughts of how I might go back in time and do it all again. I didn't appreciate some of the places and experiences I had—I treated them as just another gig at the time. And now, as I get older, I realize I should have absorbed the experiences more, gotten out of the hotel, even done some sightseeing in those incredible places. I didn't live in the moment enough—when you're going through it, sometimes you get bored with it all.

Working in recent years with Ollie Goedicke [aka D.O.N.S.] and traveling the world as a duo—we had something different that brought us to many festivals around the world. Ollie was an intricate part of my "upbringing" in dance music, for the second phase, because he brought me into the progressive house scene. We visited so many countries (for the first time), and we never knew what to expect—India and all kinds of exotic places. We've had a lot of fun and just literally laughed our way to every airport.

Your voice, your performance has been a major selling point of so many of these well-received dance tracks. Yet vocalists, in general, are no longer the center of attention in dance music—it's the producer/DJ. How do you feel about the somewhat subordinate, featured position many vocalists find themselves in today?

After "Soulheaven," I got very comfortable with the "featuring" concept. I have two opinions about it now because I come from both sides of the debate. As a vocalist, everything would be great if everyone respected each other—if everyone gave each other their kudos. Now, I don't want to put everyone in the same boat because people like David Guetta, Bob Sinclar and some others really *do* care who performs with them, and they don't want to be involved with anyone who will bring them down. They encourage the vocalist to be very engaged with the song or project and do what they do, including on-stage performances. They don't disregard the voice.

An artist who is new and trying to break into things (or even established and trying to stay in the game) tends to be nervous about asking for more. Then you have an old chicken like me who says she won't do it unless there's an "and" in the credit—so and so *and* Terri B!. David Guetta would never deny a vocalist his or her place in a project, but there are those who do just want to grab your voice.

All I can say to upcoming artists is there are moments where you pay your dues, and [in accepting a featured role] you pray the song is not the big event of your career. But when you reach the time you don't need to do that, you need to find a way to make yourself as important as whoever else is involved. Hip-hop has always been very good about that. In that genre, everyone involved is always listed. Dance music—not so much. But it is the singer who often makes a track authentic—when you remember the song, you think of the voice that was singing it. David and artists like that build alliances with vocalists that sometimes go way back and are not just a one or two hour session in the studio.

I have been blessed in my career to be at a point where I am able to say no and to be viewed as valuable enough where I can say I'm not going to just be a "featuring" name. Many artists get lost behind the featuring word. It's always better to be listed on equal footing with the main artist. But if you can't, it's not the worst thing in the world. But you should be very clear in your mind what those trade-offs mean.

You go by the stage name of Terri B!. In hindsight, was that a mistake? Do abbreviations of artist names or monikers of that style, especially in dance, reduce his or her legitimacy or ability to stand out?

That was a mistake. There's too much going on in this genre for me to start changing my name now, however. When I started out, I was divorced and didn't want to use my full name. Now that I am [on good terms with my ex], I wouldn't mind using the Bjerre name. But if I could have changed things back then, I would definitely have used my full name. I have problems even with the Terri part—people spelling it with a "y." It's just not fun. My advice to all artists is to get your name out there *in full* and identify yourself.

It's funny, when I did "Soulheaven" in Stockholm with Jerry, I didn't even want to put my name on the record at all. Why on earth was I thinking that way? I claim *everything* I write or produce now. I'm proud of "Terri B!" as a brand, but it feels like someone else, as it's really not my name.

Has being a woman, and a woman of color, affected your experience in this industry in any way?

I was very shy when I came into the business. I had such stage fright in the early '90s—I just did not want to go in front of people. I slowly built up confidence. I've been lucky. EDM and dance music gave me a career. I was there at the brink of the new DJ market, and we were ready for each other. The attraction that I had for music (music that wasn't 100 percent soulful) gave me a knack for writing trance and songs in genres like that. My audience tended to be white boys—I can't really explain it. They never made me feel like I didn't belong. I walk into a bar, and within a half an hour I am surrounded by young guys, and they all want to party with me. [*Terri laughs.*]

I don't know, I may be a black woman, but sometimes I think there may also be a young European boy somewhere in my soul. The new generation looks at me as a good vocalist—that's all that matters to them. I got older—they didn't stop calling me. I just think there's something special they perceive about me. So, I've never had a problem.

Tell me about songwriting for dance music. What elements have to be in place for a song to be a dance hit?

That's a good question. For starters, you need to be educated about the formula of a song. These elements in songwriting are the same, no matter what the genre. As a writer, you always have to be able to transport yourself into different types of melodies—childish melodies to more sophisticated ones, soulful to urban. The more talented you are at finding authentic melodies in a genre, the less likely you are to sound contrived. Also, when you're in a session with an artist and you're creating something for them, you have to be sure that there is that creative flow in place and that it feels like something they can represent.

I feel like I have unlimited ideas when it comes to creating dance songs. (Don't get me wrong—you go through periods where you don't like anything you're doing.) But then there's that shining moment when creating a track, like when Calvin Harris sings that "oooh, oooh, oooh" type of sound, that you know this is gonna be *something*. When we worked on the lyrics about being strung up like a puppet and a "thin red line" on Cazzette's "Blind Heart," I knew we had something. If you don't feel the connection and that energy like we did creating that track, fans aren't going to feel it either.

I know you can't be sure a song will be a hit, but I do feel I have that ability to identify the elements in a song that people will like. But that's not to say people of every country will respond the same. You can have that great feeling for a song, but the translation of it in another country can always be tricky. American leans urban, for example, and it's challenging in that I have to consider that when creating a package of mixes for U.S. DJs—the energy, the breaks. I have to be thinking of all that when I am writing a song.

Sometimes, however, you have to buck those trends. I've written songs where I didn't care what the trends were. I just wanted to change my voice or maybe sing a bit more intimately, not scream—and they've done really, really well. That gives me credibility in this era of electronics. "Take My Breath Away," a song I recently did with Jason Chance, is this type of track. Not super fast or overdone.

You've worked with major dance labels like Ultra, Defected, Armada, Ministry of Sound, Hed Kandi and Kontor, and you've also taken the indie label route. Have you always been savvy to the twists and turns of the business side of recording?

The day I told Luis Rodriguez I didn't want an exclusivity clause, I think I came to the table with more savvy than maybe the average artist. I loved marketing, and I once managed a hundred employees at a company—so I understood the give and take of management and how not to freak out. I also used to be a secretary, so I am into paperwork, organizing and tracking things. [*Terri points to the large binders behind her that contain her financial records.*] When I was young, I used to think about being a record label executive—I didn't initially think about singing. So, I think I am okay today because I planned and strategized long ago. I am registered with the GEMA organization in Germany (the equivalent of, say, ASCAP in the U.S.) at the highest level you can be. I will eventually retire as a writer in Germany and get a pension when I do. I always asked a lot of questions.

I know a lot of artists who have sold millions of records, and they don't understand what publishing is all about. There are basic things you have to understand with labels. Territory by territory, I like to pick and choose my partners.

When I encounter young artists, I ask them not be stupid about their careers. If you're in this industry and you don't become the next Avicii, which you probably won't, then you better understand your publishing. Europe is different from the U.S. If you don't understand this side of things and performing rights, in the U.S. and abroad, you will fall into trouble. I actually had to help an artist get residuals whose voice was sampled on a hit record (illegally, but they used a loophole)—it was amazing to me that he would never have known he was entitled to that money had we not happened to discuss it.

Every artist who knows a thing or two about the industry should be helping those who don't.

Is there a difference in the appeal of dance music in Europe compared to the U.S.?

I think in Europe, dance music has been part of pop culture and part of people's lives for a very long time. Clubs in Europe have people of all ages partying together, and it's a very unifying experience. It starts at an earlier age, and they are influenced by the older music for a longer period of time.

In America, the club music experience stops at different times for different people. But people generally stop going to clubs at a certain point in the U.S., and club life is really only a part of certain cities. I don't think people in America "get" dance music for that long—it's viewed as a kid's thing. I had one person in the U.S. describe the music as "that dance shit." I was like, thank you, well, that's what I have been making for over 25 years—*that dance shit*! But in Europe, it's not like that. Old and young—everybody loves it, respects it, and they love it for a much longer period of time.

Do you think this explains why many dance music artists, even those who have been around for many years and have number one pop hits, are not well known by his or her name here in the U.S.?

I think it comes from a perception in the U.S. that dance music isn't a real form of music—lesser than pop, rock, country, classical, hip-hop. That's changing a little bit—people like Calvin Harris are having a big effect that way. It's a kind of prejudice that exists. I think people don't realize the amount of work that goes into the best of this genre—it's not a simple business.

When Michael Jackson was making a record, VH1 and all these media outlets were showing you how he made it and took you into the studio. That doesn't happen now—we don't see that kind of marketing. Do you see Calvin or David Guetta on TV often? No. I also think a lot of dance music artists, DJs, and producers don't have the type of big personalities that make for good TV—so it's kind of a two-way street. Until they hit that side of the media, I don't think dance music artists will be "legitimized" in that way.

Racism and terrorism seem to have become a daily issue in the U.S. and abroad as the twenty-first century progresses. Do you see this affecting nightlife and the dance music industry?

If you wait a few minutes to get the information—and I do a lot of research on these acts of terrorism—you sometimes get a different picture of things. The mastermind of the Paris attacks in 2015 was from Brussels, went to a great school and wasn't always connected to Islam. He's no different from these other people who commit terrible acts because they didn't fit in somehow. I try to look at each event and understand what happened and who committed the act without globalizing the event, without automatically assuming it happened because of this reason or this religion or whatever.

Ultimately, I don't think these things will deter people from living their lives. I was partying at a bar in Beirut, and I wanted to experience this city and country. I can't think about every terrible thing that might happen. When I'm gone, I'm gone. Everybody isn't a terrorist, just like everybody in the U.S. isn't a Donald Trump supporter, and, if you think about it, the majority of people are not out to do harm.

You seem to project a very balanced mindset despite the unpredictability and tumultuous lifestyle a busy and successful international recording artist is bound to experience. How do you personally stay centered and grounded in life?

My son is 24 now, and he's been with me in this business since he was a toddler. He recently said to me that he has been watching me since he was a kid from the back seat of the car, seeing me accomplish everything I wanted to do. I think I've always managed to keep my family first. My son is my rock, and my ex-husband is still one of my best friends. They all know what my journey has been. I think I also remember what my father said to me: "You don't want to grow old and find you haven't done what you really loved." That would be my biggest regret. I think I have always kept that in mind, and these values have always kept me centered.

I know you are well aware of the many classic dance songs from the '70s, '80s and '90s we have in the pantheon of pop culture. Do you think the dance music produced thus far in the twenty-first century will be remembered in the same way?

No. We live in such a sample world now. Today, we take a whole Stevie Wonder song and put it into a production and give it a new title. Do you know how much work went into that original song? How much production? It's like we're not creating a lot of good, original material in this century. The stuff I'm hearing on Beatport now—it's unlikely I'll go back to it years from now and listen to it. Do I think Bruno Mars will still be around? Yes. Beyoncé? Yes, sure. They'll be playing "Single Ladies" 20 years from now. The songs that will be remembered are the songs that were properly composed. Adele will be around, singing the same song in a new version. [*Terri laughs.*]

Lightning Round with Terri

Favorite nightclub drink?
Just a Coke.

Craziest thing you ever saw take place on a dancefloor?
It was one of those *Soul Train* lines that people form, and this guy tried to do a big flip and landed flat on his back. He was an older guy, so it was probably a big mistake for him!

Favorite dance song of all time?
"On the Radio" by Donna Summer.

Have you ever forgotten the lyrics to a song you wrote while performing?
Oh, all of them! I am the worst—I just can't remember anything. But as a writer I am good at faking it. [*Terri invents some on-the-spot lyrics while singing a few bars of "On the Radio."*]

If you were going to consider doing a remake, what's the dance song from the past you'd choose?
La Bouche's "Be My Lover." I worked for La Bouche's producers, Ullrich Brenner and Amir Saraf, and when I got pregnant, I stopped singing for a while. That's when they found

Melanie Thornton [who became part of La Bouche]. I met Melanie just two weeks before she died. We had such a nice meeting. She reminded me of Donna Summer. It was hard to hear her records for a long time after her death.

When you're not performing or in the studio, what do you like to do to unwind?

Watch TV series. I love *SVU* and *Little House On The Prairie*. How's that for a contrast? Don't ask me to explain why in regard to *Prairie*. I can't. I just love old shows. I love period and historical programs, too, but oddly I was never able to get into *Downton Abbey*.

Terri B!'s first solo single "I'm Coming Back" hit the Top 20 of the *Billboard* club songs chart in 2016. The singer scored another hit in 2017 as featured vocalist on Rosabel's "Anthem of House."

If you weren't in entertainment, what would you be doing?

I would either be in politics or a teacher.

Bart & Baker

*Bart Sampson, Jo Baker
(DJs, producers, remixers)*

"Allez Viens" (ft. Pierre Santini
and Lada Redstar) (2012)

"Truthfully, we always thought our careers in music would be short-lived. And so, for quite a while, we only did singles and EPs. Now that we have that value as producers and songwriters, we can think bigger."—Bart Sampson

"When there is drama in life like there is now, the answer is to put more culture into the lives of people. Not less. It makes them more happy."—Jo Baker

One of the hallmarks of twenty-first century dance music has been its remarkable ability to generate new sub-genres with a rapid fire speed no previous generation has ever witnessed. One such off-shoot is called electro-swing, a format characterized by upbeat reinterpretations of catchy pop songs (largely from the American swing era) and bolstered by hip, electronic arrangements. Though updating vintage songs from the first half of the twentieth century is nothing new (think back to '70s disco groups like Tuxedo Junction, hits like 1982's "Hooked on Swing" by Larry Elgart's Manhattan Swing Orchestra and 1983's "Puttin' on the Ritz" by Taco), electro-swing has forged some highly inventive and stimulating creations using modern studio technology. The legion of fans following this style of dance music has grown steadily larger.

Among the niche market's pioneers are Paris' Bart Sampson and Jo Baker, better known as Bart & Baker. Since they came together as a DJ, production and performance team in 2005, the duo has progressively increased the profile of the electro-swing genre. Bart & Baker's sound is an ever changing one that frequently combines jazz with house and incorporates lyrics that reflect contemporary social issues. Their numerous singles, EP and album contributions to the genre, notably the Electro-Swing *compilation series, have earned the gentlemen an international following. Their support of this special brand of nostalgic, quirky, yet distinctly fresh sounding dance music has, in turn, placed the spotlight onto other artists, including Parov Stelar, Swingrowers, Tape Five and Swing Republic. Their latest album,* Only Different, *harkens back to the inspiration the pair felt at the legendary* Body & Soul *parties that once flourished in New York City. They've also indulged in contemporary house music with great success.*

Bart & Baker (Jo Baker, left, Bart Sampson, right) have been commissioned to remix some of their favorites artists, including Parov Stelar, Caro Emerald, Paris Combo, Kid Loco, Dimitri From Paris, Tape Five and Gabin.

Gentlemen, please tell me about your youth and what led to the creation of Bart & Baker. I'd love to know how you became such prolific innovators of the international electro-swing dance movement.

Bart: First, I must mention that my [stage] name is inspired by Bart Simpson. That should tell you something. I don't come from a musical background at all. I come from a middle class family. My father comes from what we call the Parisian bourgeoisie, and my mother comes from a very modest background. It's interesting that they found love and had two lovely children—including me. We left Paris when I was 10 years old and moved to the south of France. Because we lived in a very small village there, I always felt like I needed to find ways to be connected to the world. So, I listened to a lot of music and read the pop music publications I was able to get from the local news agent. My knowledge of the English language comes from listening to a great deal of pop music and my desire to understand the lyrics. (Actually, I think that's why, as Bart & Baker, we try to have depth in our lyrics. However, I know sometimes people don't care about the words and focus only on the beat.)

Around the age of 17, I also ran the French fan club for the pop band Pet Shop Boys for about six or seven years. I had a very good relationship with their record company at the time. The band was not willing to do much publicity in France back then, and I was the link for all the fans for news about what was happening with them. I printed a magazine, created some bootleg tapes—I have to say this work paid for my studies in a way. I was invited to EMI Records' offices, was given all their promotional 12-inch records, all long before the Internet.

I think that experience is linked to the success of Bart & Baker for a few reasons. One, I was what you would call a "community manager" for the Pet Shop Boys, and I have served in that capacity for Bart & Baker. I know how important it is to make the fans happy and to keep our audience interested in what we do. Second, I think the music of Bart & Baker is created in a way that is much like how it was done by the Pet Shop Boys—we try to find interesting beats and melodies and sometimes write very serious lyrics.

Take, for example, our song "Invincible." A French journalist had written an article about how young people were still having unprotected sex and how they believed themselves to be invincible. I thought, wow, what a great title for a song, and it became the theme for our track called "Invincible" (which was all about this culture of people who engage in extreme sex, take drugs and who are very lonely in their hearts). The subject of our song wasn't so obvious just by listening to it, but it is a bit clearer when you see the video. It's a very good example of a song that wasn't the typical Bart & Baker sound and style.

Lastly, getting back to the Pet Shop Boys, I think our visual presentation is inspired by the Pet Shop Boys. We are very careful with our image and presenting ourselves in a very distinctive way.

Speaking of the Pet Shop Boys, I guess I should say that I sometimes found Neil Tennant's voice irritating on some tracks (I did, however, love his voice on the *Behaviour* LP, their best album). Later on, I started to feel they were becoming too kitschy. However, he would mention in interviews his interest in jazz and described the roots of their music. I started listening to those sounds and, in turn, I discovered this other form of music, which, again, has had an impact on Bart & Baker.

Jo: My mother, Majoie Hajary, is a musician, and she came from Surinam, the Netherlands' plantation colony. She went to music school in Amsterdam and was a prize-winning classical pianist. She was a bit of a celebrity. She wanted to become a composer and studied in Paris. She met my father, married and had two children, which brought an end to her music career. My father worked for Air France, which gave us an opportunity to travel around the world. My [stage] name was inspired by my family's friendship with Josephine Baker. She was a good friend of my mother, and they used to cross paths on the same planes.

Though my mother was a classical musician, I hated classical music. When I was young, I heard this music all the time and met a lot of musicians who performed it, but I really wanted to hear something else. I discovered jazz and musicals, and I worked for about 10 years at the Folies Bergère, which helped pay for my education.

How did you come to connect with each other?

Bart: We met in 1998 at one those "record fests"—those places people go to who like to collect records. I was looking for jazz music, and someone told me there was a guy who came to these places regularly who was into jazz and also talked about the Pet Shop Boys. It was Jo. He had all the jazz background I wanted to know about, and I had all the electronic music knowledge he was seeking. We became friends and got along well, and we traveled to many places like New York City to do record shopping. So, while we were there, we attended a famous Sunday afternoon dance event called *Body & Soul*.

Jo: Yes, we'd take a plane from Paris to New York on a weekend, do our record shopping and then go to *Body & Soul*.

Bart: The last time I think we ever went to *Body & Soul* was in August of 2001. I remember that because we had coffee one day at the bottom floor of the World Trade Center, and just about a month later it was September 11th. The *Body & Soul* dance party was very connected to Club Vinyl, located in Tribeca, and it was fantastic.

Jo: It really was fantastic—no drugs, no alcohol, and it started at 2PM. It was wonderful.

Bart: I think he kept a gin flask in his pants. [*Bart and Jo laugh.*]

Jo: When I saw all these people coming to this event *only* for the music, it was just amazing.

Bart: It was, and it inspired us. It showed us that you didn't have to be super young to experience this, and the DJs themselves, Danny Krivit, Joaquin "Joe" Claussell and Francois K., weren't all that young when they played. We saw it was possible to bring together people of different generations and play a wide variety of dance music—disco, house, Brazilian, soul.

We came back to Paris and eventually formed Bart & Baker hoping to produce house music, but we were blocked from it. Many of the people in that scene were doing it from a very early age, and we had no way of gaining entry into this community without having produced any big records previously.

This was before we met the swing community.

So, as one door closed, another opened for you in the swing music culture, correct?

Bart: Yes, this niche music community was gaining interest in electronic swing, and because there wasn't anyone really involved in this genre, we took the cue and said, "We can do this!" We brought the electronic ingredient into the swing clubs. I should say, especially at this time, though the swing community loved their music, they weren't making any of the clubs rich. When we produced some of these parties, the people would bring a bottle in their bag and not buy any cocktails from the bar. Organizers quickly realized they would only make money selling tickets and not at the bar, so there wasn't much of an incentive for the clubs to have electro-swing nights and parties. What would happen is the first part of the night was electro-swing, and the second half was more clubby. But we managed to go from small loft parties to getting the swing parties into bigger clubs—places like the Moulin Rouge club.

We did this for about five years, but then we started to feel like we needed to move on—beyond the parties and more into production. I sent a CD mix to a club journalist who liked our music, and he got us a start in a cool club called Andy Wahloo, not the biggest (it held maybe 100 people), but it was one where you might see some celebrities. Of course, at first we were given the worst night of the week to play, but we did our best. We started off on a Tuesday and ended up getting Friday nights. We had no manager or assistance—only our ability to make people *want* to come back. Okay, so we were DJs, but did we produce our own songs? Not yet. Did we write our own songs? Not yet. We began to think about these things.

Back in 2010, the marketing manager of Wagram Music, a big label here in Europe, especially for compilations, saw an article about us in *ELLE* magazine. He came to see us perform, and, of course, we didn't look like the typical DJs. He asked us to propose a compilation project to him, and we came back with the track list for a collection that became known as *Swing Party*, which mixed swing with hip-hop and dance music. The album sold about 12,000 copies, which was a lot (as he never expected to sell many), and then we began curating the *Electro Swing* compilation series, which now has eight volumes. [By the time this book is out] we'll have released a "best of" set. These collections are so unique because we are finding songs that nobody else out there is proposing. We have a great licensing and digital distribution deal with Wagram.

Truthfully, we always thought our careers in music would be short-lived. And so, for quite a while, we only did singles and EPs. Now that we have that value as producers and songwriters, we can think bigger.

You produced and remixed a wide variety of electro-swing tracks for these compilations. Do you recall one of the early standout songs that exemplified the qualities of this genre?

Bart: One of our first tracks was called "Communication" featuring Slim Gaillard—a very hard swing track. It's really the roots of what we are doing now. That song is from the '40s and talks about having the telephone and telegraph—it's all about modern technology arriving in the life of a man. So that's why I think it was good that we really started with that track. The digital divide and the effects of technology were present when this song was written, and they still exist today. And our arrangement of the song really fit with the energy of the electro-swing movement.

Early on, you created interesting costumes for yourself and you developed a style and sense of showmanship that has a really avant-garde flair. Tell me about this.

Bart: We don't dress the way we do because we think it's this beautiful way to be. We want people to react to it—it's a tribute to the show business tradition. To be frank, there are times I'd love to not have to wear a white tuxedo and top hat. There's also a sense of humor in our look, as well. However, the French people don't always have a sense of humor. They think they know the rules of fashion, and they often say we are ridiculous for dressing as we do. It's funny, because the English and Americans pay us a lot of respect for the way we like to perform. But the French just don't have a clue as to why we do this.

Jo: I remember a manager we were working with said maybe we should consider changing the way we dress, especially in regard to working with major record labels. He felt it wasn't going to help the label take us more seriously when trying to interest them in an album we were developing.

Bart: Yes—what is considered an asset in a foreign country is viewed as a weakness in our own country. Recently, the famous DJ Dimitri from Paris, a friend of ours, said in an interview that he was never booked for big parties in France. All of his success came outside of this country. In many ways, that's true for us, too. And you know, we can wear these costumes for many years—we can be 70 years old, and we will be able to wear the Bart & Baker costumes.

Would you tell me about the growing fan base for and the appeal of electro-swing dance music? What qualities does it possess that distinguish it from other forms of contemporary dance music, and why has it been gaining so much momentum?

Jo: It is always a cycle. When I was working at Folies Bergère, they were playing the theme to the dance "The Charleston," tunes like this, already in the '70s.

Bart: In a way, electro-swing is a music with comfortable values. It's kind of from your grandmother's era, and there's a comfort in that. You can't go wrong with it; it makes people feel a sense of confidence. In dark times, like we often see today, it fills that need for a feel-good sound when a person doesn't quite want that aggressive sound of EDM and the more brainy music that people listen to when they want to feel more like a hipster.

How do you go about selecting the right songs for one of your electro-swing shows?

Bart: We possess a collection of about 20,000 records from the vintage period of swing, the old style, and we get all the new promos from today's labels. We listen to the songs in the car because that's the best place to tell if a song is any good. If Jo and I agree on a song, we add it to our show. For example, we heard a song called "Dazzled" by Nina Miranda, remixed in 2016 by The Cube Guys, and I said that it was the perfect Bart & Baker track. We enjoy different types of songs. I know other DJs only play music of their own or by other DJs who did a remix for them, and it ends up being very political. We try not to be influenced in that way.

In terms of the business of dance music, are you able to still make a living from recorded music—the sale of your songs and albums?

Bart: Today, our digital revenue is maybe a little over a thousand Euro a month, which for some artists is a lot. This figure is a rough guess and only from digital, not from licensing. If you have a lot of product out there but only sell a few copies of each of them, you can make some decent money. We have a catalog of over 200 tracks, including remixes, and we have released music where there is really something for everybody. But you have to think beyond just digital sales to really survive.

We also do some business on the corporate side, playing live for wealthy executives and organizations having corporate parties and the like. We don't think it's a good idea to take too much work like that because it can empty you out as an artist. We have been lucky because we haven't had a bad experience dealing with this [part of society], but we want to be careful not to kill our creativity in the process.

We don't play that many festivals either. They usually do not have good budgets to pay for us, especially in the UK. However, the U.S. is a much better market for festivals and events. We played at *Electric Forest* in Chicago, and they paid for our travel visas and treated us very well.

Jo: We also both have normal jobs, too. We never wanted to give up these jobs. It wasn't that we didn't believe in the music we were doing, but we felt it was wise to maintain this other part of our lives.

Bart: Yes! Hold your breath! Jo is a general practitioner! With our costumes, people rarely recognize us, and we rarely perform in Paris, where we work at these jobs. I work in freelance media and new marketing. That's why I'm quite obsessed with digital media. We seriously thought about giving these jobs up, but we realized keeping them gives us the independence to say no to things we don't want to do in this industry. You can easily be a slave to the music business, or on drugs because you get so depressed about bad decisions or the entourage you keep. I like the normal people I deal with in my regular job, but if I do happen to have a bad day with it, I know I can also turn to my music, perform in a cool club or create a new video. So there is a good balance in our lives, and we're very happy about that.

I was reading a book by Daft Punk, and their manager said something about the rarer you are, the more value you have. People wonder why we don't tour so much or play that often. Our dual lives give us the ability to be careful and selective about our decisions.

Tell me how the music you create that does *not* fall into the electro-swing genre fits into your plan.

Bart: When we started writing tunes, they didn't always sound like electro-swing. We thought about making another name for ourselves for these songs. But we decided no; Bart & Baker is a brand. There is nothing that says we must always do the same type of song. A good song is a good song. I understand some people may not like all our styles of production.

Do you think the increasing state of violence in our world, which Paris, for example, has experienced first-hand in recent times, is going to affect people's desire to go out and listen to this music and dance? Will it hinder nightlife?

Bart: Well, it seems like the Parisian club scene has, indeed, been affected already. We were playing the night of the November 2015 attacks. We had a few corporate events cancelled around that Christmas. But people started to talk to their neighbors and march in the streets. There was shock, but France is very resilient. I don't know how resilient we will be after continued bombings—our country could become like the war-torn Middle East, which may depress the nation. But France is a bit depressed anyway.

I think it's political and economic, in a way, perhaps because the generations are all walking very separately these days. I think people here feel very uncertain about the future. When you think the future will be super bright—when you think the future will be a civilization of leisure, as we thought in the '80s—there is less depression. As it turned out, we work even more now.

Jo: When there is drama in life like there is now, the answer is to put more culture into the lives of people. Not less. It makes them more happy.

Bart: Many of our problems are coming from friction between different types of people. We recently worked with a singer named Ashley Slater (who is associated with Fatboy Slim) on a track called "Only Different," and the song is about being different and how beautiful that is. We are very against that concept that everything has to be the same, look the same, everybody has to have white teeth and blond hair. How can you converse with people and learn if you only deal with people who are a clone of yourself? What happened here in Paris occurred, in part, because we are trying to make sure everybody is like us. I certainly don't say I hope the world is destroyed and we will have to rebuild again, like after World War II, to be happy again. But it's strange. People today can be unhappy simply because they don't have the biggest TV or car. But they do have a TV and they do have a car. You know what I mean?

I think we have to be more grateful. I try to wake up every morning grateful that we are recording artists. Jo knows a great deal about what goes on in people's lives, being a doctor, and we have many reasons to be grateful. I think this is part of what we are trying to convey with the music of Bart & Baker. I don't know that people will want to always go to an EDM party when they have been through these [acts of terrorism]. This kind of music may not cure your soul. But I think our music may be helpful.

Do you think the dance music of the twenty-first century, including the music that you are creating, will be remembered with the same kind of love that dance classics from past decades have enjoyed?

Bart: I think I have a rather complex answer for you. I believe the 2000s has been an era of super production—that doesn't mean it's great; it just means it's the reign of the engineer. People are putting so much money into making the biggest song possible, but that doesn't mean the song will be remembered. I can say that from buying records for a very long time and getting a lot of promo copies. Sometimes the power of the production is so strong, it almost makes me afraid. In my past education, I studied the Nazis. They put a lot of pressure on people by using propaganda. I think these super productions are like that. You get overwhelmed and excited by them, but you don't really know what they are about afterward. It's like a quick effect—it is overpowering, but it didn't really make your heart beat. You can still have a beautiful song today. I do believe an accident can happen.

Jo: There are 10,000 new tracks on Soundcloud every month, so obviously we don't hear them all. So there are good tracks out there that we don't know about. We just need to be positive and believe that creativity still exists—that each era comes with its own package of surprises.

Bart: Yes, it's good that artists can express that creativity with a computer. But I still hear a lot of well-produced crap, and it doesn't move me.

Jo: I guess people said that in the '80s, too. But now people are going back to those songs.

What is the power of dance music in pop culture—what makes it so special?

Bart: I had a conversation with Baker today about this. A philosopher once said that music is linked to death. We are on this planet a short time, and we need to put dance and music into our lives. Most of society's rituals surrounding death involve music and dance. We know we are going to die, and so we want to celebrate life. When someone passes, many cultures celebrate the person's life by dancing—paying tribute to his or her life. So dance music is our acknowledgment that we are going to die someday, so let's express the fact that we are alive. And what better way than to dance?

Lightning Round with Bart & Baker

What's been your biggest hit to date?

Bart: Through streaming it was the "Can-Can" theme from Moulin Rouge. That was the track that had one million plays on Spotify. So kitsch, but every time we play that in a show, everyone dances to it like they have never danced before. Our biggest digital sales hit has been "Allez Viens," which was a French translation of "Via Con Me." It features Pierre Santini, a pretty well-known movie actor who is a friend of Baker's and nearly 80 years old. We saw him perform Paolo Conte's "Via Con Me," and we thought the song would really translate well into electro-swing. He's a young man in the body of an older man, so he said sure. We added a female vocalist (Lada Redstar) because the song is a very Italian macho song, and we thought [some feminine energy] would add to the appeal. Sometimes Santini hears the song playing in different places, and he is very proud of it. I should mention that "Istanbul" was also a big hit for us—we are doing a cool house version of it for our *Best of Electro Swing* album.

What's your personal favorite of your creations?
Bart: I will always say: the last one we wrote!

What dance song by another artist do you never tire of hearing?
Bart: "Promised Land" by Joe Smooth.
Jo: "My Favorite Things" (Rodgers and Hammerstein)—any version, really.

Craziest thing you've ever seen take place on a dancefloor?
Bart: We were playing on a Russian millionaire's yacht, and it was required that all the ladies take off their high heels to go on the craft, so not to scuff the flooring. Nobody could wear shoes. Very funny for such a luxury party.

Favorite thing to do to get away from it all?
Bart: We are big watchers of TV shows, you know, TV series. We loved *The Sopranos*, *Boardwalk Empire* and *The Americans*.

One thing about your personality that you wish you could change?
Bart: I'm too impatient, especially when it comes to creativity, and I should apply the brakes probably more often. But a weakness can also be a strength.

Bart & Baker (Jo Baker, left, Bart Sampson, right) released the compilation album *Electro Swing Tribute* late in 2016, featuring electrified versions of diverse classics such as "Fever," "Groove Is in the Heart" and "Via Con Me."

Jo: I wish I didn't move my hands so much when we do our shows. Sometimes people wonder what's going on with me.

If you could be stuck in one particular year of your careers to date, which would it be?

Bart: I think when we did our first *Swing Party* album—2010. We never dreamed it could happen. I think we thought it would be our *only* record, and we felt, well, if that's it, it *should* be that one.

Bimbo Jones

Lee Dagger, Marc JB
(DJs, producers, remixers)

"Bad Romance"/"Alejandro"
(Bimbo Jones Remixes)—Lady Gaga (2009/2010)

"Music enables you to be present with your life and connect to something deeper, to feel things, to remember emotions and feel the passion coursing through your body as the textures of a song evolve. That's what it gives you! People need to re-evaluate what the exchange of energy should be with music, with everything. You have to give to get. They are just getting, without giving anything back. The industry is limping on—but again I say it's because of the beautiful artists that just won't give up."—Marc JB

"As long as we're making good product, making people dance and connecting with our fans, that's always going to be our main focus."—Lee Dagger

They've created remixes for literally dozens of the biggest names in the business (many of which went to number one on the Billboard *dance and pop charts). Among the powerhouse artists they've worked with are Katy Perry ("Hot N Cold"), Rihanna ("Diamonds"), Lady Gaga, Kylie, Kelis, P!nk and the Pussycat Dolls. They are two gentlemen who have proven over and over that the legendary production partnership of Lee Dagger and Marc JB (known worldwide as Bimbo Jones) is, quite simply, hard to beat. Their pioneering sound is ever-evolving, bright, crisp and bursting with the cutting edge power and energy dancefloors have been demanding for the past several years. As a result, Bimbo Jones remain among the most sought-after of today's DJ/producer teams.*

Bimbo Jones' original productions, such as "And I Try" (with Katherine Ellis), "I Found Out" (with Beverley Knight) and "See You Later" (featuring Ida Corr), brilliantly meld funk, house and other dance sub-genres with unique electronic creativity, allowing the pair to explore directions that Top 40 pop is often too timid to support. Following their acclaimed 2008 set Harlem 1 Stop, *they released their second studio album in 2014,* Go Naked. *The two Brits enjoy a strong friendship and an especially sharp memory for the details of their extraordinary journey. Lee, who now lives in Denver, and Marc (in London) come together on Skype to discuss life in dance music's fast lane.*

Gentlemen, would you tell me about your youth and what life was like growing up? How did you find a place in the music industry?

Bimbo Jones' (Lee Dagger, left, Marc JB, right) production skills brought them to the top of the UK National Chart for two consecutive weeks in 2006 with "Thunder in My Heart Again," a single by Meck ft. Leo Sayer.

Marc: My grandfather was a swing dance band leader in the 1940s named Jack Jackson. He worked at the Dorchester, Hilton and Savoy hotels. Back in those days, rather than going to a nightclub, the place to go was a posh hotel ballroom. He was basically the Avicii of his day. He moved into radio, which prior to him was very dry and rigid. For example, they would say, "And now we have a lovely piece by Rachmaninoff. Please pay particular attention to the third movement." My grandfather came on the air and started collecting sound effects for the program—inventing the very first sample bank and creating the first re-sampled modern radio program. This is way before anybody else—the 1950s and '60s, and I think he had something like 10 million listeners in the UK. My grandmother was an opera singer, and my mother is an artist and pianist. My father ran the largest chain of music shops in Europe called City Music, and he was a gigging musician.

When I was just four, I realized I could just make up any style of music in my head and play it like a radio—jazz, classical, rock. I also began writing songs at a very young age—at least two a day, which I have continued the whole of my life. I then went off in a few bands when I got older.

I was a keyboard player in Boney M. for a bit, which was very funny, indeed. Those guys—the band members, not the singers—were the biggest bunch of assholes I've ever worked with! You can print that—because it's about time to start saying some of these things. I'll give you an example—after one gig, a drummer from the group asked me to take his bag to Germany. It was only when I got there that I realized he placed drugs in the bag! We played a beer festival, and they positioned my keyboard under a big leak—there was a pool of water in the actual keyboard! Well, I wanted to get paid, so I was determined to bloody well play it. [*He laughs.*] It was like Blue Man Group with all the splashing!

I kept working and paying my dues, playing piano in jazz bands and at cocktail bars. I really wanted to make it in music, and I was always contacting record labels. I'd always receive flat-out refusals for my demos. It was very disheartening. So, I was looking for an avenue where I could feel some *looove* back from the music because it was so difficult back then. (It's difficult for kids now, too, but in a completely different way.) I asked a family friend, Guy Fletcher, who is now the chairman of PRS [Performing Right Society] in the UK, if he knew of any contacts. He connected me with a man named Brian Allen, who introduced me to Lee.

And with that, I hand you over to Lee to tell you his story!

Lee: The funny thing is, Marc was talking about the 1940s. My parents divorced early on, and I never had a dad when I was growing up. (I just got back from a gig in California, and seeing my son run towards me was very rewarding.) My granddad used to take me out in his old 1960s Mercedes, and he'd play the same kind of music that Marc's grandfather was into. My mind was infused early on with disco and '70s pop rock (KC and The Sunshine Band, Supertramp, etc.) and then my granddad's '40s swing music. Sadly, we ended up living in what you might call a British project for about 10 years, which was very rough. It had a very large black Jamaican population, so I was then exposed to hip-hop, soul and reggae. (Believe it or not, music from the '50s and '60s is still my favorite.)

By 1984 or '85, I was ordering hip-hop records on vinyl from America. I think my exposure to so many kinds of music was very inspiring to me. I used to write poetry in school. In 1990, I saw DJ Sasha—he was so uplifting and technically amazing—the way he would mix things so fluidly, from funky house to trance. Then I'd see Carl Cox playing techno. I became a DJ in 1991 and moved to London, where I met my wife Selina, in 1995. That's when I started taking things more seriously. Before I knew it, I started playing some of the best clubs in the UK and began getting flown to Hong Kong, Ibiza and such. I just started coming up with ideas in my head for making music, and by 2000, I knew I had enough money from DJing to make the break into actually creating music. I had also been working as an art director at an advertising company, and I gave my notice.

My wife recognized a friend of hers, who was one of the judges on one of Simon Fuller's early TV projects. The lady, Nicki Chapman, was based at a London promotions company—Brilliant!PR. Brilliant! was just about to merge with Simon's world renowned company, 19 Management. When Selina called the office, the gentleman that answered the phone told her that he was looking at setting up a management company himself, one that would specifically look after dance artists. Selina and I went and met him one Sunday afternoon in Clapham, London, and he basically set up his company to look after Marc and I. That person was Alister Jamieson, and he set up a partnership with Pete Evans and Simon Fuller—and Ambush Management was born. It became the dance imprint of Native Management and 19 Management worldwide. We were extremely lucky, but it seems like it was all fate for the three of us. Al (who we love, love, love) still manages us 15 years later!

It was a big turning point. Now that I had a manager, I decided to get myself a keyboardist so that I could express my ides quickly on a daily basis. I met Marc, we hit it off, and we began unleashing our ideas. Within a year, we were offered a publishing deal with Simon Fuller, and before we knew it, we were songwriting with loads of pop acts. That began a huge list of productions Marc and I were a part of. Marc's got that list on our Bimbo Jones HQ hard drive.

Marc: Yeah, let's have a look at it. [*He calls the data up on his computer.*] The remix folder—we're on 1,789 songs remixed by Bimbo Jones. Bimbo Jones original dance songs—390. Bimbo Jones non-dance songs—157. There's a list somewhere in here of all the artists we've worked with, too. It's all about synchronicity for us—things coming together perfectly for us because we leave ourselves open to it.

We didn't just suddenly come on to the scene. It was a real struggle and took a lot of thought as to how to do it. Today, with all the social media platforms, there's a greater chance to be seen and heard. But back in the late '90s and early 2000s, when we wanted to be noticed, it was a different affair.

We invested our life savings, literally thousands of pounds, into pressing vinyl of our tracks. Al would go to Miami for the Winter Music Conference, and we would go around to all the London record shops. Lee knew these people. We would let them have our records (and keep the money they made selling them) if they put them in the best store position. We weren't really interested in money—it was all marketing for us. After a while, the record labels started recognizing our name "Bimbo Jones." We had our first number one on the UK dance chart with Kym Marsh's "Come on Over" in 2003. That was a good mix.

We then had a string of number ones. We got a great assignment to remix Rachel Stevens' "Sweet Dreams My L.A. Ex." We remixed it, and it became a top hit in the UK and the U.S. I'd have to say, technically, that was the record that really broke us. It opened the door for us in the U.S.—we started getting phone calls, and we were brokering deals everywhere. Before we knew it, we were doing four or five remixes a week at excellent fees.

By the way, how did you arrive at the name Bimbo Jones?

Marc: We were at my mum's house—she was very kindly hosting my studio. It's a real pain in the ass to have two lads there and thumping grooves going—*um-chica-um-chica-boom-chica-um*—for hours and hours. It was lunch time, and we were watching an old black and white movie on TV. We thought we heard some character in the movie say the name Bimbo Jones. We weren't really sure we heard it right. I suggested Bimbo Jim, but Lee liked Bimbo Jones better. So we went with that.

Lee: Loads of people said that was a stupid name.

Not so stupid. In fact, it's extremely distinctive. Let's look at your process. So, when you guys decide to create a dance mix, what elements of the original song need to jump out at you?

Marc: I'm just going to digress slightly before I give you that answer, because it ties in. I'm picking up from the point where I met Lee and I was bashing my head in trying to get my music heard. I had the studio know-how and Lee was actively DJing—I'm talking amazing DJing. I loved listening to him. He was playing The Cross in London, a magical club.

Lee: It was the best club!

Marc: Going from being shrugged off by A&R people at the labels, we figured we could play our tracks out live at the club. I would be near the main floor, literally with a clipboard, watching the audience's reaction to our songs. The way the sound changes from the studio to the dancefloor is absolutely phenomenal. In the studio, you can hear every detail. In a night club, you can hear the kick, maybe one synth, and a vocal that sounds like "oh-oh-oh-oh." That's it. There's so much noise and screaming in a club, you can't really hear any other details in a song. That's when I realized all this extra stuff we were putting in our tracks had to be stripped out. Our sound didn't just happen—it was born on the dancefloor after lots and lots of testing. So you have the drums—amazing! Then the bass comes in—this is just sublime! Then a piano or synth or vocal comes in. It builds on simple foundations, but every part is so good on its own. Together, they create this monster sound. The less you've got, the bigger the sound is.

So, we get a remix gig and the parts come in—like a vocal a cappella on an MP3 today or, back in the day, attached to a hard drive in a briefcase handcuffed to a security guard. In the old days, these parts were worth so much money because if they leaked out, it was over—all the marketing, everything. Anyway, the first things we listen to are the vocal and the speed because that has a massive bearing on how the track will pan out. In the early 2000s, we were creating hard house and trance—136 beats per minute. These days, it's down to 120 or 125. That's where most of our remixes are now.

Do you ever disagree about how to approach a song?

Lee: Yeah, we do. But it's never anything serious. Over the years we've come to know each other so well and can operate trans–Atlantic. I might tell Marc what I'm loving about the clubs these days and another day Marc might have a different idea.

Marc: Lee and I are highly synchronized. If you took a picture of us any given day, there is a high probability that we are wearing the same color t-shirt. We are very linked together. I knew when he was going to move to Denver there would be no problem.

You seem very enthusiastic yet still humble about your accomplishments, but I imagine it must feel very empowering to help artists gain traction in their careers with your mixes. You've worked with so many of the greats.

Lee: A lot of people don't realize that over the years we've actually broken a lot of artists into the pop market. The labels would approach us and ask for a remix for one of their up-and-coming artists. Many times, a radio station, like KISS-FM in London, would only play a song if it was a Bimbo Jones remix. Over the years, we were able to help launch several artists.

Marc: The essence of what we do—we're so joyful when we make music. We're so full of passion for what we're doing that we enjoy the process tremendously, whether we are remixing or producing our own songs. The club atmosphere is completely dependent upon the music—that's what drives it. I think one of the reasons Bimbo Jones has been successful over such a long term is that our music creates such an uplifting atmosphere. It really affects people, and they love it.

Lee: We've had some incredible opportunities to work with amazing people like Rihanna, Madonna and Lady Gaga. We also managed to get in contact with Cyndi Lauper because we wanted to do a mix of her '80s hit "Girls Just Want to Have Fun." I had a gig at Sydney Mardi Gras and kindly asked Cyndi for the parts so I could play a new Bimbo Jones update of the song. She sent us every single part of the song, including her dialogue on the track. We've also worked with the vocals of Candi Staton, Earth, Wind & Fire and so many others.

I also was invited to Cyndi's hotel in Beverly Hills, where we discussed music and new projects for over four hours. After this meeting, Cyndi then decided to fly to our London headquarters to work on some initial ideas for the *Kinky Boots* [Tony-winning Broadway show] project! We also wrote together a hot new dance track called "It's True" (Bimbo Jones and Cyndi Lauper).

Did you know we were also approached by MGM Studios to work on the 2009 movie version of *Fame*? We did a version of the theme song—it was like Bimbo Jones meets quirky, electric Deadmau5. It worked so well, and it's a great story—we need to write a book one of these days ourselves. We have so much we could talk about! [*Lee's wife Selina calls out in the background.*] My wife says we should let *you* go on asking the questions! [*The gentlemen laugh.*]

Okay, then onward! Do you ever get intimidated by a well-known artist's legacy in dance music and the pressure that whatever you produce for them has to move that star forward?

Lee: I always pay respect to whoever they are. But I have had instances where you must also respectfully assert your ideas. For example, I had to go to Cyndi Lauper's hotel room and say that one [of the songs we were working on together] was amazing and that we had some inspiration for this *other* element that could take it to the next level. You have to have the balls to say that, to be honest and not be intimidated. I love the histories and heritage of some of these artists—definitely. And we are there to work with them to bring out their best—and in turn they bring out the best in us.

Marc: I think it's become a very level playing field between us and the artists we work with. They come to us because we have something to offer, and we want to work with them because they have something to offer. It's always a win-win. But that's not to say I'm not thrilled by what they've already done.

Cyndi was incredible—she's one of the geniuses walking the planet today. We worked with her on a main track for the musical *Kinky Boots*. It didn't get used in the end, but it almost made it. I remember we were in the studio writing lyrics with her, and she suddenly said, "Guys, stop! Stop! Sit down. I'm going to give you a master lesson in writing lyrics." She took us right back to the basics. She is formidable with her knowledge and so generous with sharing it with fellow musicians. I would say she is one of the few artists I've worked with where I felt that formidable sense—but *not* intimidation. I felt her *genius*!

Cyndi Lauper is the type of vocalist and artist that audiences still eagerly buy into and follow. But in today's dance music culture, other singers have lost some of that ground, standing in the shadow of many DJs and producers. What's behind that shift?

Marc: I think it goes way back even before this example, but look at Black Box's songs—they were sampling Loleatta Holloway and showing a performer in a video who wasn't the real singer (they were showing Katrin Quino). The world has been smoke and mirrors for a long time, and what is happening now is another form of that. I really don't like it—I think it's super disrespectful. When a DJ/producer collaborates with a vocalist, they sometimes end up putting it out under just their name. I actually think this is insulting. So many artists in music today have this unsung team behind them—ghost writers—the people truly responsible for the samples they borrow and such. I think you have to give credit where it's due. But it's the nature of the world today. It's more about brand than appreciation of an artist. I've put a lot of artists up there, and then discovered they weren't the people really responsible for the passionate and ground-breaking music that I loved.

Lee: The tracks Marc is talking about—it's not always just a little funky guitar hook that's borrowed, it's a major chorus or something. I don't know why it has shifted the way it has. I was on a music panel with a real genius, Grandmaster Flash, not long ago. He was an amazing pioneer among DJs, and I imagine it's built up from his day. Now I see Guetta and Tiësto on marquees in Las Vegas. But like Marc, I still tip my hat to the artists.

You're both DJing at today's top venues, and you're in the position of taking the spotlight as on-stage performers yourselves. Does that come as naturally as your talents in the studio?

Lee: Personally, I love it! I have been very blessed over the years to have DJed all over the world—from Australia, New Zealand, South Africa, Hong Kong and the U.S.A to all over Europe. You just reminded me of something—another fun fact. I think our very first performance was at the Glastonbury Festival in England in 2005. Most people start off in a small venue, but ours was this huge gig. There were 150,000 people there over four days. We saw where we were going to perform and thought it was all amazing. At 6 AM, however, the heavens opened up and our tent was struck by lightning. It actually burned down. All this trash started floating by.

Marc: I've been on stage performing since I was 15. I was at a boys' boarding school in the UK, a bit like Hogwarts—very strict teachers, too. I was part of a thrash-funk metal band called Vivid and got a gig on a school night. I put on my stage clothes, escaped by the window of the school, got picked up and did the gig in front of 300 people (all smashed out of their brains), came back, crawled through the window and got the telling off in the morning. Back then, I was petrified to perform. But after doing so many gigs over the years (and since 2000, DJ gigs inspired by Lee), I now *love* being on stage. I remember being at Voodoo Lounge while Lee played and saw everyone feeding off the energy of the DJ. So now, when I'm playing, I feel this magical feedback!

Lee: I agree. I have to pinch myself that I have shared a stage with Carl Cox, Kylie, George Michael, Adam Lambert and so many others. To be in front of that crowd and to get the people going is amazing.

Tell me about a remix project that you've worked on that really stands out for you.

Marc: My two favorites, still, are P!nk's "Sober" (2008) and a record by Systematik in the early 2000s called "I Want to Know What Love Is," a remake of the Foreigner classic.

With Systematik, I remember we thought, "How on earth are we going to do this? This could kill our careers." You have to level everything with being cool and underground, but you want to be commercial and accessible as well. So, we got the a cappella and put it over this killer, funky track—it all came together. The whole process to get there, though, was really time-consuming, and we made loads of mistakes until we found something that worked in the limited palate we had. Back then, you had to work so hard to make these tracks work around all the technical inadequacies you were dealing with. But that particular remix, coming from a really challenging concept, came out brilliant. It has the most wonderful bass line and guitar. I could dance to it day and night.

Lee: I'm looking at Wikipedia as we're talking and the list of songs we are credited with remixing. You really do forget a lot of them, and they all have a story connected to them.

Marc: I know people are probably most interested in the biggest name artists, like Lady Gaga. Her record company loved us, and we always ended up on her CD singles. Between Gaga, Britney, P!nk, all these big artists—I realize we've done practically everything that has moved through the global hit charts. We probably had more remixes pressed at that time than anybody else. Lady Gaga is more accessible to a gay crowd in a gay club, and the reason her label loved us was because those DJs actually favored and played the Bimbo Jones mixes. It's just my hypothesis—but maybe we helped to some degree with breaking her into the gay market worldwide.

Lee: I actually went on eBay and bought [a special 12-inch picture disc of Lady Gaga's Alejandro]. I'm really honored that we are connected with her. Sometimes our remixes aren't used by some artists. That may be because a band simply hates remixes or some such reason. I should point out that sometimes a remix may be on YouTube, and the fans say they think it's better than the original. The artists don't always like that.

Another favorite remix of mine is "First Time" by Sunblock (featuring Robin Beck) in 2006. That was an amazing project. There's so many we love—Pixie Lott, Natasha Bedingfield, Miley Cyrus. Obviously, some songs are a bit more cheesy than the others, but we are still very proud of our work. We also did an unofficial remix of Coldplay's "God Put a Smile on My Face"—it has drums very similar to the intro drums on Rachel Stevens' "Sweet Dreams." We didn't have the parts to Coldplay's songs, but it's still one of our very favorite remixes.

Lee, I wanted to mention your recent success apart from Bimbo Jones with your smash on the *Billboard* dance chart during the summer of 2016, "Drink the Night Away," featuring Bex. When is it the right time to work separately from each other?

Lee: We've been together for so many years, we thought we would explore doing our own little bits and projects as well. Bimbo is the main hub, but we're very comfortable doing things on our own, when the time just feels right. Lee Dagger featuring Bex/ "Drink the Night Away" got to number seven in the *Billboard* Dance Chart, which isn't bad considering I only just moved here to the U.S.A.

For those that don't know, I bagged my first *Billboard* number one under Lee Dagger featuring Inaya Day back in the fall of 2014. The track was called "Shelter Me." I have a whole plethora of other songs that I have written over the years with the likes of MC Lyte, Leo Sayer, Djs From Mars & Bam from the Jungle Brothers, Crystal Waters, Chris Cox, Jade Starling and more—and I'd love to see them get released.

Gentlemen, how are you coping with the changes in how dance music is monetized today? Can artists continue to create music when it appears to be so undervalued?

Marc: From the first days of Napster, we have a whole generation worldwide that expects music to be free. Back in the '80s, I think the average person's expenditure on CDs was about $60 a month. That was money that the record industry got to live off very nicely. Despite the change, I think the outlook for the music industry is very positive. You can't exclude anyone who can't afford to pay $60 a month from listening to music. We have to bring the new generation slowly into the new monetization and collection systems. Maybe this sounds a bit technical for a Bimbo Jones interview, but my prediction—and my predictions are always right [*he laughs*]—is the music industry is going to be just fine.

It's just like when Lee and I were getting into remixing—many people were getting out of it. Before we came on the scene, they might pay as much as a quarter of a million dollars for a remix. As soon as they dropped the payments (and Lee and I didn't mind; we were getting paid well with the number we were doing), everyone started moving into real estate. A message to anyone reading this book who is an aspiring music producer/DJ/artist—if the music industry looks bleak and there doesn't seem to be much money around, this is your chance to get in front of the cue when it all kicks off again. And it will, but it will take time.

Thank goodness the passion of artists is so strong it keeps the whole scene alive. Frankly, with the limited amount of money in the record industry now, the labels have no proper funds to pay for remixes. Many remixers are doing it for free to get DJ gigs. DJs are playing for free to gain a following and get more remix opportunities. So, the whole thing has gone up its own behind. It's only through the love, dedication and passion of the artists that dance music stays alive.

It's interesting to me that this new generation seems to expect [artists] to give up their lives to be creative and yet make no money from it. It's interesting that they place no monetary value on what these people do for them.

Music is so special—sorry, Lee, I'll be over with this rant in a second.

Music enables you to be present with your life and connect to something deeper, to feel things, to remember emotions and feel the passion coursing through your body as the textures of a song evolve. That's what it gives you! People need to re-evaluate what the exchange of energy should be with music, with everything. You have to give to get. They are just getting, without giving anything back. The industry is limping on—but, again, I say it's because of the beautiful artists that just won't give up.

Lee: We've learned to carry on, as Marc says. You have to stand tall and plow on. As long as we're making good product, making people dance and connecting with our fans, that's always going to be our main focus. I believe if you create a solid fan base, the people will follow you and support you.

Marc: We're not lying down like old dogs—we're turning it up, baby!

Lightning Round with Bimbo Jones

Have you ever worked for hours and days on a track and accidentally lost everything?
Marc: No, never! Every five minutes, we save off. Nothing is lost; everything is archived.

Your favorite dance track of all-time (with which you were not involved)?
Marc: Junior Jack's "Thrill Me."
Lee: Oh God, there's too many, but you've put me on the spot. I love emotional tracks like "The Age of Love" by The Age of Love (Sasha's mix). But I have just too many favorites to pick one. I also love piano house anthems such as Bizarre Inc's "Playing with Knives."

Craziest thing you ever saw take place on a dancefloor?
Marc: A girl slipped over and whacked her head on the edge of the stage. I thought for sure she had killed herself. Literally, she just got up and kept dancing like it never happened. Oh—that happened to me, too. I was at a Tommy Boy Records party in Miami, and it had been raining. I was talking to Tom Silverman, the founder of Tommy Boy, I slipped backwards and landed on a pool table filled with water, my back and trousers were soaking!
Lee: I've seen sex and marriages take place. I don't know. I did a gig in the Hamptons and everyone thought my wife Selina was Lindsay Lohan at the time. I remember being at Mardi Gras [the gay pride celebration in Sydney, Australia], and two gay men were walking towards me (I was with the singer Leo Sayer). I didn't want to break them up and said, "I don't wanna break the love!" I sang it to Leo, and Leo suddenly started singing it back to me in full voice—"Don't wanna break up your love…"

Coolest celebrity party you ever attended?
Lee: In 2010, we worked on an album (which won a Latin Grammy) for Sergio Mendes, *Bom Tempo Brasil* and also *Bom Tempo Brasil (Remixed)*, featuring the single "The Real Thing." We had suggested Sergio record the remix album. He was such a gentleman. He introduced us to everyone, took us to his jacuzzi, then to a restaurant for an amazing dinner, then a sound check at the Hollywood Bowl, and then sat us next to Burt Bacharach's people. Two guys from London, getting all this star treatment!
Marc: After his show, we went back to his house, drinking beautiful wine from the Napa Valley, discussing Bossa Nova music and Tom Jobim. Oh my goodness, what a dream! And then, at the end, he takes us and just a handful of people to his piano room. His beautiful wife, Gracinha, joins us as he sits at the piano. He gave us a private performance. This is just one moment in my life that was like an out-of-the-body experience. So much emotion—unbelievable.

Worst job you ever had before becoming famous?
Lee: Working in retail for Donna Karan. [*"That was the worst?" chimes in Selina.*] Yeah, it was the worst because of the awful money it paid. But I did get to meet interesting people

The prolific team of Lee Dagger (left) and Marc JB (right), aka Bimbo Jones, have shared their remix and production talents with The Killers, Lady Gaga, Rihanna, Kylie, Melanie Amaro, Rita Ora, Tom Jones and Annie Lennox to name but a few.

such as Michael Hutchence, Steve Martin, etc. Previous to that, in the town of my birth—Bath, UK—I used to work at a family-run burger bar called Schwartz Bros. This was when I was 18. It was horrible scrubbing down the grill, but we played a lot of our music cassettes while we worked. We'd change our clothes afterward—still stinking from work—and go to raves in the middle of Oxford, where everybody was equal and loved to dance. No VIP nonsense back in those days.

Marc: For me, it was being a cocktail pianist in the hotel bars, constantly having cigar smoke blown in my face.

Mind you, there was a really nice one—The Milestone Hotel—and I was playing in a small room there. There was a big commotion outside, and in walks Shania Twain with her entourage. She had just finished playing the O2 in South-East London. She sat down, but her people kept bothering her, so she shooed them away. She just chilled out and relaxed, listening to my piano-playing for an hour and a half. Then she just said thank you and walked out.

Ferry Corsten
(DJ, producer, remixer)
"Barber's Adagio for Strings"
(Ferry Corsten Remix)—William Orbit (1999/2000)

"It's interesting to see how things have evolved, and I can't help but think now that knowing less is somehow better."—Ferry Corsten

The trance-fused hit dance tracks of Moonman, System F and Gouryella, released in the late '90s and throughout the 2000s, share one thing in common—the progressive, creative vision of Dutch producer and DJ Ferry Corsten. His early worldwide smash "Out of the Blue" (1998), under his System F moniker, was a Top 20 hit in the UK and a major influential track of this transitional time, but he has since broadened the scope of his art to include other forms of electronic dance music, including progressive house. He's had numerous awards bestowed upon him over the past 17 years and was nominated twice by the International Dance Music Awards in 2016 for Best Trance DJ and Best Trance Track (Gouryella—"Anahera"). Ferry has remixed tracks for many top pop artists, including U2 ("New Year's Day"), The Killers ("Human"), Tiësto ("Kaleidoscope") and Miguel Bosé ("Eso No").

Ferry is a star DJ by every measure, who has performed with the biggest names in the business, from Alesso to Markus Schulz, and he continues to play at major events and venues across the globe, including Tomorrowland and Madison Square Garden. Corsten's drive to move forward continues to make him one of dance music's most exciting artisans, and his knack for tapping into the emotional power of the genre seems virtually limitless.

Tell me how you discovered your passion for music when you were growing up?

As a young kid, I was always interested in music. There were some kids on the

"My goal is also to have the listener identify the remix as a work by Ferry Corsten. It needs to have my fingerprint on it, for sure," says the producer/DJ, who launched his career with the single "Out of the Blue" by System F in 1998.

street I lived on that told me about this radio show I should listen to—it was called *The Soul Show*. I am sure other Dutch DJs will reference that show, as well. It was very influential for my generation. It was the mid-'80s, and they featured all the latest music being played in the discos. I was about 10 or 12 years old. This music sounded very different from the usual Top 40 stuff, and the cool thing about it was a feature where they'd broadcast mixes that people sent in. The challenge was to get as many records as possible in that mix in 15 minutes. I thought, wow, that was so cool. I realized I needed two turntables, a mixer and a recorder. I saved up for them, and, through trial and error, I learned how to do it.

Fast-forward a few years later, in my first days of clubbing, I met these guys who had a small studio. That led me to a shift from putting mixes together to actually creating my own music. In a nutshell, that's how it all started. Music was so important to me early on—while my friends were out playing soccer, I was mixing and creating new sounds.

What was the appeal of dance music for you?

Just before my days of clubbing, somehow I got a tape from someone that had some of the first acid house mixes on it. For me, it was an "oh my God" moment. As I started hitting the clubs, I began hearing tracks like 808 State's "Cubik" and all these really noisy records—all when hip-house began shifting to more pure dance stuff over here (but it was all called "house music"). It was so new, there weren't a lot of sub-genres yet. I don't know—it was all just very inspiring to me. Everyone was doing new and different things, especially compared to today.

How did your professional career evolve from this?

It began as a hobby, but I just started making some music with the gentlemen that owned the studio. I was able to bring the stuff that we were making to A&R managers from record labels, who were also my contacts at the record stores. After dealing with a few "no" responses, we finally got a "yes!" Whatever money I got, I put it back into buying new equipment and saving for my own studio. Eventually, I started to understand what type of sound the labels were looking for. I was still in school, but I started releasing my music left and right, and earning a decent salary from it.

In 1996, I made a track under the name Moonman called "Don't Be Afraid," which was, for my repertoire, one of the very first records we'd call "trance" nowadays—a big synth melody. Because of that track, which entered the Top 40 here in Holland, I was able to get some remix jobs. It was my first modest success.

The real breakthrough, a track which I still play today and which was a hit all over the world, was called "Out of the Blue," released in the end of 1998.

"Out of the Blue," which came out under the moniker System F and was a massive instrumental dancefloor hit and Top 20 track in the UK by 1999, was an extremely exciting sonic adventure. It was a trend-setter in many ways for the new century. Would you tell me about the origins of this composition?

In Europe, we had gone through this very influential period of Italo-dance or Italo-disco—very synthesizer-based music. I guess I was influenced by that four-to-the-floor sound, and sounds of the '80s in general. So if you listen to this song, it has this synth-melody and a big snare drum sound that is reminiscent of Italo. I'll also admit that just having new equipment, especially in the late '90s, worked really well for getting inspiration.

I was one of the first people here in Holland to have the Roland JP-8000 modeling synthesizer—it was one of the first to have that super-saw-sound in it. I'd joke that it sounded like a beehive in a way.

Yeah, when you have a melody that meets the right pre-set, the right synth, it can *really* be amazing. That became the sound of System F.

Having had this enormously popular and commercially successful track under your belt, how much pressure were you under to keep reproducing that sound?

In general, your fans tend to want to keep you where they discovered you. Record labels want to keep you with the type of song or sound that makes them money. On the other hand, I've seen artists follow up a hit with another song that sounded exactly the same, maybe a two-note difference, and it's a complete flop.

In the case of "Out of the Blue," the follow-up single was a vocal track called "Cry." It has a bit of a trance sound, but it was way more in the piano-house vein. It really didn't have nearly as much of that stadium sound as the previous hit. The label was very reluctant to release it as a follow-up, but we pressured them. Luckily, it scored pretty well—the UK Top 40 as I remember.

I have always said that doing more of the same is an easy way out—the same old thing with a different melody. I think for longevity, it's important to show the world what you are capable of, what you can do. It's not like Madonna released 50 songs that sounded like "Vogue." Every song was different. Fortunately for me, I was producing music under a variety of names besides System F, so I had my other avenues to create music in different styles.

For example, my decision to step back into the studio under my Gouryella guise was something I felt a lot of pressure about. I know what those old records mean to people, myself included, so I needed it to be 100 percent authentic. It had to have that feel and energy that only a Gouryella record does. That journey from "Anahera" to the most recent single "Neba" was a long road, and it's fair to say that I'd built my own sense of pressure on what was needed to be done.

So the pressure is there in dance music—I guess it's all about how sensitive you are to that pressure. In this business, you have to weigh your options.

How has your production method evolved since those early days?

In those days, I had no clue what I was doing. I just did what I thought was right. I didn't know how to mix very well—I just knew what felt right and good to me. I could feel that rush, the excitement, when it all fell into place. Back in those days, hardware was very expensive, and I made the most out of what I had.

Fast-forward to today, I am infinitely more knowledgeable about music and mixing—how to make a song sound open and how to let it breathe, yet keep it exciting. But I'll be honest with you—there are times when I wish I could turn it all off and go back to my first days. In those first days, I was so limited in what I could do—it was all in the momentum. You created, arranged and were *feeling* those tracks—mixing took 15 minutes, putting it on the table and leveling it, and that's it.

Today, the options are endless. You have to be so much more decisive now about when enough is enough—deciding the track is good as it is. With all the plug-ins and software out there now, you could keep tweaking a track for months and months, maybe years. You have to know when to stop. And yet, while I am continually evolving my sound and techniques, I still believe in that same sentiment that can be found in my older records, which definitely continues to play a pivotal part in my music today.

It's interesting to see how things have evolved, and I can't help but think now that knowing less is somehow better.

Would you say that all the sub-genres in dance music today are legitimate—in that they represent solid new creative tangents?

Well, if you look at all the genres in electronic music now, they are not so much music-driven as they are technology-driven. Dub-step and all that. You don't make the best dub-step track if you just come up with a great melody. It's all about the weird effects and the crazy stuff going on with the beats and bass. It's not really about melody or music—these sub-genres are often more about the freaky sounds you can create. That's how a lot of audiences are wowed today. Technology has brought about a lot of new styles of music, but it's also brought a lot of limitations, in a way.

Let's talk about your remix process when you are working with other artists. What elements have to be present in a song for you to be intrigued about the prospect of remixing it?

When I hear the word "remixing," I really think of the traditional way. I always try to imagine receiving a 24-track tape and re-editing the original. Of course, that's not what an artist wants today. They want your involvement as a producer—to pour your sauce over it, if you know what I mean. I always want to take elements from the original track and basically stick to the original as much as possible. My goal, though, is to make it *better* than the original. I know many remixes don't sound anything remotely close to the original, but I always strive to keep that original integrity.

My goal is also to have the listener identify the remix as a work by Ferry Corsten. It needs to have my fingerprint on it, for sure.

Would you give me an example of a track that you feel best represents your personal goals when it comes to dance music?

I'd say a great example was William Orbit's "Barber's Adagio for Strings." I was invited to pick a track to remix from the album he had done, and I selected that piece. I remixed it in an "Out of the Blue" style. Funnily enough, I restored a lot of the strings [Orbit] had taken out. Another one was a remix I did a few years ago for U2 of "New Year's Day." It was the full song, but instead of utilizing rock guitars and drums, it's electronic stuff. But it's still very close to the original.

When you work with such high profile artists as William Orbit, Public Enemy and many others, do you feel a sense of pressure to live up to his or her reputation when creating a remix?

Yes, in a way. It may be an artist I've grown up with or looked up to for years. You definitely start working on a remix like that with shaky hands. There is some pressure. But then you switch off those emotions and think for a minute—why did they come to you? They want your sound! So you do the best you can. It's a natural response to be nervous, but you think about the job at hand, and you bring them the sound they want.

Is it a different experience to collaborate with another DJ in the creation of a track?

Well, everyone has their own way of working. When I worked with Armin van Buuren, he had his own interpretation—it was very different from my own. Yet the combination of our two views coming together in one track, such as "Exhale" (2001), is what makes it so interesting and so cool.

I collaborate a lot with Markus Schulz, and he definitely has his own ideas about music and how it should sound and, in his eyes, how the crowd will react to certain things. I do, too. But when you collaborate, you must be very open-minded. When you do tracks like these, that's exactly what you want to happen—to have two worlds come together. It won't work—how can I say this—if you're stubborn and you don't want to let the opinion of the other artist into the mix. What would be the point of getting together?

My most recent collaboration (Event Horizon) was one with the German producer duo Cosmic Gate. The three of us have known each other for many years and have spoken countless times about doing a record together, but for one reason or another have never managed to get around to it. When we finally did, it had been such a long time in the planning it just felt natural. We know each other's styles and sound very well, so it kind of swiftly glides you through the first pace of the creation process with some ease.

Is there a great deal of competition between DJs when they aren't collaborating?

There's *always* competition. Everybody is looking for the attention. But you must accept that and realize it just keeps you sharp and moving forward. It makes you push the envelope, I guess. I view it as a good thing. I think you feel it a lot more if you haven't sufficiently created your own identity and style—if you're just copying others or cashing in on what's happening right now. If you're that type of DJ, I don't think you'll ever really get anywhere.

In your opinion, when did the DJ really become the focal point of dance music, as opposed to the vocalist, for example. Why did that shift occur?

Wow, that's a great question. I can only speak for myself, but when, for example, I started playing in the UK, with my initial success there, I noticed everyone wanted to watch the DJ. It's almost like you were the maestro conducting an orchestra—when I raised my hands, so did the audience. It was kind of weird. I think it's just grown from there, especially as the DJ became more of a producer. The DJ ended up becoming the pop star. Also, I think the shift—and I say this respectfully—from DJs who just played music to DJs who became creators of music changed the audience's perception of who they were and their [prestige] increased.

What's your measure for success—what lets you know you've accomplished what you set out to do with your music?

That's such a hard question to answer. Radio, sales—that's what everybody wants. I also look at *why* I made the track. Was it for radio? Or was there a more artistic purpose? If I'm able to get on radio with something I intended as an artistic creation, well, that means the track will reach so many more people. I've tried to focus on radio success at some points in my life, but it doesn't really satisfy me—not really. I don't know—when I get messages on social media from people saying a track I made changed their life, I think I feel like that's it. Radio success will come when a track surfaces, but feedback like that has more impact with me.

I'm also very intrigued by the way music is consumed today. Streaming is such the dominate force with releases nowadays. Watching a record I've made, say "Hyper Love" (which to date has had over eight million Spotify plays, or "Heart's Beating Faster" which has had three million-plus plays on Spotify) pick up a more organically grown amount of support definitely gives you a sense of accomplishment.

I think of the frenzy of enthusiasm that existed among your fans for your long-awaited Gouryella release 'Anahera' and I wonder—how does it feel as an artist to simply see a huge crowd going crazy over one of your tracks?

Yeah, well, that's amazing! Especially when it's with a record like "Anahera." I'd spent a good few years feeling I had another Gouryella single in me just waiting to come out. So when you go through that whole process of getting into the studio, putting down that first note all the way to playing the track in front of thousands of people, it's a really emotional journey you have with the record. Then you see the crowd losing it. I have to pinch myself. It's an incredible feeling.

Lightning Round with Ferry

A dance track you are hot on right at this moment?

Alex Di Stefano—"From Heaven to Inferno" (Original Mix)

Worst experience you ever had in a night club?

Having a huge crowd chanting and having an amazing time, only to press the stop button by mistake. I felt like the biggest idiot.

Favorite form of social media?

I'm actually not a major poster on social media. I'm pretty private about my social life, but out of all the social media, I do like Instagram the most. Every once in a while I do like sharing with people what I enjoy doing and what I'm really awed by.

What personality trait do you have that would probably surprise most people?

As everyone knows, I produce my own music and can spend hours in the studio mulling over various sounds and beats. There's a Dutch saying—"mierenneuker"—which, when loosely translated means, ant fucker. [*Ferry laughs.*] But seriously, it means nitpicker—and I guess that is what I am.

Ferry Corsten has produced and remixed for Justin Bieber, Moby, Faithless, The Killers, William Orbit, Duran Duran and many other top artists. In 2017 he released his hit single "Live Forever," featuring Aruna.

Single biggest advantage of being a dance music star?
   Being praised by lots of people—hey, I can admit it. That always feels good!

If you weren't a DJ/producer, what would you be?
   I started producing at a young age, and my parents were always very supportive but told me that I should at least get a degree if all should fail. So, I would have been an engineer if I had not been a DJ/producer.

Chris Cox

(DJ, producer, remixer)

Kelly Osbourne—"One Word"
(Chris Cox Club Mix) (2005)

"I heard my mix played at these massive parties in Ibiza, and British DJs who would never touch my pop stuff were playing it. I had one of that summer's biggest records, and it really just came from me playing around in the studio with a bass line on my Juno 106 synth."—Chris Cox

Chris Cox, a native of Nevada, has lent his remixing and production skills to well over 600 dance music records, and that number just continues to grow. He rose to fame as one half of the production duo Thunderpuss beginning in the late '90s and through a series of solo endeavors that got the attention of clubs and radio. Cox earned a Grammy nomination in 2004 for Cher's "Love One Another" and has worked with some of the biggest legends of the genre, including Donna Summer, Britney Spears, Jennifer Lopez, Janet Jackson, Whitney Houston, Christina Aguilera, Michael Jackson, Katy Perry and Rihanna.

Cox's infectious mixes incorporate a wide range of irresistible elements and styles, including disco, house and tribal beats. Among his most prolific endeavors have been Enrique Iglesias' "Be with You" and "Hero," Madonna's "Die Another Day," Britney Spears' "Don't Let Me Be the Last to Know" and "I'm a Slave 4 U," and Kelly Osbourne's "One Word." He has amassed over 50 number one Billboard *dance and club chart hits and produced the number one dance/electronic album* Hannah Montana 2 Non-Stop Dance Party *in 2008. He's also a world-class DJ who has headlined parties and festivals in Paris, Rio de Janeiro, New York, Las Vegas, London and Montreal.*

Chris Cox is a two-time IDMA Award winner in 2000 and 2002 for "Remixer of the Year."

Chris, please tell me about your early days, growing up and how you came to connect with dance music.

My connection started pretty much by playing in a band in high school (sax, guitar and percussion mainly) and actively buying music in a small town setting. When I saw *Saturday Night Fever*, it completely changed my structure of reality. It seemed so exciting—the lights, the loud music and the beat. So anytime there was a school dance, I was the first one there, and the last to leave. I listened to a lot of old disco. Music became a driving force in my life, whether playing it for friends or listening to it on the radio.

I got several college music scholarships, and I ended up attending in Las Vegas because, at the time, they had an excellent internship program. I ended up getting a full scholarship for playing sax. As I was studying, I started DJing for a mobile music company—conventions, weddings and all that stuff. At the same time, I started being a radio announcer on the University of Las Vegas' radio station KUNV, initially beginning on the jazz programming side. I moved very quickly from jazz to the alternative programming, mainly because that's where all the action was—way cooler parties, and the music was fun! I started getting into the '80s British music sound and new wave. So, I was studying music in the daytime, and at night I was playing more and more parties. Eventually, I DJed a few KUNV nights at a massive Las Vegas club. The nightclub owner really liked the way I DJed and offered me a spot to fill in for the resident DJ for two weeks. Well, they ended up telling that DJ not to come back from his vacation, and I had my first regular club gig.

Everything changed from that point. It was during that year that I *really* started getting into mixing. I joined a record pool, and I started getting these great promo vinyl releases—great stuff coming out of New York. I was completely enamored by New York City. I was a "credit reader" of vinyl for as long as I can remember, and I became more and more aware of re-edits and remixes for the clubs and who was doing them.

Who were some of the key remixers of that period to whom you were drawn?

Well, Shep Pettibone was my main man—he's the reason I am remixing today. I loved what he did, the music and the artists—Madonna, Janet Jackson—the big pop artists he was handling for big dance mix productions. I was paying close attention to Clivilles and Cole (before they were C+C Music Factory), Eric Kupper, a key engineer (I knew I'd love whatever his name was attached to), David Morales, Frankie Knuckles, guys like that. From the UK, I was into Phil Harding from the PWL camp.

When did you begin your professional career as a remixer?

During college I was selected to be a member of an all-star collegiate band that got to go on a summer tour and perform throughout the UK. One night while in Edinburgh, Scotland, a group of us went to a nightclub after our show. That was the night I discovered house music. I heard this super-repetitive song come on—it was very redundant, weird and low-fi, but I went crazy over it. I asked the DJ what it was. This Scottish guy shouted over the track, "It's scous music!" I had no idea what he was trying to say, with his heavy accent. "Like where you live—in a 'ouse!" My brain finally clicked. "Oh—H-O-U-S-E music!" I asked who the artist was on this particular record, and he said it was Steve "Silk" Hurley. "Silk, like a shirt!" Turns out it was the song "Jack Your Body," and I went to the nearby Virgin record store and found it. I started buying all these records (not appreciating that they were all imports from the U.S.—I didn't realize that at the time).

So, by the time I was in my senior year at college, I was on the radio six nights a week and interning at an NBC affiliate. I had really gotten into music programming on the computer, as well. I was loving house music—the club environment—and wondered what I could do with that. That's when I thought maybe I could be a remixer, combining all the elements I was learning. I had to really work hard to learn how to do it (because nobody in Vegas knew how to do that kind of thing). I basically taught myself and crossed paths with Hot Tracks, a DJ remix service that started in the '80s in San Francisco. As a DJ, they'd give you access to records via a subscription service. They'd supply you with a compilation of key tracks on the club scene, remixed each month. By sheer luck, the owner of the company had the same last name as me and happened to be in Vegas. He was looking for a new producer to create their remixes, and my name came up (which totally stuck with him). He asked me if I could remix, and I said yes (even though I was far from an expert at this point). I basically lied my way into the job.

Suddenly, I was hired as their producer. I quickly learned how to create extended versions and do reel-to-reel re-edits. I started meeting all the promoters and record label people (all of whom were in New York). That's the long story of how I eventually got connected to the record companies and began my professional career as a producer of commercial releases.

What was your big breakthrough remix record?
Oh, yes. It was the extended mix of Paula Abdul's "Opposites Attract." That became a number one single. They sent me all these outtakes from the session, and my mix was created with just tape editing. It was on Virgin Records, and when I read my name on the label with a credit for editing, it was the most amazing thing in the world to me. I always dreamed of seeing this happen for myself. Paula had just broken out as a star, and MTV was on fire. I was still in school at this point, so for me it was just the coolest thing ever!

Chris, can you tell me a bit about your experience working during your years as one half of the Thunderpuss production team (which also featured Barry Harris), '97 through 2003?
The Thunderpuss years were certainly a crazy time. After the one-two punch of [our success remixing] Whitney's "It's Not Right, but It's OK," followed up with "Sexual" by Amber, the work phone started ringing, and didn't stop for several years. I didn't really get to feel what was going on at the time because I was working non-stop in the studio, plus Los Angeles wasn't featuring the same kind of musical style that was lighting up the east coast.

I would get reports from label people or promoters that a certain song was played at a big party or on the radio, and it was great to hear those things, but then I would return to a small, windowless room to continue programming and mixing. DJ touring started during this period as well, so it became very normal to work seven days and upwards of 90–100 hours per week. The whole period is pretty much a blur.

It really was a unique time that can't exist in today's music industry. The remix budgets were crazy, the stars were huge, the sales were at an all-time high, and the amount of projects offered was staggering.

Over the years since, you dramatically added to the roster of artists for whom you personally created remixes—name-drop a few of the most significant stars for me.
Britney Spears, Christina Aguilera, Katy Perry, Cher, Madonna, Rihanna, Gwen Stefani, Celine Dion, Enrique Iglesias—yeah, there are a few. [*Chris laughs.*]

Did you ever feel a sense of pressure that your work had to live up to the reputations and past accomplishments of these artists, who were all dance-floor icons?

You know, in the beginning—no. I don't know if it was confidence at the time. I think I just wanted to make records so badly that I didn't care what I had to do, or what might happen. If I now listen to some of the stuff I've done in the past, I think it's God-awful. But back then, I was learning as I was going along. In the beginning, I was still a fan of some of these artists, and the only time I remember feeling pressure was maybe when I was working on his or her project after they came off a really big previous hit. The label would come to me and offer me a ton of money to give them *another* big success. When I [thought about it] in those terms, I started worrying about fucking up and living up to what came before it. But if I stuck with that way of thinking, the record wouldn't come out that good.

I try now never to think of expectations. Every record I do, I listen to it later and think, "Why didn't I do it this way?" I always see improvements that could have been made. The best thing one can do is make the best possible record *at the time you're doing it*, but not for "business" purposes.

Whenever I took projects because of the paycheck or for what I thought was a good political move, it just never turned out to be as good of a record as when I'm in the studio and I simply love what's coming out of the speakers. I love it when I can't wait for somebody else to hear something I have created—like when I was a kid and I'd jump on my bike to take a 45 record over to my friend because I wanted him to hear how cool it was. Yeah, when you bring in the baggage of expectations, it's just too much pressure. Then you over analyze. Nobody knows what's going to work in a song. You can try to recreate moments of gold from the past, but that's no guarantee. You can hire all the same people that created a past hit, and some can do it again, but most of the time it's like trying to win a lottery. You just go in the studio and do the best possible work you can.

My goal is always to do my best and it be good enough to have the artist or label come back to me for another song. I'm always looking at what's next. I just want to be able to keep doing what I'm doing.

In your experience, do artists (even very hands-on individuals, like Madonna) generally let you do your thing?

Madonna definitely has a say in everything she does and has to sign off on all of it. She is very involved. The same goes for Janet Jackson and Cher. Then there are artists, at least on the remix side, who don't even know it's happening. It's all done through management or the label. When you are working in the studio with the artists directly, it becomes a much more collaborative process.

I've heard my share of stories where artists can be like task masters and things like that. But usually, the biggest stars out there use a collaborative process and realize that no one person can do it all on their own. They recognize the value of a team effort. I can tell you, for me, the only time it really can get weird is when the business people get involved and start saying things like, "We don't think this will work at Top 40 radio, and it's gotta be better." It is the music business, so you *do* have to consider the financial stuff—and the business of staying in business. But generally, when you mix those two worlds, you sometimes end up with a crappier product.

I would imagine remixing is a personal experience for you as you infuse your soul, perhaps an identifiable style and your own reputation into an artist's track. How much of a balancing act is it to inject your own creativity into a song envisioned by someone else?

I think that's the thing that's kept me employed. Because I was a musician first, I didn't stumble across my sound. I have a varied musical background, and I enjoy playing off of many styles. People have told me I have "a sound," but I don't really hear that in myself. How do I phrase this? As far as remixes go, I believe my purpose is *not* to make it all about *me*. My purpose is to serve the artist and the song so that it will be played in another market. So, if you're Rihanna and your song leans towards hip-hop, you get a remix done so that people in a dance environment will get turned on to it. I may change chord structure and take some liberties with it, but I try to retain the essence of the song. It's my interpretation, and if I'm lucky enough to be taken on their coattails a bit because I made the version that's the hit, that's not a bad outcome.

When you encounter a song that is far removed from the dancefloor and are asked to make the track work for that environment, like a melancholy ballad by Adele, for example, is the challenge greater?

The key that will make any song work on a dancefloor is whether or not it's a good song in the first place. A really good song can be translated to any style. In the late '90s and early 2000s, the biggest dance hits were remixes of big ballads. Subject matter is an interesting component. A song like Adele's "Hello," which is so melancholy—that is a good description—if you've got a dance club or fun environment in mind, it is a bit more challenging.

For that matter, I don't care for super socially conscious records either. It can be a good song, but if the lyrics are a downer—well, it can affect the energy on the dancefloor. You can do a remix, but if the lyrics are getting through, it's like, "This is a bummer!" That doesn't mean every song needs to be "dance-dance-party-party." But, in my opinion, certain thematic elements just don't work that well.

As a DJ/producer/remixer today, how do you cope with the rapid fire emergence of sub-genres and ever-changing tastes and trends?

That's a really good question. Without a doubt, it can be challenging! Let's say a new style comes along—Dubstep, TropHouse, whatever—I'll be interested in it and will dive into learning the techniques that create it. But I often wonder, if I come out with something that reflects this new sound, does it look too desperate? There are guys in the business who, whatever the style or genre that's hot, will be right on it. One way to look at that is to say it makes you relevant. The other way is to say it's a bit disingenuous. In a way, it was like back in the disco era when people like Rod Stewart and the rockers started releasing disco records. There's this weird dichotomy. You want to be marketable, and if you do the same thing all the time, people get sick of you. But if you jump too quickly to adopt the new sounds, you can lose your consistency and style. Does it then look like you're that old guy who tries to hang out at the young people's party?

I will try to use some of the modern coloring and elements and combine them with the classical aspects of a remix so that it bridges the gap with today's ears, but I have never been the one who just jumps on the newest thing. Yeah, sounds change way too fast now.

Marketing is so fast, and that sound can burn out just as fast as it came up. I've heard it happen many times—a sound comes on like gangbusters, there's one truly amazing, innovative record that's got that sound, one or two copycat records get through after, and then suddenly the flood gates open, and then everyone jumps to the next new thing.

And, yeah, the sub-genre creation process—just look at the classifications on Soundcloud. The minutia of it is insane. It's exhausting to keep up with, so you pick and choose the ones you want to invest time and interest in.

To some degree, it appears as if you've kept remixing and Djing as your top priorities, as opposed to concentrating on original productions. Why is that?

I wrestle with that issue almost every day. I initially wanted to be a rock star like everyone else. I know I need to do my own thing (in addition to working with others), but I'm not sure what my own thing exactly is just yet. It's like the impressionist comic who does a million voices, but then the public asks, "Who are you?" I've been struggling with this issue a bit.

I've completed a lot more original stuff than I've released, and I think part of that may be based simply in fear in general. But I don't know if it's what I want to do. I like working in music—the remix thing gives me a clear-cut end game. But when you become the creator of the project, what's your motivation—to express something in yourself, to get gigs or to get a message out? I get overwhelmed with those possibilities.

As we speak, I'm working on an album. I played some tracks for another producer, who thought they were great and asked what the problem was. Is it a confidence thing? Or am I more comfortable being behind the scenes, in the studio or in the DJ booth? I'm not sure. For some reason, in my brain, I think it's a huge commitment to release something of my own and say "this is my artistic statement." I wrestle with that every day.

Chris, your experience goes back to the days when vocalists were the primary focus of the dance music spotlight. As recently as 2016, you remixed "Ice," the comeback single for the heritage trio The Ritchie Family of "The Best Disco in Town" fame. Things have changed quite a bit for vocalists with the rise of the DJ/producer in the twenty-first century. What's your take on it?

Let's take disco. In most cases, you had a producer putting it all together, building this amazing arrangement and putting all the components together—and a singer who came in and did the recording in two or three takes and leaves. The person who did the heavy lifting, even back then, was the producer. That was the person with the vision. I recognize that people bought the records for the voice, talent and star quality of the singer as well, but it was the productions that built fan bases for people—like Giorgio Moroder and Quincy Jones. In dance music over the years, the truth is it wasn't usually the singer's vision that gave birth to these recordings. There was already a song written, and it needed a female (primarily) to deliver it. Over time, the recognition has now shifted to the producer. I don't think it means the death of the singer, but I have to say there's a lot of really crappy singers coming along in this century. And I should note, in a few cases, the singer has remained the star. In dance music, the DJ has moved from being like one of the guys in the band to the forefront.

As I said, I don't think it's the death of the singer, but with the way music has been marketed and sold over the past 15 years or so, the dynamic has changed. After years of selling the vision in music, it's now gotten back to selling the brand, selling the product. With that, the singer has lost his or her value. The singers who get the most attention today are the ones who have the biggest infrastructure attached to them. She or he doesn't have to be a great singer—they just have to be someone people will like and talk about. Artists are really trying to find fans that will spend their money on a live show, merchandise, movie, or whatever. Real artistry comes out, regardless, but the industry, the machine, is not in the business of selling real art.

We're talking about all these shifts that have taken place this century. In your opinion, what's the biggest change that has occurred overall in the world of music?
I'll tell you one thing that's changed, and it's quite remarkable. You can have a direct connection with an artist now. When I was growing up, buying records and going to concerts, these people were *gods*. You would see their picture on a record album jacket, and the only connection you had with them was to maybe write a letter to their fan club. You saw mainstream music press, but these stars weren't on TV all the time, and there was some mystery about these people. Generally, you'd hold their records, hear them in a club or on the radio, and see them once in a while on a music TV show or at a Grammy telecast or something.

Now, with social media, you know where they go for coffee, you see what they had for lunch, you see their tattoos, their pets, you can even see the inside of their house. We never had that access in the past. There was once a mystery, a magic about these artists. They'd release their new record, and you'd see them for a time—then they'd disappear until the next one. In the past, you may have only heard rumors about them—now you see naked pictures of them! They are no longer larger than life—they are human. Now Rihanna can say she likes a movie, and if you like it too, and you can tell her you saw it, and then she can "like" your comment—you get what I mean? That's kind of weird!

The filter has been taken away. That can be good in some ways, too. But it also makes these artists, well, not as cool—at least to me. You're not a rock star anymore—you're just eating your lunch like everybody else. The focus is so much more on that regular stuff, not the music. The music used to be the lifeline to the artist. Now it's about the social world of the artist, and the music is very, very secondary.

"You should never meet your heroes," as the saying goes.
Oh, I use that quote all the time! I've been pleasantly surprised after meeting some of my heroes, but often incredibly disappointed. And not because they did anything wrong usually. It was because of what I attached to them. You listen to a song and love it for 20 or 30 years and build this mindset up of who this person is, and then you see them snapping selfies outside The Gap—and, wow, the magic is gone!

So, you have met your heroes and had some amazing personal experiences in dance music. On a positive note, is there a highlight that stands out as the most memorable?
There are actually a lot. One was connected to the Kelly Osbourne record, "One Word," in 2005. It was one of my biggest hits as a remix, but the significance was so interesting for me. I was a massive Ozzy Osbourne fan as a kid. He was a really big guy for me growing up in a small town trailer park. Getting this one degree of separation from one of my idols was incredible. Plus, it was one of the biggest British records I was ever connected with. I heard my mix played at these massive parties in Ibiza, and British DJs who would never

touch my pop stuff were playing it. I had one of that summer's biggest records, and it really just came from me playing around in the studio with a bass line on my Juno 106 synth. It turned into a very special year for me.

I'll add another—my Whitney Houston remix, "It's Not Right but It's Okay" from 1999. That set off the next 10 years of my life. I finished the remix in November of '98 and started getting reports that it was turning into a hit by January. Nobody was playing it LA, where my studio was located, so it didn't feel real for me yet. But I kept hearing that the DJs in New York were loving it, and it was starting to move up the charts.

So my label partner and I at the time, Jeff Johnson, went to Cannes, France, for the annual MIDEM music convention. We took a side trip to Rome and were walking by rows of clothing shops on our way to visit the Vatican. I heard my Whitney mix coming out of a store, and I ran in to ask to clerk where the music was coming from. Through broken English and some rapid hand gestures I found out that she was playing the radio. This was the first time I ever heard it played in public. How cool! We go out that night and heard it again from another shop—it was wild being on the other side of the world and seeing the impact of the song beginning. For me, the track ended up having a way bigger footprint than I ever could have imagined!

I met Whitney at the after party of a VH-1 divas special she had done. We didn't have a personal connection, but she was very gracious, and I know she was well aware of the remix's success.

I'm curious—do artists generally come back to you and thank you for creating a remix that got their song noticed?

It happens from time to time, but it's funny—not a lot of artists do that. I had that experience with Christina and Enrique, but it occurred in a more general setting. But there was one time where an artist specifically reached out to me to say thank you—maybe the *only* time directly. One day, I got a phone call (on my first cell phone), and it was Donna Summer! Her husband made the call and put her on—I had never met her before, but I had just completed a production of her track "Love Is the Healer" from the 1999 album *Live & More Encore*. It ended up going to number one on the *Billboard* club chart. I pulled my car off the road to experience this incredible moment with no distractions. She told me she loved what I did for her record and the production—it was a phenomenal moment. She was all over the radio when I was a kid—a superstar. Everything about her was amazing. For her to call just to say she appreciated the work—I was floating for days.

I also got a call from Janet Jackson, but it's a rare event. Independent artists tend to do that more, and now with Twitter and such, you get more of a response from the actual artist in the form of a Tweet or a posting. But it's not like your phone rings after you do the jobs.

As great as getting a call like that is, I think the biggest acknowledgment you can get, as I mentioned earlier, is to get called back to do another project.

So much of the dance music from the '70s, '80s and '90s has stood the test of time and remains embraced by those who grew up with it, as well as by younger listeners. Will the dance music of the twenty-first century enjoy the same fate?

Because there's such a massive amount of dance music out there now, and so much compartmentalizing of everything, I think it's much harder to achieve the same groundswell and impact you had in decades past. Dance music in the past, the '70s, '80s and '90s, had that massive worldwide groundswell. Today, that kind of thing doesn't happen in the same way.

There will be songs people will remember, songs that transcend pop culture, or cultural milestones like Lady Gaga, etc. There are the dance music bombs that went off—Daft Punk in 2007, Lady Gaga in 2008, Black Eyed Peas & David Guetta in 2009—they all became mainstream. But, I think the music that stands the best chance of being remembered will be the songs that a person listened to from high school through college. It's pretty much a six to eight year window when the average person devours music passionately. After people get married and have kids, being in a club or dance environment (and music in general) may still be an occasional outlet—but the passion they had often moves to their new priorities.

Dance music in the first part of this century will be remembered by those people who experienced it during those six to eight years. Music is a time machine when you're older. Everybody, however, will be remembering different things. Dance music also found its way into so many other genres in this century. There are many songs that are going to get lost in history, but the impact of the music, the scene, the style and production *are* going to be remembered.

Lightning Round with Chris

A dance track you never get tired of hearing or playing?

I want to say two—M/A/R/R/S' "Pump Up the Volume" and Inner City's "Good Life."

Craziest thing you ever saw take place on a dancefloor?

Probably the first time I played Mardi Gras. The DJ booth was way above the floor. Over the course of those hours, I saw every type of sexual act between every type of person you can envision. Guy-guy, girl-girl, multiple guys-girl, multiple girls-guy, and I literally saw this very graphic porn flick unfold before me for something like 10 hours.

"I think it's a huge commitment to release something of my own and say 'this is my artistic statement.' I wrestle with that every day," says Chris Cox.

How important are lyrics to a dance track today?

I admit I'm not a lyrics guy and don't listen to them much. I have often said "boys like beats, girls like words." People who are more feminine seem to be drawn to lyrics, more masculine to beats. That may sound like a generalization—and it is, but that's what I've noticed.

What tests your patience?

Stupidity and repeating things multiple times.

What advice would you give an aspiring DJ?

You have to realize you must work harder in this business than anyone else. Number one, nothing comes without it. You must commit to spending tons of time learning and perfecting your craft. Overnight success is very, very unlikely. Number two, don't be an asshole! You have a better chance of surviving if you're a decent person.

If you weren't a DJ/producer, what would you be?

A comedy writer—maybe for television. Maybe a stand-up comic, but I don't think I'm depressed enough. But I'd definitely be doing something in comedy.

Darude

Ville Virtanen
(DJ, producer, remixer)
"Sandstorm" (1999/2000)

"The only thing I wanted to see happen was for me to burn a CD [with 'Sandstorm'], take it to my local DJ buddy and see the crowd go crazy over it when he played it. That was my dream. Let's say I upgraded my dream a few times since, but that was all I wanted at the beginning."—Darude

Finland's Ville Virtanen (better known as Darude, a moniker that first evolved in his youth after playing Leila K.'s 1996 hit "Rude Boy" numerous times at a friend's party) set the success bar almost impossibly high at the dawn of the twenty-first century when he somewhat unknowingly unleashed the smash hit "Sandstorm" upon the masses. Selling reportedly over five million copies and reaching chart-topping positions around the world (including the U.S., where the song originally reached the Top Five of Billboard's *dance chart, and duplicated the feat a year later in a remixed version), "Sandstorm" became a highly influential and iconic electro-dance track for a new generation. Although his fame is permanently attached to this colossal, swirling, driven nugget of melodic and relentless energy, the artist has continued to expand his career. Today, he is widely regarded as a live performer and DJ, and his résumé includes dozens of compelling and crowd-lifting trance, progressive, electro and big room house tracks. Among them are "Feel the Beat," "Music," "In the Darkness" and "Beautiful Alien" (the latter from his 2015 album,* Moments*).*

Ville, would you tell me a little about your youth and your first exposure to music?
I was the first of three children in my family—I've got a sister who is 11 years younger and a brother who is five years younger. My dad is a carpenter and mom was an accountant. My dad is here in Finland, and my mom lives in Spain. I grew up in a very small village, just 900 people—a lot of agriculture and farming there. We were not farmers, but we had a little patch of land where we grew our own potatoes and carrots. My family, in a way, wasn't really that musical. My mom and dad listened to music, though. I didn't start making music myself until I was 19 or 20 years old. I had the regular music classes here and there in school, and like just about everybody else, I had a Casio keyboard at home that I noodled around with. But I never took lessons or anything—I was more interested in ice hockey at that time. Not that I didn't like music or studying it, but hockey was my priority.

I remember, looking back, that I was a little more into music than most other people

Darude's smash hit "Sandstorm" is reported to have achieved gold status in digital sales in the U.S. in 2010.

I knew. Everybody listens to it, but my buddies would like to just go and hang out. I did that, too, but very often I would go home and listen to local or Finnish national radio that would have a dance music show on Friday and Saturday nights. I would come home and listen to it, with my finger on the [tape recorder] pause button to try and record songs.

It sounds like a normal background most anyone might have had. It's interesting that such a typical youth gave rise to the massive hit "Sandstorm" and a prominent career in dance music.

My whole musical education was listening to radio. I think I'm such an average guy when it comes to music—I know I have an ear for it and have talent (I'm not bragging, but of course I can recognize that)—but I'm not sure why things happened the way they did or why "Sandstorm" was the hit that it was. I am an average guy, and I made something that resonated with average people. If I made R&B or rock, I suspect it still would have been music that the average person could relate to. It just happened that because I did not study any other form of music, electronic dance music was the only thing I could start making.

By 1995, I knew a few guys who were making music with computers, and I watched from the side what they were doing. At school, I found more buddies who were into this music, and I got to experience it more. I soon realized in a trance or house music song, there's a separate hi-hat, there's a kick and bass. I started hearing and identifying the different layers, and that made it possible for my brain to dissect and analyze them. A good song is not only the melody that you whistle. I was able to analyze the other aspects of the tracks and start creating them myself. With computers and samplers, if you create a bum note, you can correct it. You can change speeds and things like that. This all gave me the opportunity to start making music.

Tell me about the creation of "Sandstorm."

"Sandstorm" wasn't the first track I created, but it was the first one that was [commercially] released. I'm a better keyboard player today than I was back then (but I'm still not any sort of wizard). The song was a combo of finding keys and playing melodies and a lot of programming—meaning drawing notes with my mouse. I would know that a rhythm should go in a certain direction and place notes where I wanted them. Any errors, I would just fix them, like the note needed to be C instead of B, or it was in the wrong time position. That meant tons of repetition, listening to the song again and again. In the beginning, I didn't think of myself as a musician—I was just tinkering. I always thought you needed to be a great live instrument player or singer to be a musician. But then I realized it was a skill to be able to move the notes electronically till it starts sounding good. And also what to keep and what to take out of a song.

It sounds as if with "Sandstorm" you may have accidentally stumbled upon something remarkable, not necessarily pursuing it as part of your career plan.

Oh, I was totally a hobbyist with it. I wouldn't have called myself a producer. I had one synth, a computer and some software. I didn't even have a studio. I made "Sandstorm" in my little kitchenette, so-to-speak. I studied telecommunications and worked at an Apple-authorized retail store and repair shop. I never graduated [from college]—that's the only bummer about all of this—I was napping too much during school and going home to work on the music.

This brings to mind one thing. Often people, aspiring musicians, will ask me for advice. My first response may not be very original, but it's very valid—*don't quit your day job*. The point is that nothing kills creativity and fun more than having to think of money or other pressures and shit. And then, when you are in a position that your creativity becomes your source of income, you have to detach yourself from the pressures of the world. When you create, you cannot create shit to meet your rent. It must be genuine.

Why did you call the track "Sandstorm"?

The track wasn't called "Sandstorm" initially; it had a working name—or rather a couple of them. A little sidetrack—I made the original demo version. The version you know of this song was made and produced together with Jaakko Salovaara (aka JS16). He was the man who found me and signed me to his record company. The final sound you hear on "Sandstorm"—a huge piece of the credit must go to Jaakko. The commercial form of this track that became a hit was made with him. I wouldn't have gone anywhere without his help at that point.

So, Jaakko was my partner in crime, and when we finished the track we started writing down cool names on a piece of paper. It's an instrumental track, so there was no lyric that we could utilize to come up with a name. If you're into electronic dance music and you happen to know a synthesizer called Roland JP-8000 or JP-8080, if you take it out of the box, hook it up and turn it on, take a look what shows up on the LED display—the first sound is called "sandstorm." We actually used that sound in the track. It may seem like an unimaginative way to come up with the title, but tell me the song doesn't sound like a sandstorm.

It was the perfect title, and the song was a breakthrough techno-EDM track. The track has sold an extraordinary number of copies, reached number one (or at least the Top Five) in numerous countries, gone gold or platinum in several territories, and enjoys literally a massive cult following on Vevo and YouTube. Could you ever have imagined it would achieve this kind of success?

No, not at all. It doesn't really matter in a way, but someone downloaded my original mix of "Sandstorm," and it has something like 50 million hits, or some crazy number like that. I could have asked for it to be taken down at some point, but I don't want to—it's just such a good number! [*Darude laughs.*] I don't mind. It's been posted up there for probably over a decade, and at some point YouTube started showing that clip first, if you looked up "Sandstorm," ahead of my own channel. Maybe it's because it has the most views.

Not to put myself down, but, again, I never really considered myself a musician, and I wasn't really thinking of sales or numbers when I made "Sandstorm." The only thing I wanted to see happen was for me to burn a CD, take it to my local DJ buddy and see the crowd go crazy over it when he played it. That was my dream. Let's say I upgraded my dream a few times since, but that was all I wanted at the beginning.

The track came out when it was still possible to sell solid unit numbers in the CD market (and even the 12-inch single market, where it was the best-selling title of the year in some territories). If I may pry just a bit, does a song of that magnitude, coming out at that time, set you up for life?

If you mean purely from royalties, the answer is no, probably not. I have a wife and son and the regular expenses people have. But, on the other hand, "Sandstorm" started my career and gave me my name. I've done four albums, 15 singles and 30 or 40 remixes, so I don't view my career as being just "Sandstorm." But it is fair to say that it is still the track people will remember, if they remember only one thing. In that way, it still helps to pay my salary.

The song is played everywhere, but I don't really benefit from any of that. I live with my family in a normal house in Finland we built two years ago, and "Sandstorm" is one of the reasons I was able to do that. I'm one of the lucky guys—there are so many talented people who I know who are holding two or three jobs in addition to making music. It is really hard to make money in this industry.

"Feel the Beat" was a powerful follow-up that did extremely well, but I wonder how much pressure you felt to live up to the magnitude of your debut.

Every track, remix, whatever, that I've done since "Sandstorm"—there are so many people who will say "it doesn't measure up or come close" to my first hit. Even if there are positive comments made, there is sometimes a back-handed way of saying them, and, inevitably, comparisons are made to "Sandstorm." I'm pretty much okay with the fact that it is highly unlikely I will make anything that successful again. The reason, again, is that that track became a phenomenon. It's become connected to sporting events, and I didn't make that happen. I made the track, but none of that extra stuff was planned—not then and not even afterward. When the track became a hit, I didn't go to hockey arenas or NFL games and ask them to play my song. It's actually a good thing for me to remember so that I stay grounded, meaning I made the track having fun, with no thought of how it would become so big.

Many of the tracks from my first album, *Before The Storm*, were in the process of being made before "Sandstorm" was a hit. "Feel the Beat" was the perfect follow-up (and some people still think it sounds the way it does because we were trying to duplicate the success of "Sandstorm"). We actually had the same gear we'd been working with on "Sandstorm" (we liked the JP sound and the drums), so it really wasn't a copycat. It was natural. The whole album was just a flow. We didn't feel any pressure creating it—we knew we had good energy throughout the set, although the compositions were each unique. The only thing we felt pressure about was the rush to get the album done and out after the first two singles took off. Time-wise, our UK and Finnish record companies were pushing us to get it out and take advantage of the momentum. We weren't against that, but we were the ones in the studio who had to create this music.

The second album, *Rush*, in 2003, put a huge amount of weight on our shoulders. When we began making the music for it, we decided, screw it. The first single, "Music," wasn't exactly a "fuck you," but it was sort of that we weren't going to even try to make a commercial hit again. Instead, we went hard. That was the point—if it wasn't a hit, we could at least be proud we made something hard, energetic, and you can hear we didn't try to copy "Sandstorm" just to make money or think of chart positions. That was the key thing for us, and it was quite a relief.

In addition to "Music," I also wanted to ask you about a rather unique track you produced—"I Ran (So Far Away)" from 2008, featuring vocalist Blake Lewis. You don't indulge in remakes often, but this track, originally by A Flock of Seagulls from 1982, was quite powerful, bringing new life to a vintage dance classic. Why this song?

So, I had a friend who had a record company, and the credit for the idea of doing the song goes to him. He actually had original elements of the song, and permission to use the original vocals. He asked me if I wanted to do a remix of the track, and I was interested. I knew it had been a huge hit, but I did not remember it from my childhood. So it wasn't probably a big song in Finland, but I was familiar with it. Unfortunately, we had a disagreement about how I would go about making the remix, and I didn't see the point of continuing with the project.

Two or three years later, I met with Blake Lewis, a vocalist from *American Idol*, Season 6, in Seattle, where he was working in a club. I loved his voice and happened to mention doing the "I Ran" track. He was eager to sing on it and did a great, great job—sort of sounding like the original but doing it in his own way. It was about two years after discussing my buddy's remix project, so I felt I wouldn't be stepping on his toes to release it. I really grew to love the original song—it's a really catchy track to begin with.

I've been very, very careful about doing covers and remakes. I would hate to make one where people say it's a horrible version, doesn't do the original justice, blah, blah, blah. In this case, I felt I was true to the original but added a good amount of my own twist, too, and Blake's voice was perfect. It didn't end up being a big commercial success, but I've received so many compliments for it from the true Seagulls fans. So that's what matters to me most.

Speaking of critics, many accuse modern dance music and EDM of being cold and soulless. I assume you disagree?

My short answer is yes, of course. Let's look at Ed Sheeran—my image of him is a man's voice and a guitar. How does he compare to, say, Metallica? Is Metallica worse or better? I guess what I'm saying is, it doesn't matter. Whoever is listening will make their own decision. Right? So you have two men singing and playing guitars, but coming from completely opposite ends of the spectrum. In the same way, we have EDM or a fluffy dance pop track at one end and some minimal techno or dubstep at the other. Both stir people and move them, but which is better?

When I am at a club that plays minimal techno and it's a great place with a great sound system and DJ, I feel something. When you are at a big club and that space around you is filled with 100, 1,000 or 10,000 people going nuts to the music, whatever type of dance music it is, you feel something. It might be that you then play that same track in your car or something and you don't get anywhere with it. Atmosphere, the setting you are in, has a lot to do with how much of a connection you make to the music.

You know, I am a Coldplay fan. I don't know all their tracks, but I think they are brilliant. Take the song "Fix You." I hear it on the radio, the regular album mix, and I like it. But when I see them live at Wembley and something like 40,000 people are singing to it and everybody is pretty much crying happy tears, I start weeping, too. It's such an amazing vibe. Nobody can tell you that experience is any more or less emotional than the techno experience. It's all situational, where you feel the whole thing. I think people can say EDM is cold and clangy, but I believe even the most minimal techno can affect you in a very deep, spiritual way if you are in the right situation listening to it.

Is a similar connection made between your creativity and the vibe you get, whether you are in the studio recording or the DJ playing live for a crowd?

I started as a music-maker, and I didn't know I would be a live performer. When my career took off, I did live performances, but not as a DJ. I started doing DJ work because there was a demand growing. Who is this Darude guy? I found a booking agent, and all of a sudden, I just started doing it. Being both a DJ and a performer is the best thing—like perpetual motion. I'm in the studio getting goosebumps about a track or a kick drum or a hi-hat. But then I get to put the track together and play it for a crowd. Their response, whether good or bad—I may feel differently—feeds my urge to go back to the studio and work more. If I see the crowd goes nuts, I know it works. That either makes me want to make the track even better, full-on, or make another one.

I guess it's okay to admit my tracks are usually on the mark. It's been a while since I had a track that got a shitty test run and didn't work out. But if something isn't getting as strong a response as I'd like, I will analyze the arrangement, the melody, the build-up—and that prompts me to get back to work. Again, when I am in the studio, alone or with somebody, there is the artsy side and there is the purpose side. Being the DJ, you see the crowd's reaction to certain things—like how a snare roll builds and builds or how the pitch bend works—and that all feeds the cycle of making a great track; it goes round and around. Of course, I play other artists' music, too, and I am inspired by those tracks as well.

Is it challenging for you to still be an innovator of dance music, as opposed to a follower of trends?

Good question. I actually believe I am both, meaning I listen to new music all the time for new tracks to spin in my DJ sets, in addition to my own productions. Every time I hear something great, there's always a bookmark made, a mental note about it. It's either in my brain or written down. It's a dangerous thing to say because people misunderstand what I mean, but I want to "re-do" it. I want to copy it, but not to duplicate it. Then, the next time I'm working on something, I am copying the vibe I got from what I heard. Musically, I want to avoid copying someone else's work, but I want to create that same feeling. Sometimes it means I end up making a progressive house track, or some other sub-genre, and sometimes I change it to another style, like old school piano house, trans, whatever. I'm definitely a follower—I'm not ashamed to admit that. I take my influences from everywhere. But I try to be very careful not to directly copy stuff.

One of the greatest compliments that I got when my *Moments* album was released in August of 2015 was that in some tracks, I blended two or three genres, and people said it made them forget about what genre they thought they were listening to. That's very cool to me. I literally went between genres and influences and mixed them up in many of the tracks, not caring how it might be classified. I'm not saying that makes me an innovator, but I think that reflects my innovative side.

You give the impression of someone who doesn't get caught up in the competition that pervades the music industry. I refer, for example, to the ranking of DJ popularity.

From my side, I feel no competition—none whatsoever. I make music, Avicii makes music, David Guetta makes music. If our tracks are played, the crowd likes them or they don't. Of course, I want people to like my music, but it has very little to do with what David Guetta does. I want other DJs to make great music—first of all because that helps all of us in the industry. Secondly, I can play their great music if there's something I like and if it fits my sets. So, personally, I feel no sense of competition with anybody.

The only time I can say there is a sense of competition might be when my booking agent tries to get me in a better position on a line-up. Those things *do* matter, like if you play first or last, or before this guy or that guy. But I try not to take part in that kind of thing; I have my agents and managers handle it. When I meet other DJs in the green room or exchange messages with them on social media, it is always very friendly. I have a great deal of respect for those who have been in the business for more than a couple of years—I know they've done something right, and I know how hard it is to maintain your profile and keep up.

Are you observing any changes in the club scene, any contraction of the dance music culture?

I was talking with some buddies about this subject recently. I started touring in the U.S. in 2000, 2001. I usually average 40 or 50 gigs a year, and 20 or 30 are in the U.S. Last year was one of my busiest in a while, and the U.S. has been one of my biggest markets for a long time. Early on, I never really understood when people said dance music in the U.S. was very underground. Especially in the big cities—I'm not saying my shows were always sold out, but they were packed. Then I realized the U.S. is such a large country, there were enough people to support even specialized music like house and trance, so I didn't see that dance music was underground. But then, about five years ago, when EDM started exploding everywhere, your average type of person started filling the events and clubs, not just [devotees].

That said—and I don't expect to see EDM's popularity decline any time soon—I do see pockets arising where people are becoming increasingly particular about who they are going to see. Especially in the U.S., I see people emerging from their period of gateway drugs, pop-dance and EDM, and now are looking for something a little deeper. This all might be affecting [club and party event] attendance, but in terms of the whole U.S., I think you can expect the world of EDM to go on for decades.

I'm curious—where are your biggest markets here in the United States?

Interestingly enough, New York hasn't been that big of a trance city. But I've played New York, places like Webster Hall, a number of times, and it's been good. My best places are on the west coast in general—Seattle, Frisco, San Diego, LA, Orange County. Florida, the Tampa and Miami areas, have also been very good. I've been to over a hundred cities in the U.S.

We are seeing terrorism have an effect on large and small scale shows and events, increasingly causing people concern about attending. Have you been able to wrap your head around this threat?

It doesn't affect me exactly—how do I say this? If I had a show scheduled in Paris right after the attacks, I probably would not have done it. In other ways, it's a thing we artists *do* think about. In practice, after Paris, we make a point of understanding where a venue's exits are during our soundcheck. Literally asking where the closest exits are and if they are always open. Simple things like that. But at the same time, when I play a club, the thought of such a terrible event is not in my mind. Flying back and forth—not really then either. You know? The threat is there, and it's in the back of everybody's mind really since 9/11. But as far as the huge festivals go, the organizers and local police are affected tremendously. Should something happen at an event I am playing, it would be absolutely horrible and terrifying. But I feel like it is so important that we don't shrivel up and die because that threat is out there, out of fear. Then it's over, and they've won.

One of the saddest things about all of this—and I'm not particularly religious in any one direction—but I feel for those people who are being discriminated and shat on because of this. Normal people, whatever their religion, do not [commit acts of terrorism]. They mind their own business and live their lives. It is extremists who are doing these things. That creates so much more than the deaths that occur—it creates the shit that spreads everywhere, to innocent people who are not involved. It's a crazy world we are living in— I know my thoughts are not the deepest or most original about it—but I think a lot of people feel the same way as I do.

How challenging is it to maintain stability in your family life with the demands of being a dance music star?

Nothing is difficult about it other than time. The cool thing is, my son, who turns seven shortly, is very much into music. He's probably better at playing the piano now than I've ever been. So, we've got that taken care of early. Nobody forces him into music—he plays on his own and has an amazing teacher nearby. He understands on his own level what daddy does. I've been in a good position in that I get enough gigs, with some ability to choose them. As a family, we have a general rule that I am not going to be away for more than two weekends at a time. I don't want to be gone longer than that for myself, and I don't want to do that to my wife and son. But he understands that I don't have a nine-to-five job and that while my job is making music (and that's fun), there is also a huge responsibility to our family unit. My wife helps me quite a bit with the business side of things, and my son gets to see the working side of his parents. Also, we live in a normal kind of neighborhood and interact with our neighbors. So my son is exposed to many different angles, and I try to be there for him as much as possible.

Lastly, what do you think makes dance music so great, despite the critical bashing it has taken over the decades?

It's funny you should say that—I know what you mean. People have said dance music is druggy, frivolous, this and that—and definitely that it's so easy to make. At the same time, especially in the U.S., some people have no problem with Woodstock and the rock scene of the '60s and '70s, which probably had more drugs (or crazier drugs) than dance music ever gave rise to.

I don't know. Absolutely, go to a dance music event and you will find ecstasy or whatever drugs. But try going to a rock concert. You'll see them there, too. Visit, I don't know, a plumber's shop and who knows what the person has in their blood? It doesn't matter—it's a horrible stamp that's been put on dance music. Some think that DJs and producers are responsible for that part of dance music. Yet vodka is the strongest substance I've ever had. Wait, maybe it was a contact high because I was in a room where everyone was smoking weed. Otherwise, I've never done drugs. The drug thing, to me, is such a stereotypical stamp placed on dance music.

But getting back to the core of your question, dance music is important because it is a huge piece of pop and music culture, in the past and today. It has united so many people—which may sound like a cliché. But that cliché came from truth. You see a club with 200 people—you won't often see a fight; everybody's dancing and taking the music in. A big festival—again, generally a very peaceful experience. And someone like Armin van Buuren playing a beautiful trance song, and 70,000 coming together, moving to the beat and feeling that power—what's cooler than that?

Lightning Round with Darude

The dance song that you never tire of hearing?

Chicane's "Saltwater."

For what do you have no patience?

Well, we touched on it earlier. Intolerance—people who hate or condemn someone or something without knowing the subject matter.

What personality trait do you have that would probably surprise most people?

Oh wow—that I'm not rude. [*Darude laughs.*]

Favorite food to eat after a night of clubbing?

I don't do it often, but it's gotta be a hot dog—a street corner hot dog.

The best time to use social media?

Dude, that is a very valid question! It

Darude has won a number of prestigious awards that include two German Dance Awards, a Dance Star Award, and the U.S.A. Golden Turntable DJ Award. He is a three-time Finnish Grammy Award winner.

sucks for me because I'm in Finland, which is seven to 10 hours ahead of U.S. time. The other way around for Australia or parts of Asia. So I have to say nine or 10PM my time (afternoon in the U.S.) is the best time for me.

Extended versions or radio edits?

[*Darude laughs.*] Extended versions, of course.

If you weren't in entertainment, what would you be doing today?

I know I would still be working at that amazing Apple repair shop. I liked it there.

Inaya Day
(vocalist, songwriter)
"Can't Stop Dancin'" (2002)

> "I notice that a lot of people who listen to dance music may not be church people. But the dancefloor is like their church, and the DJ is like their minister."—Inaya Day

The list of dance songs made in this century that feature the rousing voice of Inaya Day is extensive. What began as an opportunity to record a couple of house tracks in Germany with Mousse T. (think "Horny '98" for starters) soon became a full-time career for the New York-born singer. She possesses an uncanny knack for lifting spirits with her soulful and gospel-fused vocal power, making hits like "Movin' Up" (DJ Mike Cruz presents Inaya Day and China Ro), "Can't Stop Dancin'," "Nasty Girl," "Do the Right Thing" (with Quentin Harris) and "Rapid Fire" ("Rapido") (with Giangi) signatures of the modern age house movement. Her 2016 single "One Night in Heaven" was a near instant smash on Billboard's U.S. club chart. And while distinctly American, Day has forged a strong international following that illustrates her remarkably broad appeal. Most importantly, the singer has no plans of slowing down.

Inaya, let's start with your youth and how you came to connect with music. Did you discover your voice early on?

My mother enjoyed singing, and I remember one of the first things she did with me as a child was to take me to choir rehearsal at church. I have been hearing music ever since. My cousin, Solomon Roberts, Jr., is the leader of the group Skyy, who had the 1981 hit "Call Me." We are actually meeting later today—we're finally going to be putting out some dance tunes together. When I was a kid, I would hear Skyy rehearse down in my aunt's basement. In church, I joined the

In addition to being an accomplished singer, Inaya Day has written songs for Bootsy Collins, Randy Crawford, Robin S and Missy Elliot.

kids' choir. I would get annoyed because they would kind of sing out of tune—I couldn't understand why they couldn't sing a song correctly. I'd tell my mom I didn't want to sing with the kids—not realizing I, too, was a kid. Eventually, they started letting me lead and do solos. I even sang in the mirror, holding a hair brush, singing Michael Jackson and Chaka Khan songs. That all became part of my psyche and part of my being. But I never thought I would actually be a singer when I grew up. I thought I'd be a veterinarian or a journalist.

In junior high, my best friend heard me sing "Home" from *The Wiz* and started crying. I said, "What is wrong with you? Why you trippin'?" I have to laugh—she said, "You can really sing! I'm gonna tell!" She told our seventh grade music teacher, who made me sing the song. She wanted to know why I was hiding this "gift." After a while I was singing in contests, but I started to get banned from them as a competitor because everyone felt I had some kind of advantage. That's when I started to consider a future in singing. At twelve, I had a lead role in a musical, and later, after doing Off-Broadway and a Broadway National Tour of *The Wiz*, I found myself in Germany doing musical theater.

How did you come to connect with Mousse T. and Boris Dlugosch, the creators of your first major dance hits, including the smash "Horny '98"?

I was performing in a German language production of *Little Shop of Horrors* around 1995. I didn't speak German at all, but I was good at mimicking. By doing that, I gradually learned much more German—at least well enough to understand it, even if I wasn't completely fluent in the language. I was able to carry on business and have light conversation. The assistant director of the show was a friend of [music producer and remixer] Boris Dlugosch, and he told him I could really sing. He encouraged us to work together. To appease his friend, Boris invited me to Hannover (I lived in Düsseldorf at the time).

It turned out he had a skeletal track (which was the foundation of the song "Keep Pushin'" [later to be credited to Boris Dlugosch Presents BOOOM!]).One of the label owners asked me to sing encouraging lyrics like, "if you keep moving forward, you'll make it" and stuff like that. So I started singing until I got to the line about keep pushin' on and that things are gonna get better. Producer and musician Mousse T. (Mustafa Gündoğdu) was also there, and he encouraged me to keep going with that theme. I embellished and built on it—all in that churchy way. They really liked my voice, but I just basically wanted to be paid and get back to Dusseldorf.

The theater production went on hiatus, so I went back to New York. I remember I was vacuuming my carpet and the noon day master-mix show comes on the radio, 98.7 KISS-FM. I suddenly realized they were playing the "Keep Pushin'" song I had recorded in Germany! I was on the radio—"Yay! Wait—hold up!" I worked out the particulars with the guys, which led us to doing a follow-up ("Hold Your Head Up High" in '97), and that led to "Horny" in '98, which was produced by Mousse T. I said, "Okay, God, I get it. I'm supposed to do dance music." I had to tell my agents to stop sending me out on auditions for musical theater because this dance music thing was getting too big, and I just didn't have time. I wanted to see where the music would go.

You sound as if you quickly became very comfortable with dance and house music, and the long line-up of hits that followed seems to back that up.

Yes, I really did. With dance music, you're not constricted by a certain type of lyric. People are more apt to feel what you feel, when you sing honestly in this genre. If you are honest in your delivery, the audience grabs on to it. I was singing from my soul, like the positivity of "Keep Pushin'" and "Hold Your Head Up High." "Horny" was a fun song because it was really meant to be a double entendre—the horns, you know? It could have been called "The Horny Song." The risqué verses were created and sung by Emma Lanford [and Nadine Richardson, aka Hot 'n' Juicy]. I sang the hook and harmonies.

I'm definitely comfortable with being called a dance music artist. After all, it is one of the things that I am. I've been in the genre for 20 years. It's a constantly changing genre. How can I have disdain for it? It's a blessing. It used to be just house music, now there's nu-disco, EDM and so many sub-genres that you can experiment with. I'm grateful to be in it. People could just as easily say, "Oh, she's old school." But they don't—in this genre they let me grow and evolve.

You've also written a lot of great songs for a number of prolific artists, including Randy Crawford, Bootsy Collins, Missy Elliot—and I believe you collaborated on some level with Michael Jackson.

With Michael, I created and arranged background vocals for his song "Ghosts" [1997]. Mousse T. did a remix and asked me to help with the backgrounds. Mousse told me the worst that would happen is that Michael would discard what he didn't want and would keep what he liked. Michael kept just about everything I did for the song. What sucked was that I was in Germany and Michael was far away in LA, so I didn't get to meet him. But he sent a fax that said, "Please tell Inaya I love what she did with the song." So every time I saw the video in Europe, I heard my voice with Michael Jackson's, and that was extremely exciting.

In terms of dance music, people tend to dismiss the lyrics of many songs as being too frivolous. How do you view the role of lyrics in dance music?

I notice that a lot of people who listen to dance music may not be church people. But the dancefloor is like their church, and the DJ is like their minister. I see people put their hands up and shake their heads shouting, "Yes! Yes!" Having powerful lyrics in dance music, the kind people can grab onto, really makes a difference.

One particular gentleman contacted me on Facebook telling me he came out to his parents, and it didn't go well. He said they wanted to kick him out of their lives, and he drove away as fast as he could toward a wall. He was blasting music in his car, and the song "Keep Pushin'" came on—the whole theme of things getting better and pushing yourself to the top. It got him to stop the car, and he was able to pull himself together, telling me I'll never know how much hearing that song meant to him and that it saved his life. Wow—it makes me realize there is something valuable in what I am doing, in what I am singing.

I know you have strong faith and a solid church background. Has that created any challenge for you when it comes to embracing the gay community?

I see no problem at all. Honestly, I don't think it's anyone's business who a person loves. It's between that person and the one they love. We are taught that God is love and love is God. Period. How do you then condemn a gay person—how do you say someone is going to hell because he or she simply loves someone? That doesn't make sense to me. I don't get it. There's something getting lost in the translation.

Let's talk a bit about Prince, who we lost not long ago. You've covered some of his iconic repertoire with very popular renditions of "The Glamorous Life" (originally performed by Sheila E.) and "Nasty Girl" (originally performed by Vanity 6). How do you feel about this incredible artist, and how did you approach the challenge of interpreting those hits?

As I said, I listened to Chaka Khan, Rufus and Parliament-Funkadelic a lot. I love funk music. I was influenced quite a bit by that because my older sister played it often. I have a funk band with Cheryl "Pepsii" Riley, and we've been singing together with that band for about 12 years. I would sing "Nasty Girl" a lot, putting my own twist on it. I'd perform it, and so many people would say to me that I needed to remake it. I decided I *had* to re-do the song before someone else did. I went back to Germany with Mousse T. to finish someone else's project and asked him to make a loop for me of "Nasty Girl" because I wanted to record it. He agreed, but wondered how easily he would find the original record. It turned out I spotted it on a pile of records he had right there and held it up! He said, "It's a sign! It's a sign!," and as soon as we finished the other session we laid down the track. He worked on it further while I went back to America. When I got back to Germany, our version just blew up. It crossed over to pop. I think my success reinventing the track just comes from my love of funk.

I encountered Prince very early in my career at a club called Nell's in New York down on 14th Street. Prince dropped by the club a lot, and I was there one night when he came down. He walked by, and his bodyguard was just a pace behind him. But it gave me just enough space to slide in, and basically I was face-to-face with Prince! Prince says, "Pardon me!" I responded, "No! Pardon *meeeee!*" He just burst into laughter, and I put my hand out to allow him to pass. He goes to the other end of the place. A short while later, we cross paths again, and I said, "Oh!" He shook his head like "this girl is nuts." I was stalking him I guess. [*Inaya laughs.*]

I met Prince again about three years ago at the Village Underground, a live music and comedy club on 3rd Street. I was at home in bed when the owner of the club called (I played often with the band there) and told me Prince was coming down. I dragged myself down there and it was packed, and Prince was indeed there. To my surprise they made an announcement that Inaya Day had arrived. I was like, "No! No! No!" The band started playing "Nasty Girl" to coax me up on stage, but I was so afraid he wouldn't like that. I started singing it, and at first Prince just looked at me. Then he started swaying from side to side and bobbing his head. Then he stood up and started the step touch. At the end, he nods his head and gives me the okay sign. Yeah, like, "Aiight, you did that!" The owner said Prince told him he loved what I did with the song. How validating is that? It means even more to me now that we have lost him.

I couldn't believe the sad news. It was shocking, and I still don't want to face it.

I think most of us felt the same way. You share something else in common with Prince. You've been at the top of the *Billboard* dance chart several times, seven to be exact at this point in time. When you reach number one on that chart, how much of a game-changer is it? Is there pressure to deliver more hits of that caliber?

Oh, yes, there's definitely more pressure. The number one's are wonderful notches in your belt that raise your profile, just as they raise the money you can ask for to perform.

Take my new song, "One Night in Heaven." It came in the chart at number 49. Next week it will climb to 36 I'm told. We're promoting the song, and because this track is so new from me, one sometimes takes a lesser fee to get it out there. It's important to be in front of a big crowd and be able to show them what we've created. But once it hits the *Billboard* chart, you don't have to compromise as much—especially if you've hit the chart numerous times. The other advantage of having number one hits is that you can say no thank you when an offer isn't "right."

In America, the *Billboard* dance chart does not translate that well to sales. In Europe, if you hit the dance chart, you'll see that reflected in sales. Australia, as well. The U.S. *Billboard* dance chart helps, but more as a promotional tool. Any big chart like that gets the masses to notice someone. It gets the attention of promoters, and it does still make a difference.

What kind of changes have you observed in the dance music industry over the past 10 years?

Dance music is DJ-focused now. The DJ is the star. For my song "One Night in Heaven," it's Toy Armada & DJ Grind featuring Inaya Day. Meanwhile, they are the newcomers and I am the veteran. Now, why couldn't I present a song and feature someone else? If I did, the first thing people would want to know is who produced it. Who's the DJ involved? That's the focus today. Look, everything changes, and it's just their turn. And that's fine. I just try to work with DJs that understand and appreciate the type of music I do—the vocal house—and the vocalist is important in this style of music. Toy Armada & DJ Grind work well with me because we work together. The show is not them with their hands in the air and turning buttons and knobs. They want an artist to convey the power of the music and draw people in. The fans like our banter and camaraderie. It's a package. A lot of DJs want it to be about them, and nobody knows who the singer is.

A few years ago, a track was released by a DJ that sampled Etta James, and it was a big hit. But her name wasn't in the artist credit. I felt it was disrespectful because, my God, it's Etta James. You need to bow down. Placing more attention on her name might have helped his sales. (I realize he probably didn't need any help because the song just blew up anyway, thanks to her vocal.) But I think it's important to really include the other contributors to a song.

A lot depends on the artist, too, the vocalist, especially in terms of conducting business and watching out for yourself. I happen to be both an artist and a business person. I have my own company, Ny-O-Dae Music. I won't participate on a record and allow it to go out without my name on it. That's not going to happen. Other artists may need to get a song out there, or they may be new, and they will allow themselves to go uncredited, even if they don't like it. Or they don't realize what they can negotiate. As the old saying goes, people can only do to you what you allow.

What is the most surprising thing you've discovered about being a business person? Were you able to comfortably move yourself into that role?

I think my personal trials and errors in the music industry helped make me a good business person. I made contractual mistakes in my youth, but thank God none of them ever broke me. But I still lament some of them to this day. For example, I did a sample CD and sang a number of words or phrases—they just told me to sing them any way I wanted.

I recorded those bits in Germany for someone who was putting out the CD in Japan. I didn't think it would go anywhere—I got paid for my session and that was it. A few other well-known singers were doing it, too, so I thought it was all good.

A few years later, my sister sees a Discover card commercial and hears someone singing on it that sounds just like me. She asked me if I had done the commercial, and I said, "I wish!" Eventually, the commercial gets up to New York and I heard it. It was from that sample CD I had done, and there was nothing I could do about it! So I learned along the way. Now I put those protections in my contracts. And I try to help other singers avoid the mistakes I made.

Much of dance music, like the rest of contemporary pop culture, is youth driven. Do you focus on this at all as you project your identity into the scene?

Not at all. I really just am myself. Luckily, I look pretty young. Ultra Naté and I were going to Shelter, another club here in New York, and I had on my Capri pants and sneakers. She said, "What's with the skateboarder look?" I said, "Hey! This is my style. I'm feelin' this today!" [*Inaya laughs.*] I dress the way I want, and I love it.

Do you notice club culture contracting?

Yes, I do. All over the world it's happening. It may be economics. People are reluctant to flip $20 or $30 or even $10 at a door like they once did—and buy the drinks, which are ridiculously expensive. And bottle service—I hate that nonsense. It may be governments—you know that old saying, "Nothing good ever happens after midnight." The drug culture got out of hand for a time, and many clubs were being shut down right and left. There were sometimes brawls or gunshots at clubs. Some people even got killed. It may have started to make nightlife unappealing for a lot of people. I'm not sure.

I used to tour all over Australia two or three months out of the year, during our winter, which is their summer. My agent over there said it's gotten very dry—the clubs are disappearing. The same is happening here. However, I do notice, even abroad, that festivals are gaining momentum. My opportunities to perform at large events like that are increasing. Whatever changes in dance culture, we as performers just have to adapt and become part of that change. That's how you stay alive. You open for somebody else if necessary. But to be there is to grow. In this business, truly, out of sight is out of mind. But if they see you and they think you're great, the word spreads. And you know, I think it's important just to go to some events, whether you are performing or not—be seen. You can meet many people who may say they have a track for you to record or another event for which they'd like you to perform. That's how you stay in the game.

What's on your bucket list?

An album! I have over 92 singles and have never done an album. Frankie Knuckles once offered to produce an album for me—the godfather of house music! He produced and laid down about six or seven songs. He left this world before we could put them out. Eric Kupper, who was his musical partner, still has all those tracks. He's going to master them and trickle them out. "Not Over Me" is going to be released soon, a duet I did with Ultra Naté. There's another duet with Frenchie Davis and another with Valerie Simpson. Once the singles are out, we'll release the album or an EP. Also, I want to do a Christmas project. It's not a "Jingle Bells" project—you'll see; it's kinda dope! I'm also about four or five songs into a funk-rock project. And I've worked with the amazing Jocelyn Brown on a project.

I'm a firm believer that when you've reached the mountaintop of whatever you've been doing, you don't have to become complacent. You try something else. So much to learn! There's so many genres I want to explore. I can feed my live band monster, satisfy my house music track monster and never be bored or feel that I can't spread my wings. It's funny, I literally have enough house music songs recorded to last the next three years! Maybe five!

We've had so many amazing dance classics come out in the '70s, '80s and '90s. You were right in there with 'Horny.' Do you think dance music of the early twenty-first century will be viewed in the same light, say, 20 or 30 years from now?

Not at all. There will be a few—a favored few. But not like in decades past. David Morales and Barbara Tucker threw a party not long ago, a reunion for The Ozone Layer, a club from a while back in New York. Just about every song he played everyone went ballistic over. You remembered them instantly and went crazy. Somehow, I can't believe way off in the future we're going to hear someone say, "And now here's blah-blah-blah from 2008!" What will they play and will anyone really recognize it? I'm not so sure. I also hear songs I call "pots and pans music." To me, it seems like a collection of sounds with no melody, no hook and nothing to hang on to. It has no soul or depth. I can't imagine anyone saying, "I remember where I was when that song came on!" There's too few songs in dance music today that really make an impression.

I joke about it, but 2016 seems to be the year of the remake. Are they out of ideas? Imagination? But, hey, we recently released "One Night in Heaven," the song by M People, so I'm part of it, too. But it was a great song, so we reached back and tried to refresh it. Yes, it's a remake, but I think it's good for people to hear a song like that today. Maybe, they will understand better what a great song sounds like and what we mean.

Regardless of the point we find ourselves within the evolution of dance music today, there's no denying the powerful effect the genre has on people. What is it about this music that makes it so powerful and popular?

Simple. It's freeing. The best dance music sends people's hands into the air, makes them scream and run to the dancefloor. It's so liberating, and—I know you've heard this before—but you can take your problems to the dancefloor, and it releases you from all of them for a little while. That's what it does for me!

Lightning Round with Inaya

Craziest thing you ever saw happen in a nightclub?

Oh, easy! I was at a YMCA, where they were having one of those classic dance music parties. One guy became so overwhelmed by the music, he jumped down from a balcony in an attempt to do a split landing on the dancefloor! Seriously! Everybody gasps as his leg goes *arrrrrggh*! It twisted the wrong way, but he still raised his arms, ignoring the agony, like "ta-da!" I shuddered when I saw the way his leg was twisted!

Have you ever been mistaken for another singer?

Ultra Naté! There she is again. We're the same height, about the same complexion, and in the '90s we both had short blond hair. I would hear, "Excuse me, are you Ultra Naté?" "No, I'm I-n-a-y-a D-a-y!" Even her mother said I looked like her!

The dance song you never get tired of hearing?

"Follow Me" by Aly-us from 1992. It's one of the biggest house tunes ever, and they play it all over the world.

True love or $10 million?

True love, of course.

Have you ever forgotten the lyrics to one of your hits?

Yes! I mumbled lyrics to a song at The White Party this year. The lyrics were taped to the monitor, and all I had to do was look down at them. But no, I got excited and instead started shaking the hands of fans and had no idea what I was singing.

Inaya Day returned to *Billboard*'s club chart early in 2017 as the featured singer on Joe Gauthreaux's hit "The Urge in Me."

Favorite food to eat after a night at the clubs?

White Castle hamburgers! Murder Burgers!

Online shopping or in a store?

Definitely online. I hate shopping in stores. I love getting new clothes, but hate the process.

If you weren't in entertainment, what would you be doing today?

I'd probably be a veterinarian, which I mentioned was an interest early on. Love animals! I've had so many kinds—three guinea pigs, gerbils, hamsters, newts, all kinds of fish, cats, turtles. I think that turtle is actually older than me, and it's still going!

Deepend

Bob van Ratingen, Falco van den Aker (DJs, producers, remixers)

"Catch & Release"—Matt Simons
(Deepend Remix) (2015)

> "In the past, so many dance songs didn't have a real song structure—just an intro, a breakdown, a drop, a second breakdown and an outro. And now all the DJ/producers are looking for genuine song structure—a verse, a bridge and a chorus."—Falco van den Aker

> "We get a lot of requests to remix tracks, but we can't do what we did with 'Catch & Release' with every song. It's not like a formula that you can apply to everything."—Bob van Ratingen

Deepend, the Dutch DJ and producer duo embodied by Bob van Ratingen and Falco van den Aker (both born in the late '80s and friends since the age of 10), know how to make people feel good. Their roots were firmly set in deep house, and their first bootleg remixes caught on like a wildfire, taking the sound of the tracks they chose to refashion in fresh and unexpected new directions. They justifiably called themselves Deepend—perhaps because an unexpected depth flows through their original productions and remix work like some crazy, glowing ectoplasmic energy. In just a few short years, millions have felt it.

They've scored a series of major international hits, including a successful remix of July Child's "When You Call" (2014) and their inventive take on American pop singer Matt Simons' hugely popular smash "Catch & Release" in 2015. Deepend's work caught the attention of Armada, the influential recording label home of DJ/producer Armin van Buuren, and now the two are being taken quite seriously as important innovators in contemporary dance music. Bob and Falco will, it seems assured, be moving the genre forward in fascinating and exciting ways in the decade to come.

Gentlemen, would you tell me about your youth and to what musical influences you were exposed early on?

Bob: I didn't really come from a musical family. My parents didn't play any musical instruments, but I had grandfathers and aunts who were really into music. They played the violin and piano. Falco and I met each other in primary school—a long time ago it seems. I listened to a lot of rock-oriented music in those days too, like Eric Clapton.

Falco: I had a similar background. My parents didn't play any instruments, but I defi-

In 2015, Deepend (Falco van den Aker, left, Bob van Ratigen, right) released an official remix for American pop singer Matt Simons' hit "Catch and Release." The track stormed the charts resulting in number one placings on Hype Machine and top rankings on iTunes charts in more than 40 countries.

nitely grew up with music. The radio was always playing. My mother tells me when I was a little boy I would sit on the back of the vacuum cleaner and sing the songs with her as she was cleaning. I was really into drums, too. I'd use the pots and pans in the kitchen to simulate drum-playing. But I have never actually played a musical instrument.

My parents played a lot of old soul music (Solomon Burke, Ray Charles, Otis Redding) and a lot of disco.

How did you come to form your professional and creative partnership?

Falco: It really happened very naturally. Bob and I met in primary school, and then we went to high school together. At that time, we really were into R&B and hip-hop music. We started hanging out after school and began downloading music production software on our computers. We just started experimenting with beats—just for fun. Over the years, we were able to progress to more professional productions.

Bob: Yes, it started out as fun—definitely as a mutual hobby. Then we really discovered dance music. In 2010, we decided to try and begin creating this kind of sound.

So many young people were doing the same thing at that time. How did you get yourselves noticed?

Falco: For us, it took off when we did what you would call a bootleg remix of a Passenger's track called "Let Her Go." We liked the original version and decided to post a house version of it, posting it on our Soundcloud page. At that time, we had about 100 followers—really just friends and family. When we uploaded the track, it went viral. Normally, we'd only get maybe 100 plays. But that song got over 15,000 plays in just one day. It was just luck through the Internet—you post something and it kicks in, you know?

Bob: DJs started playing it in their sets. It was a big surprise for us. It was not our plan to be noticed like that. People discovered it, and they liked it. So we started to create more bootlegs and reworked songs by Bill Withers, like "Ain't No Sunshine." We did a "summer edit" of it, and it was played all across Europe. That really got us noticed.

Falco: We started getting a lot of support from DJs and through Soundcloud. We started getting local bookings as DJs, and then we started going regional. Our connection to DJ and producer Armin van Buuren happened around 2013. We had finished creating two [original] tracks and sent them to the Armada label, which was Armin's record company. On Soundcloud, you can see who is listening to your music. We had seen that Armada had listened to our music and sent them an email saying we saw they were listening to us, and we wanted to send them some new stuff we were working on. We figured it would be very difficult to get their attention, but we sent the tracks in anyway. A few hours later, we received a response that they actually wanted to sign the tracks!

Bob: We couldn't believe it! It was really amazing! It was a big step for us to be signed to the Armada label. That resulted in our first international booking—in the UK, Leeds. We played with a huge Armada banner behind us, so they were really branding us as their DJs. It worked out really well.

Falco: People started to notice us. A big booking agency (the same one that Armin was signed to) approached us, asking for a casual conversation. We were so nervous—we couldn't sleep the night before. All the major DJs were signed with them. They felt we were on the right track, even though we didn't have a big hit on the charts yet. They said they would be interested in picking us up if we kept going in this positive direction.

What quality do you think they and others see and hear in your music that's setting you apart from the pack?

Falco: It's so hard for us to say. At that time, maybe three years ago, EDM and deep house were really big, but people were increasingly moving into the trend for more melodic tracks—we were producing that kind of sound. Our first single on Armada was called "Turning It Back"—it was a really laid back song. It did very well—and we weren't even playing [as DJs] that much anywhere at the time.

Why did you decide to call yourselves 'Deepend'?

Falco: It's a funny story. We were looking for a good name—Falco & Bob didn't sound quite so cool. A guy who was into branding helped us find the name. There were a few words that were being used to describe our music: warm, deep, progressive, etc., and he came up with Deepend. We thought it sounded really good.

Would you tell me what your process of creation is like—how do you work together to develop a dance track or a remix?

Bob: A remix is a bit easier because you have source material to start with. We get a lot of remix requests now (especially since our recent hit with Matt Simons, "Catch & Release"). The most important thing for us is that we are hooked by the *original* song.

When we play the original, if we are into it, we have immediately something like 30 ideas of what can be done with it. We usually start with the bass line—we'll be humming that the minute we hear the original version. We "feel" what we have to do with it. We'll get the vocals and all the elements and start working on it.

Falco: Yes, and often we start working on it separately. Bob lives in Amsterdam, and I live about a two hour drive away from him, so we begin with our two separate versions of the song—then we start to combine our efforts. Quite naturally, we are able to combine the best of both our versions. The funny thing is our tastes are so similar it's almost scary. We'll go to a festival and the DJ plays a song, and I will know Bob will like the track, and he'll know I will, too! We have a lot of friends that are into music, but they all tend to have different likes. But with Bob, our tastes are really the same.

You mentioned the Matt Simons' hit track 'Catch & Release' a moment ago, which you expertly remixed into a chill dance club and radio success late in 2015. As we speak, it has well over 125 million hits on Spotify and it's still on their chart. Matt is more of a singer/songwriter artist. Is it challenging to shift a song that originally falls more into the easy-listening pop category into the dance setting?

Falco: No, it's not really difficult as long as we feel the vibe of the original, as I mentioned. We can take it from there. For us, that song was really refreshing because it wasn't a typical dance vocal. We added our style, which brought the song into new territory—in between genres. That's what makes Matt Simons so interesting. His fans who appreciate him as a singer/songwriter really dig our remix—and they may not even be into electronic music. And even those who *are* big fans of electronic music are digging our mix of the song. A project like this also expands our audience and Matt's.

Bob: We get a lot of requests to remix tracks, but we can't do what we did with "Catch & Release" with every song. It's not like a formula that you can apply to everything.

Are you able to tell me, in your experience, how artists like Matt or, say, Mike Posner ("I Took a Pill in Ibiza") are reacting to having their original songs converted into this pop-dance-electronic hybrid? Is a dance mix, simply put, somewhat essential to prosperity in pop music today?

Falco: Yes, I think so. I think you are seeing a lot of artists use this strategy, and there's no question it helps them a lot.

Bob: Dance music dominates radio now, so to be mainstream, having alternate dance mixes helps [if you want] to have a hit.

Falco: Dance mixes will generally give you a much stronger reach. Yes, singer/songwriters will have their core fans, but today, for example, everyone knows Matt Simons because of our remix. It helped him reach a much bigger audience, and the mix added this refreshing quality to his song, which already was a great track.

We know Matt very well, and with him (and other artists like him), it's a two-way street. He too has to *feel* the remix, just like we have to feel the original version. They went through five or six remixes by others (all rejected) before Matt's people came to us to try it. The other remixes lost the whole feeling of the original song. Matt is very picky, and he should be.

**It's interesting what you are saying about these artists and how they may [reluctantly] be shifting into the dance genre. Dance music, too, is shifting. In the past, so many dance songs didn't have a real song structure—just an intro, a breakdown, a drop, a second breakdown and an outro. And now all the DJ/producers are looking for genuine song structure—a verse, a bridge and a chorus. They want radio songs—real songs. Singer/songwriters can deliver that. We are all meeting in the middle somewhere.

EDM, possibly the most dominant style in twenty-first century dance music culture, has been critiqued by some as being cold, noisy music. So, are you saying there's a shift now to stronger melodies, lyrics and—soul?

Bob: Yes, maybe the best way to describe it is a shift towards—emotion. The last five years have been about one big kick drum sound—just a hard, in-your-face sound. Melody is definitely returning. We're seeing that in our bookings, too. We are getting prime-time slots that used to be filled by EDM DJs. During our first Ibiza season this past summer, normally all the big names like David Guetta get their own big night at the clubs. But increasingly, DJs like Kygo are also playing those venues. We were invited by Guetta to play one of his parties. It's a good sign.

Today, you can't rely just on singles and remixes to prosper in the business of dance music. You have to be a performer and be able to entertain with your personalities and images as DJs. You certainly have the technical and creative talent, but how naturally does this other side come to you?

Falco: Well, you're right. Selling, or rather producing, music tracks is really just a promotional tool. Radio airplay can generate some income, but 90 percent of your income comes from live performances. I really like the combination of being a producer and DJ/performer. We started as DJs and then became producer/DJs. But we weren't performers—we were working safely behind our decks. We weren't grabbing a mic and dazzling the audience. But I can say I definitely like performing—I don't think I'd enjoy this as much if I was just a producer. But we definitely had to adjust to the performing aspect.

Bob: Yeah, like two months ago we were playing a main stage for 25,000 people. We had to grab the mics and get out there—we were so scared. We like it and are learning, and you get more confidence as time goes by with every show. But I would never say we were natural-born performers either.

You definitely seemed to have gotten the hang of it in the video for your party single "I'm Intoxicated."

Falco: Yeah, that was a lot of fun. But it's definitely two different worlds—the kind of nerdy technical world of producing and the fun and excitement of performing. We're learning how to get better at it every day.

I'm curious why there are still so few women producer/DJs in the business.

Falco: I think the producing side of things is less appealing to a lot of women. You *have* to be a producer to be a DJ now. I don't personally know any women who produce music. I can't really explain why this is—I actually think it's a little strange.

In terms of DJs, have you observed a lot of competition—by that I mean aggressive competition and rivalry?

Bob: No, I haven't. It is actually a very nice scene—especially in deep house and especially in Holland. There's a lot of sharing, and it's a lot of fun.

Falco: It's like we are colleagues, not competitors. We know most of the DJs in our country, and we often have big group chats. We plan nights in Amsterdam and get together for chicken and beer, discussing management, bookings, contract information—we help each other with everything. We give each other production tips and music. And labels like Armada—they will have a party every so often so that we are more like a team. We don't see that kind of negative competition.

We've spoken with DJs from other countries, who definitely say there *is* that sense of negative competition, fighting—and everyone is on their own. But in the Netherlands—you make good music, and if you do, you don't have to fight over it.

A great deal of popular dance music seems to come out of the Netherlands. I've been observing that since the '70s. What is it about your country that makes it such a great place to produce such uplifting music?

Falco: Maybe there's something in the water? [*He laughs.*] I think Dutch people are very down to earth. If you were to ever meet Armin van Buuren or Tiësto, you'd see they are very normal guys who happen to be living a rock star's life. Yet every day they go home to their families and live a somewhat normal life. I don't know—maybe it's that we are a small country, so we help each other. Dance music really kicked in here during the '80s, and we all grew up with it. You can drive through our country in like three hours, and there are something like 500 or 600 dance festivals here annually—it's everywhere. I guess that's pretty healthy, and, as a result, Holland is a natural [epicenter] for dance music.

Do you find there is any difference between audiences from different countries in terms of their reaction to dance music?

Bob: Oh, yes. For instance, the Dutch crowds are really tough to please. They grew up with dance music, and they've seen all of the best DJs and performers. So, it's really hard to entertain them. In Germany, in Berlin, the underground is very big, so you can play more groovy, non-commercial music. In France, however, you must play the most commercial tracks out at the time to get the crowd going. It's actually fascinating for us to observe these differences.

Falco: Whatever the gig, we try to arrive an hour or so before we go on to hear what other DJs are playing and to see how the crowd is reacting. That way, you can determine if you need to be playing a more underground style or whatever. And you can figure that a younger crowd will be into more commercial music, and an older crowd will like it if you play a wider range. You'll know by the first three tracks you play where to take things.

What's the biggest sign that you might be losing the crowd?

Falco: [*He laughs.*] They are standing still on the dancefloor or playing on their phones.

Bob: Or they are just standing there, staring at us. It doesn't happen to us much anymore, fortunately.

Falco: That's also the job of the DJ. We don't play pre-recorded music sets. We play based on audience reaction.

I dislike having to move on to this next subject after speaking about the joy of people's enthusiasm for these dance music events. But there's a dark side to these big crowd gatherings that has, unfortunately, become a grim reality of life today. Such parties and events are now the targets of acts of terrorism. How has this affected you?

Bob: These are terrible, tragic events. And they are affecting the industry. We have felt the impact already with the loss of a number of booking requests.

Falco: We received a lot of requests to play places like Lebanon, Egypt and other areas, but we were advised to avoid them. We played in Brussels the week after the 2015 attacks in Paris. There was a major lockdown, and the streets were empty. You could feel tension at the party. It's strange—we weren't always thinking of this before, but now we are always checking where emergency exits are located.

Airports are now just as scary. I traveled to an airport in Amsterdam, and it's like I almost ran through the arrivals area. I want to get through security as fast as possible. You just want to get out of the airport as quickly as you can. You see all the military guards with huge machine guns. It's definitely scary. You're more and more aware of the risk, and now you must learn to live with it. It's no longer in just what you might call "high risk" countries—it's everywhere.

Bob: We played at Tomorrowland, one of the biggest electronic music festivals in the world held in Belgium. The security to get into the event was as rigorous as at an airport—60,000 people or so all checked-in that way. Security, machine guns, dogs—it was crazy.

Drug use has played a major role in how an audience responds to dance music across a number of decades. Is it a consideration when you play your sets?

Falco: Yeah, you see it a lot at the festivals. But it doesn't affect how we play.

Bob: It's more that you can see how the drugs are affecting the people's response to the music. They may close their eyes more and things like that. But it isn't a consideration for us when deciding what tracks we will play.

You are making tremendous strides forward in your music and your momentum is clearly building. Where do you want to go with your music and careers?

Falco: We are still primarily considered DJs, but I like that many other DJs become actual artists. For example, Robin Schulz, David Guetta—they go far beyond just being DJs. They release albums and singles and do so much. That's our goal too. We'll do some good remixes and original singles, and our long-term goal is to get a really great original album out there. A Deepend album with a variety of styles. We don't play house music—we play *Deepend house music*—a much broader genre. We'd like to incorporate hip-hop, too.

Bob: I'd love to also see us do a tour for such an album project. We recently saw Robin play one of his tour dates—it was amazing. We are starting to think about all these things for our future.

You remixed Robin Schulz's "Heatwave" (featuring Akon), another hit during the summer of 2016. Do you study artists like Robin in such opportunities as this—do you look at these people as mentors in a way?

Falco: Absolutely. The show Bob mentioned—we went with our manager, and it was like a study trip. We carefully watched everything and analyzed every aspect of the show and performance afterward. We can learn so much from these artists—but we also see ways we can do things differently, so that we build our own identities.

Have you been able to maintain a social life so far?

Falco: We get time home during the week—it's Friday and the weekends that get crazy! But we can maintain our lives.

I know you're both very young, but I wonder—do you ever look at yourselves and what you're doing and see yourselves as part of this great dance music lineage that goes back to artists like Donna Summer, Gloria Gaynor, Martha Wash, Nile Rodgers, Giorgio Moroder and so many other legends? Do you think of yourselves as carrying on that great tradition?

Falco: Oh wow, no, I never did—not until right now that you describe it that way! But hearing you say that, it actually *is* kind of amazing to be a part of such a big movement. It's an honor.

Bob: Yeah, I don't think we ever thought of that. We just make music that we like. But it is very cool to look at it like that.

What do you think is the core appeal of dance music—what has made it so popular over the past four decades?

Falco: It's the groove—it's even that repetitive character in the music. There is something special about getting sucked into a dance record! That's the power—the four-to-the-floor kick drum, the loops and the grooves.

Bob: Its power is really amazing—when you see something like 60,000 people at a festival all in the same groove because of a dance song, that's pretty amazing!

Lightning Round with Deepend

The dance song you never tire of hearing?

Bob and Falco [*speaking at the same time*]: "Pjanoo" by Eric Prydz.

Falco: That track really got us into dance music from the start. Super uplifting—and we still play it in our sets sometimes.

Do you remember the first time a stranger recognized you as a member of Deepend?

Falco: It was only [early in 2016] that it happened for the first time—but it's happened often since then. It was the first time we were in the U.S.—California. We were having breakfast at a little bar in Venice Beach, and a guy came up to us and recognized us both as Deepend.

Bob: For me, personally, it was at a deep house festival in Amsterdam—I was there as a visitor, not playing, but someone in the crowd asked me, "Hey, aren't you with Deepend?"

Craziest thing you ever saw take place on a dancefloor?

Falco: Oh, it was in 2015. We were playing in Switzerland, and there was a very overweight guy giving a terrible pole dance in the middle of the dancefloor, in the middle of our set. He really scared people—girls were running out of the club. He didn't have the effect he was going for. [*They laugh.*]

What's the biggest downside of working in dance music?

Bob: The traveling. Not that you are seeing all these amazing places—that's one of the best things. It's the fact that you can spend 12 hours in a plane to get there. A while back, we played Malta. On the way back, our flight got delayed in Rome due to a strike. It took about 13 hours to get back to Amsterdam, which normally would have taken about three.

Falco: Traveling is one of the hardest parts of DJ life. When you have four or five gigs in five days in five countries—it's brutal.

Deepend (Falco van den Aker, left, Bob van Ratigen, right) released the hit single "Runaways" in the spring of 2017, a collaboration with Sam Feldt, featuring Teemu.

What artists do you currently like to listen to in your spare time?
    Falco: I really like DJ Claptone from Germany.
    Bob: Kygo—he's riding the current wave in tropical house music.

Best website or social media outlet for promoting dance music?
    Falco: For us it's been Facebook, believe it or not. We reach the most people through it.

Dirtydisco
Lajos (Louis) Polgár (DJ, producer, remixer)
"Shake Your Banjo" (2015)

"It's great to mash-up current styles with '70s and '80s disco music. I don't think the sounds are really all that different. There is a heritage line you follow—it mixes quite naturally with today's fashionable sounds."—Dirtydisco

Standing considerably over six feet tall, the Hungarian DJ, producer and bodybuilder known as Dirtydisco (aka Louis Polgár, and not to be confused with UK act The Dirty Disco or US production entity Dirty Disco) is a rising star on today's European dance scene, and he's hard to overlook. In recent years, Polgár's been scoring a series of international hits and remixes with tracks such as "Hallelujah" ("Miami 2 LA"), "Bass Dunk" (featuring Charlotte Devaney and Fatman Scoop), "Die Hard" and "Shake Your Banjo." He's been gaining a growing reputation for his unique brand of high-energy, which deftly melds Eurodance, house and pop-disco sounds. That power is evident in his DJ sets and his remix productions, both of which are earning him accolades across the continent. His appeal is now reaching far beyond the borders of his native country, and he looks to continue to build upon that momentum.

Dirtydisco is a true multi-tasker, enjoying a growing career as a DJ/producer that is expanding beyond his home base in Hungary.

Louis, please tell me what it was like growing up in Hungary and how you first connected to dance music.

Our family ran a little bar, and as I was growing up, I spent quite a lot of time helping out there. We had all kinds of contemporary dance music playing at the bar. I was always into music, especially the rhythm aspect. I had gotten into drumming very early on.

Why the name "Dirtydisco"?

That was my very first idea, so I stuck with it.

Can you describe the nature and energy found in the Hungarian, Polish and European music scene you work in today?

The popular music found in this part of Europe is very energetic and commercial sounding: catchy melodies, lots of good vocals and brutal grooves. As far as "politics" in dance music is concerned, all the DJs around here are quite selfish, unlike in the western hemisphere. There is no tendency to really help each other out. In Hungary particularly, there is a lot of confusion lately as the national media has been dominated by unprofessionals appointed by the Orbán regime who don't know or care about the tastes of the masses and the dynamics of the local music market.

How did you first become involved in professionally creating dance music and remixes?

Although there were many great tunes out in Hungary, there was a lack of playable club versions. That's what made me start creating remixes—so that I could play them on my DJ gigs. I was always connected to music via the basic rhythm, and I put myself into the world of remixes via carefully selected, powerful groove structures.

What's your measure for success or satisfaction when you create a remix or an original song—chart position, sales, people going crazy on a dancefloor?

All three count, but maybe the best measurable reaction comes from the dance-floor crowds.

Do you approach remixing other artists' work differently from creating your own original work?

"Yes, definitely there is a different approach. For one thing, it is a different setup with a tune that already exists. There are a lot of elements—key, leads, etc.—which you need to appreciate as you bring your own vision to the track. For some reason, I actually enjoy it more than creating an original song. And, for me, there is also the element of a challenge—you need to at least equal the quality of the original with a remix, and it's always nice to come up with something that's even better.

You seem to appreciate the retro sound of old school disco in your work ("Rocky," for example). How much does classic disco influence your EDM creations?

It's great to mash-up current styles with '70s and '80s disco music. I don't think the sounds are really all that different. There is a heritage line you follow—it mixes quite naturally with today's fashionable sounds.

I was also a fan of action TV series growing up as a kid; they influenced my world view quite a bit. It's nice to pay homage to something that has meant a lot to you. Not to mention people love what's already familiar to them, as long as it's not too worn out. So these older songs, like [my interpretation of Dr. Alban's] "Hallelujah (Miami 2 LA)," are part of the masses' DNA. Present them in just the right way and they can relate to your vibes more easily.

How difficult is it to balance the creative and business sides of your enterprise?

I am fortunate to have a friend/manager/partner-in-crime named Zoltan Foldes, who I work very closely with. We share all the duties. He chips in on the creative side, but mostly oversees the business side of things, which allows me time to create the music.

How quickly do styles and trends generally emerge in dance music? Is it challenging to be an innovator of these styles as opposed to a follower of what other artists are doing?

Styles and trends in EDM/dance have a certain somewhat detectable way of behaving. They mostly move in a circle—everything comes and goes in circles. Some sounds, grooves and musical structures are out of trend now but will move back in soon enough. It is a lot easier to follow trends, but that has a lesser payoff. It's great if you can have your own unique sound and build it into whatever you're working on right now as a trademark.

There have been a number of dramatic changes in the world of dance music over the last 10 years, including the diminished ranking of the vocalist, as the DJ/producer took the spotlight. What are your thoughts about this trend?

This is the new world order. DJs became the top producers. Any artist *should* be able to adjust his or her ways to this, but not all can. Why and how this came about would probably fill a book in itself. I have always been a DJ and was inclined to produce, so there was no conflict on my side about going with this trend. When an evolution like this comes along naturally, I believe it's perfectly okay from a revolutionary standpoint.

That said, sometimes I will say that the talents of the vocalist are just used by the DJ/producers for their own progress. The vocalist profits way less and can't turn this job into an opportunity to build his or her brand. I think it has a lot to do with the decline of the record companies, who were largely responsible for building the careers of vocalists as worldwide brands in the past, and they definitely aren't doing that any more.

Do you see any challenges for DJs, now that they are the center of attention?

Sometimes, DJs (for better or worse) feel the need to produce when they are not really capable of the job. With this type of DJ, we have a problem. Also, in some very visible cases, the opposite is true—a great musician and excellent producer tries to sell himself as a DJ. But he is just too introverted, lacks the energy and poise, or is incapable of handling that situation. There, too, we have a problem. Sometimes when they play their sets, they can't even tell if a song is any good or it fits their set or not. This causes a lot of confusion, not only in the DJ's heart or in the industry, but also in the perception of the public. They see people who are famous but can't DJ and think that it's somehow okay. (It is *not* okay.) They hear music that's been put together badly by someone who is established in the clubs, and they don't quite get it but accept it.

How are you coping with the other dramatic changes in the business, such as streaming and dismal digital sales?

The main income source for artists, DJs and producers in dance music now comes from live performance—having your tracks released and made available on streaming services must be viewed [strictly] as subsidy income.

Which has more impact on the success of a dance track these days—social media exposure or word-of-mouth from the clubs and dance music festivals and parties?

Both are quite important. What you really need is very good quality and original music (which I reckon is about the top five percent of all music produced), and it will go all the way. For that you need talent, and lots of practice—and sometimes to get influence from the right people. I can tell you this is extremely difficult to find, especially in Hungary.

What satisfies you about DJing?

Meeting the crowd has always been the most important thing for me. There is a lot I gain from their energy and a lot I have to thank them for. There are always new pieces of music in the making, and we, as DJs, need their feedback!

As a DJ, how do you manage the saturation of music available—the literally hundreds of tracks that come out each day?

There is a lot you must pay attention to, and it's a matter of discovery. Your audiences have definite tastes and they discover music, your fellow talented DJs discover good music, and some very good specialized top labels with good A&R departments let you know about some good tracks. You have to pay attention to what trends they are dictating and whether there is also a pulse in the nation or a scene, a certain fashionable music style that is gaining momentum, etc. Then you have to decide whether or not you can build the given tune into your regular repertoire or not.

In past decades, drugs (the crowd being high) often played a huge part in the mood of the room and how a DJ will play. Is that still the case in the twenty-first century?

Drugs, I think, still play a similar role. But it also depends on your style. And I really believe that good music, and how exactly and by whom it is presented in the club, can have a special hypnotizing, drug-like effect on its own—if its selected carefully and played right at the right time.

Acts of terrorism are becoming a risk to consider when one thinks about engaging in nightlife activities (ex. the Paris attacks in 2015, the Orlando shootings and the Nice attack in 2016, etc.). Do you think it will deter people from clubbing and going out to dance as time goes on?

Everyone loves to party and will continue to love to party! The party that is most secure—probably the bigger, more established, traditional clubs, places and festivals where security is higher—will have the advantage here. I am also a security expert, so it is my job to know this.

How difficult is it for you to maintain a healthy personal life with nightlife and the running of your business?

Okay, as with any other profession (even with a nine-to-five office job) there is a lot of risk of becoming unhealthy if you're not paying enough attention to your body and mind. Speaking for myself, I love to work out, I eat right and keep a very healthy lifestyle going in general. I don't smoke, no alcohol—and I just love what I do. I might be the exception, though, among DJs. [*Louis laughs.*]

What's been the highlight of your professional career so far and what do you want to still accomplish?

We have had some really great international successes lately—our first number one track in Poland, an official remix for UK DJ/actress/top model Charlotte Devaney featuring Fatman Scoop, and some nice gigs under our belt. I look forward to having even more number ones, more remixes for top artists and even more international gigs.

Do you think the dance music of the past 17 years will one day be viewed as fondly as the classics of the '70s, '80s and '90s?

It seems to me that music (in general) which was produced in the previous century might have a better life expectancy. Again, this trend of music now becoming a social thing (without record company professionals telling us what's hot or what should be considered memorable) may ultimately be the deciding factor. But, hey, there's still a lot of talent out there, producing some great stuff and a lot more diverse music than ever before.

What do you think has made dance music so great, so valuable over the past four decades?
It addresses massive crowds, it is commercial when done right, and it is easy to digest.

Lightning Round with Dirtydisco

What is one track that never gets old for you no matter how many times you hear it?
3 Drives On a Vinyl's "Greece 2000."

Diana Ross or Beyoncé?
Diana Ross.

Best thing about Hungary?
The culture, the food, the diversity. I *loooove* Hungary—it is my home country!

Best decade in dance music—'70, '80s or '90s?
The '90s.

Craziest thing you ever saw take place on a dancefloor?
There was this featherweight Chinese guy who was doing something wrong, and the big strong security guy lifted him straight up with one hand, raised him over the crowd like a flag and carried him out!

Best thing to eat after a night of clubbing?
A hot dog.

Favorite activity outside of music to unwind?
I like to enjoy the sauna, jacuzzi and movies.

Dirtydisco's "Shake Your Banjo" was an international hit and number one commercial track on Polish radio.

What is the biggest mistake a DJ can make?
Disregarding the crowd.

If you weren't in entertainment, what do you think you'd be doing?
I am also a security expert as a side career—I love it as much as I love DJing!

D.O.N.S./Warp Brothers

Oliver Goedicke (DJ, producer, remixer)

"Phatt Bass" (2000)—Warp Brothers vs. Aquagen/
"Phatt Bass" (2016)—Wolfpack & Warp Brothers
"Big Fun" (2014)—D.O.N.S. and Terri B!

> "Perhaps the meaning music has for me is deeper than for some others, but when I DJ, and the second I stop thinking and just play the music, it is for me—maybe it sounds silly—nirvana!—D.O.N.S.

Late December 2014, was a monumental point in Oliver Goedicke's career, better known by his DJ moniker D.O.N.S. and other incarnations, such as Disco Nation, Brain Twins and Tranquillo (and more). Despite a long history in twenty-first century dance music, including a partnership with Jürgen Dohr as the legendary hard house duo the Warp Brothers (whose smash 2000 hit "Phatt Base," credited to Warp Brothers vs. Aquagen, was recreated by Goedicke to much acclaim in 2016), the inventive producer and DJ hadn't ever conquered the top spot on the Billboard dance chart. That changed with the release of D.O.N.S. and Terri B!'s version of "Big Fun," a reinvention of the classic Inner City club track, which became a number one smash on the dance survey of the all-important music bible.

For Goedicke, it's another high point in a series of amazing adventures he's experienced in dance music (notably the trance and hard-trance sub-genres), an outlet that has allowed him to tap into the very core of his passions and which harkens all the way back to the funk and soul roots of his tumultuous youth. Possessing a vivid memory for the events that have shaped his career, Oliver clearly appreciates his high ranking in dance music today and discusses his journey during a touring break while in Germany.

Oliver, would you tell me what life was like for you growing up and how you first came to connect with music?

That is the first time someone has asked me that question! I was always waiting for it, and I know I will end up giving a very personal answer. I can't separate my private life in my youth from what music means to me. The fact is I had a very turbulent childhood—extremely turbulent—dominated by a lot of severe violence and sad and traumatic family dramas. I grew up with and spent a lot of time with my grandparents in France. They were very well off—which made me, in part, a bit spoiled. That was the stable part of my life because they were amazing people. I also spent time with my aunt and uncle and my dad. My dad was a really crazy guy—his history is a book and movie in itself—and my sister and I were in the middle of a scenario which was definitely not suitable for young kids. My mom, who is an adorable person, finally got us out of this mess. My grandparents tragically died shortly after she regained custody over me and my sister. Until that day, there was always this back and forth thing going on. I remember when I was little my stepmother or stepfather fighting with my parents. When it became too loud or violent, I took my tape player and headphones and pressed them so hard against my ears to suppress the violence I was hearing and witnessing.

At a very young age, music developed a very high meaning for me—it was very important. My uncle was a man of color (his father was Jamaican) and was crazy about music, so I was always exposed to records for as long as I can remember. My family always had music in the background—I guess you could say they were like posh hippies. When things turned really bad—many times to a tragic level—I escaped into music. For me, the most important thing in my life has always been music.

Specifically, I started out with soul and funk, not the typical AC/DC, ABBA and Depeche Mode type of sounds. I was listening to Kraftwerk at the age of 12, James Brown and Miles Davis—and I loved it. When things fell apart for my sister and myself in such a sad way, I started recording cassettes. I had a very cheap turntable to record these cassette compilations. In 1980–81, when I was 14 or 15, my father lost custody of us, and I went to live with my mom. I was very shy, but I started inviting other kids to house parties in my mother's apartment. She was very open-minded. I had two Panasonic turntables by then, with no pitch control, and I'd mix records by Zapp, Bootsy Collins, Curtis Mayfield and artists like that. I didn't talk much; I was a kind of nerdy kid. These parties gave me confidence, and at some point there would be something like 100 people there—the cool kids.

I wanted to connect to more DJs, although I wasn't intending to become one. One day, a guest at one of my parties asked me if I wanted to play music for an event at a Hamburg

D.O.N.S. and Terri B! reached the top of the *Billboard* club chart in 2015 with "Big Fun," their first number one record in the U.S.

rowing club. He wanted me to play rock and pop, not necessarily the funk and soul I favored. Of course, I said yes, and it was very successful—my first paid gig at the age of 14. From there, I started doing more of them. At the age of 18 I got a job at a record store—it was rather a well-known store where DJs from all over the world, from all the cool clubs, came to shop. I spent a fortune there, more than some DJs. They had a basement where DJs would listen to records, and they invited me to come down there and listen to music. I was shaking—this was like the holy grail of music for me. A girlfriend of mine (she was a successful model) was with me one day in the store, and it was she who told them I would be a good person to work at the place. They told me if I got over my shyness and started talking, they would give me a job. I turned out to be the best salesman they ever had. When I spoke about music, I lost all my inhibitions and sold so many records. (This has stayed with me to this very day—I don't care so much about making money; I just want music in my life.)

Keep in mind, I never really was a pro DJ with good equipment up until this point. A few meters from my mom's home was the number one club in Hamburg (and I believe it was in the Top Five in Germany). It was called Trinity (later renamed Offline) and was a reconstruction of Studio 54 in New York. Some people still say it was the best club in Germany—ever! The record store was sponsoring various nights at this club. One night, the resident DJ (who was paid DM 2500 a night) was unable to play. They came to me and asked me to do the job. Naturally, I said yes, despite the fact that I didn't know how I would do it and had never been in the club. Now I was exposed to professional DJ gear, turntables with pitch—everything. I started playing at 10PM, and the night lasted one hour longer than average. The next day they called me to book me for Fridays and Saturdays (and, I swear, they fired all the resident DJs) and paid me DM 600, which was a fortune for me at the time. I became the resident DJ (which caused many other DJs to quickly hate me). I bought my first professional equipment.

In 1986, at around the age of 20, I kind of decided to run away from the stress, fear and anger I felt in Hamburg. After two years of being the resident DJ at Trinity/Offline, being asked to play the same stuff all the time—Stock Aitken Waterman, Rick Astley, Kylie—I was getting very tired of the scene. I thought, you know, I'm not a service bitch! I have to play music people like, but my heart has to be in it—and it wasn't like that anymore.

When a friend suggested we move to New York at that point, I agreed. We moved to 72nd Street, where I quickly became the biggest customer at Downtown Records. I started buying soul, funk and dance records, 1,000 or 2,000 of them over time, and resold them to people in Germany. I was able to finance my stay in New York that way. I eventually returned to Germany and got another residency (and promotion job) at a top club there for 12 years. I was voted one of the top three DJs in the nation regularly. After that, I wanted people to dance to music that *I* created. So, by 1993, I had to learn how to become a producer.

From there, I believe you launched your professional music-making career as D.O.N.S. and as part of the Warp Brothers. How does this phase kick off? Oh, and would you please tell me where the moniker D.O.N.S. came from?

D.O.N.S. used to mean "design on sound"—there's a story attached to that. I was a resident DJ at a club called Traxx (a venue that made it to the Top 10 of the worldwide best clubs ranked by Playboy International), and someone approached me to supply the music for a fashion show video that involved Versace, Cerruti and other upscale designers. They wanted hit songs, and I selected the music for the video. However, they used these songs by people like Whitney Houston without securing the proper permissions, and they got sued. After that disaster, they then approached me to produce new music for the video. Once again, I had no idea how to do that, but I said yes. I was paid very well and went to an engineer/musician friend of mine, and we produced 30 tracks in one week's time. We delivered it, and they loved it. The video won some awards, which brought me to the attention of many music publishers. That led to a music publishing deal for me for a crazy amount of money—I think it was something like DM 750,000 for nothing really.

There was a track I made where we used a sample, and a record label heard it, called me and asked if we could do it in a trance style. I said, again, yes—I always say that whether I know how to do it or not. (I had done a remix for Modern Talking's "You're My Heart, You're My Soul" previously, but it was terrible—*dreadful*.) They needed it by tomorrow for one of the best-selling compilation albums in Germany called *Trance Nation*. We worked on the track for 20 hours straight, boosted up the kick drum on it and remastered it on DAT tape the next morning. The record label, Kontor, was just starting, and they loved it. "This is a fucking hit!" they said. The song was "Drop the Gun." They wanted to sign me to a record deal, so we needed a name. I looked around the studio and saw a record called "Sound Design" by Todd Terry, who I loved. We didn't want to take that exact name and get into trouble (back in the day, legal situations could be more drastic than they are today), so we called ourselves Design on Sound. D.O.N.S. If I knew how the Internet would develop, I would never have chosen this name because of the dots in it. The name gets spelled all kinds of ways, and it's very hard to Google it, but that's what we chose.

Our second release was "Pump Up the Jam," which was followed by the Warp Brothers. I had been doing so many productions that by 1997 I decided to quit a day job I was holding (which was in an investment/financial company—stocks and bonds, things like that). I opened a huge studio and really started my own little empire in Hamburg.

The Warp Brothers, your collaboration with Jürgen Dohr, produced some big hits at the turn of the century. "We Will Survive" and "Phatt Bass" reached the upper echelons of the pop and dance charts in various countries in 2000. Do you recall the background of "Phatt Base," which became connected with another popular group at the time, Aquagen?

Those two songs you mentioned were made about six months apart. I was DJing at a house and techno club, where I met a man of color—he came into the club, and there was some excitement surrounding him. After a while, he approached me to ask if I would play some Reggae. The dancefloor was still empty at this point (as it was very early in the night), and so I played some tracks for him. He danced out there all alone. He thanked me and introduced himself as Wesley. Seconds later, another DJ came up to me and asked if I knew who that was. I didn't. It was Wesley Snipes, one of the biggest emerging stars at the time with a movie coming out that was to be called *Blade*. I didn't care about that sort of thing—fame or money. I just thought he was a nice guy. Some time later, I actually happened to watch the movie *Blade* by coincidence, and I heard a song playing during the now infamous bloodbath scene. I was so taken by the song and the fact that I recognized the bloke I was chatting to some weeks back, I had to have the rights to it. It was New Order's "Confusion."

I asked New Order for the rights, and they were fine with that. My idea was to do the track with an amazing vocal—this would be the foundation of "Phatt Bass."

A guy (he was just an ordinary guy with a deep voice and no singer) named Jack, who may have since passed on (not 100 percent sure, but he was already way over 60 and chain-smoked), handled the original vocals, according to Jürgen and my text briefing. They were not pitched at all; these were the original vocals. He was smoking two or three packs a day and drinking whiskey, and the sound just worked. Jürgen and I finished the track and brought it to the Dos Or Die label because Kontor didn't want to take it. Dos or Die's label owner loved it, but claimed he had another track by Aquagen that was very similar (and he wanted to merge our tracks). To this day, I don't believe Aquagen *really* had a song that was that similar—but who knows? I never dared to ask them. [*Ollie laughs.*]

I thought this was fishy, but Dos Or Die was one of the biggest labels in dance at the time. (It later went bankrupt in 2003, and they failed to pay us a lot of royalties for our first singles. Eventually, I secured the rights to the label name.) So, anyway, I agreed to the deal, but I wanted our name on the credit first—Warp Brothers vs. Aquagen. He agreed. It ended up being helpful because Aquagen was very famous back then, and nobody had heard of us obviously. The radio version of the song—I must admit, I hated it. We did a much more underground version that I much preferred, but I had to acknowledge that it was the radio version that became the hit—Top 10 in the UK, a gold record in Denmark, a *Billboard* dance chart hit in the U.S., etc.

That song was followed by "We Will Survive," and we started touring, which lasted for about 12 years.

I notice that many of your productions are highly original and very reflective of the time in which they were released. Other tracks seem to pay homage to great dance songs of the past, such as "Jack to the Sound of the Underground" and "Pump Up the Jam." You even worked with the legendary Jocelyn Brown on a remake of "Somebody Else's Guy." Some critics look at remakes as evidence of a lack of originality in dance music. What's your take on making new versions of classic dance tracks?

Of course, the past always has an impact on the present. Even Elvis Presley had hits with cover versions. Covering has been around forever and is not that bad. I will say, there is a certain kind of pressure in the music industry. If you deliver something, like my original song, "Drop the Gun," and it's a hit, there is pressure to follow it up. And record labels have a lot of say in what you do next, as well.

I did a version of "Pump Up the Jam" in 1996, yes, but I took just one element from it and reversed it by reversing and looping the lyric about the jam pumping. It was a very deep original track, but then Kontor Records approached me in 2005 and asked for a more commercial version—and so we delivered them a smash hit record, even bigger than my previous version. Later, my hit with Terri B!, "Big Fun," a remake of the Inner City hit song, was voted by *DJ* magazine as one of the Top 25 cover versions of all time. I remember hearing Frankie Knuckles playing the [original] song at the Tunnel. It blew me away when I first heard it, back when I had no money and didn't speak English, living in New York City.

I feel I managed to bring new creativity to my cover versions. Covers actually take me longer to create than an original because if it's going to come out badly, I don't want to do it. I cover songs that have a meaning to me. It's not just because the song was a hit back in the day. I'm not saying I don't think about that at times today, but back in the early days, the song had to have a powerful connection with me. Take "Cokane," written by Lester Bullock of Dillinger, which I remade in 2002 with the Warp Brothers. It was one of my uncle's favorite songs and one of mine when I was a teen. Jocelyn Brown—I saw her perform her original version of "Somebody Else's Guy" when I booked her at my club, and I saw the crowd all raising lighters as she sang it. It touched me long before I remade the song with her. I can say the same thing about working with Gloria Gaynor on "Supernatural Love," although this was not a cover. She had a great influence on me when I was younger. (Unfortunately, that song was a complete flop, except in Eastern Europe. I'm thinking of revamping it.)

So, I don't believe cover versions are a bad thing if you contribute something new to the original and if you bring your own vision to it. I will tell you, I don't even mind if someone samples one of *my* songs, as long as they have the courtesy to ask.

As you mentioned, in 2015 you went to number one for the first time on the *Billboard* dance chart with a new version of the song "Big Fun," featuring Terri B!. How did it feel to reach this achievement and how much of a game-changer was it for you in the dance music business as a DJ or producer?

I was really happy (and still am) about that number one. The *Billboard* chart is one of the most important club charts worldwide, but it wasn't really a game changer. It kept my name in the circuit and was good for social media buzz. In terms of business, things didn't change much.

Let's talk about vocalists. Today, the DJ is the star and people buy into their presence far more than the singer. Why do you suppose things evolved this way in dance music?

I believe this can be explained by one word—money.

We've gone through a big decrease in income from record sales, which dropped off tremendously. My first record ("Drop the Gun") entered the Top 100 in Germany at number 100 for only a week, and while I may have considered it a flop [in terms of the charts], it still made 40,000 Euro. Now, you go Top 10 on iTunes, it's a hit, and you get a few millions streams on Spotify, and you make 2,000 Euro. That's a generalization, but you get the idea. Today's singers can't get as many live performance gigs, so they jump from studio to studio to try and make money recording. Maybe the song isn't that great for the singer's image, but for 2,000 Euro, they take the job. They can pay their rent, repair their car, etc. When you start doing so many recordings for DJs, you begin to lose your identity. If you lose your identity, it becomes very hard to market you. Singers are important for a production, yes, but the appreciation of their work has declined.

Singers have to make a living and take job after job with the DJ/producers. The profile of the DJ went up faster and faster, as did their fees, and the singer's fees stagnated or even decreased. The correlation between the work and the person's input changed. Some DJs don't even go to the studio anymore—they have their engineer handle most of the work. I don't think there's anything bad about that. I can't imagine Puff Daddy goes into the studio on every track he's involved with and says I want this or that.

There was a time when clubs booked many singers who were becoming connected with David Guetta, Armin van Buren, etc. But that only lasted a short time because the model of singing on stage alone is pretty dead, at least for now—but things can, of course, always change. Nobody (of the younger generation) is that interested in seeing a singer with a microphone anymore. The younger generation wants the overall experience, rather than quality. I don't even think they care about the music as much as the experience it generates, especially on all those pimped-up, mind-blowing festivals with productions that could put rock star shows to shame.

The kids of today don't talk anymore—they are chatting with each other on WhatsApp and Snapchat and filming themselves on the dancefloor. Twenty years ago, if I played a record at a festival that another DJ had already played, they'd slaughter me. "How lame is this guy? Wasn't he listening? Why did he play the same record the other DJ played?" Now, if you *don't* play the same hit record over and over again, the people lose interest, and they don't even dance. They want to be entertained by what they know, by fireworks and whatever distractions that can be produced. They want to be on Snapchat, Instagram, Twitter while the music is playing. That's okay—I get it. They just want the energy. But at the same time, it doesn't support the quality of the music. Maybe that's why kids smoke less and less, as smoking would require a third hand to text. [*Ollie laughs.*]

So, is there a formula that dance music is operating with today, or is success in this genre just a matter of luck and the result of good staging and theatrics?

I think success is always 70 percent hard work and 30 percent luck. So, no hard work—no luck and no success. None of the big DJs today just popped up out of nowhere. There's a story behind their success that people don't generally know. That said, I do think there is a formula at work here—if you have the financial backing to succeed. Without mentioning any names, I am sometimes amazed how bad some of the music produced by very successful people can be. If I were in their place, with the kind of money they have to work with, I may not be able to guarantee a number one record, but I can guarantee a quality track. Sometimes they release shit records simply because they are providing music to consumers who are completely uneducated about music. DJing is about educating people with music. If a DJ plays 40 hit records in two hours and doesn't surprise his audience once, he may be successful, but he's *not* creative. That's just my point of view. Listen, I've had those nights myself. There are nights where you just can't do it. And then there are sets where you try something new and the night becomes amazing. But the formula for [quality] dance music remains the same—good songwriting.

Usually, instrumental tracks (with either no vocals or barely any) don't become worldwide hits, like "Children" by Robert Miles. That song was one of the exceptions—a strong melody, no vocals but still a huge hit. In the end, the song always comes first. With electronic music, the dynamic has shifted. What is a song if it has no lyrics or vocals? Or it's as simple as throw your hands up? Where's the song structure? Today, you often have easy, cheesy melodies, and kids like it. If you want a commercial radio crossover hit today, you quickly call the best songwriters and publishers and produce whatever playback is necessary just to support the songwriting using a template. With EDM, you don't even need the best production. That's songwriting today.

We are experiencing a very challenging time today where acts of terrorism are striking at the core of dance music—the places and venues where people congregate to express joy and experience the power of this music on a larger scale with others. Do you see this threat damaging the future of dance music and its culture?

I've already seen the impact of this based on my travels. I was in Paris when the attacks occurred in November of 2015. I was with my girlfriend, running to get to my French manager's flat to be safe, after we left a restaurant where one of the owners was shot at Bataclan. Things like this touch me, but they don't scare me. I think I'm a very convinced democrat, and the beauty of this life is that you can say what you think and do what you want—as long as you don't harm other people. I am reluctant to respond to this violence by retreating, as terrorists want.

Today, few artists will perform in Turkey for example. The clubs there are empty and dead because they are such a big target, and Russian tourists were kept away by a public order (which, at the end, is a development based on politics that created terrorism). But terrorism wants to destabilize social structure by spreading fear. I go to Turkey; I play there. I play Istanbul. I was in a cafe in Morocco just one week before it was blown up by terrorists. I remember sitting there and noticed they had gas tanks sitting exposed to the public and wondered why they would take such a chance in a place like this. One week later, someone blew himself up in that area. I am sure many artists can say they were close by or in recent proximity of events like these. I know some DJs won't use certain hubs to change flights and won't use certain airlines, so I know terrorism is having and will continue to have an impact on dance music culture in some way or another. Just look what happened in Florida.

That said, the festivals are still jam-packed. So people are sending a message—they wanna dance, they wanna party—regardless.

Do you think the dance music produced in the twenty-first century will be remembered in the future as fondly as, say, the hits of the '70s, '80s and '90s?

Maybe not in as vast a way as the music from those past decades. There are some songs from the twenty-first century that I am sure will have long term impact. Avicii is making his mark, as are David Guetta, Calvin Harris, Lost Frequencies and the like. They are globally successful. However, I don't think today's generation will embrace this music with the same importance that we did from previous generations. This is the difference.

I look at myself—I still want to tour because it's in my genes to deliver music to the people. I have been DJing for 36 years, and I have no plans to retire from something I love. I stepped back a bit from all of it in 2010 because of some more serious health reasons and producing obligations, but the passion in me has never lessened. Every generation says the music of their time is better than what is out there now. I think in 10 years it will be the same. The youth of today will say in the future that their music was better. In the end, I think every generation is right.

But I must say that the consumption of music has changed so much because of technological progress over the past several years that it's almost become like fast food. Dance music is now like a can of Coke. You open it, drink it and throw it away. So the life expectancy of a dance track today is very, very short. You won't even hear a dance song today that was a hit just six months ago. Yet dance hits from earlier decades are still around and still being played. And they will be around 30 years from now. But I would argue that 90 percent of the hits from this decade won't be around 30 years from now.

I think in some ways dance music has lost its authenticity. Perhaps this is a little too esoteric, but I have a theory that as everything became digital, dance music sold its soul. There is no musician playing a guitar. There's no drummer drumming. It's all from a computer. I am very sure that people hear that and, subconsciously, the body feels the difference. Evolution causes us to adapt to it, perhaps, just as we adapted to how fast things move now. To be honest, I watch a movie or TV show and don't like most of them because they cut in and out so fast I can't even tell if the actor is any good. The film or show doesn't give me the chance to experience his or her acting because you never see the person for more than a few seconds. This is why I think our current actors and music artists have less impact than past generations and why we still talk about De Niro or Deep Purple and AC/DC.

Let's consider the lighter side of your experience in dance music. You have a great memory, so I am sure you can recall at least one of the crazy experiences you've had in the business?

Seriously! Some crazy shit happened, but these are stories for the time *after* I'm retired. Only three words: sex, drugs & rock ′n′ roll! [*Oliver laughs.*]

Well, there is one story I can tell you, but the club, location and people involved have been changed (*or not*). I was playing in Miami, and a very close (and well-known) DJ friend of mine appeared during my set on stage. It was a small-sized club holding about 500 people, jam-packed and with a crazy vibe. He was obviously off his tits, and when I tried to tell him that he had to leave, he told me that he wanted to show me something. I was kind enough to ask him what it was and faced him. Suddenly, this knob head grabbed my hand and blasted a full pack of cocaine on my hand and then pushed it up in my face. It was winter time in the DJ booth! Security finally took him out. My face was powdered white, and people on the dancefloor, along with me, laughed their asses off. Some people actually tried to lick it off my face, but I was faster, cleaning the shit from my skin, as I don't like drugs at all!

Can you tell me what you experience when you create, hear or play a great dance track?

It's the biggest heart-opener you can imagine. Perhaps the meaning music has for me is deeper than for some others, but when I DJ, and the second I stop thinking and just play the music, it is for me—maybe it sounds silly—*nirvana*! When I see the people so happy, even crying because of the music I shared with them, I am perhaps closer to tears than even them. [*He laughs.*] I'm so happy. It is such a release and such a calming experience— I guess the best way to put it is I am really in the moment. I'm not thinking of the past, worrying or wondering about the future. I am just enjoying the moment. I'm in balance with myself. I feel united—in perfect unison with my energy centers and my thoughts. I've had experiences DJing where I thought I could die now and that this gig was worth every minute that came before it. This is what music does for me.

It makes it very hard to manage me—it can be very frustrating for my manager when I'm willing to play a gig for free simply because I want to do it. I am very business-minded, but I love what I do, and it's not always about money.

Lightning Round with D.O.N.S.

Name the dance track you never get tired of hearing?
Stardust's "Music Sounds Better With You" (1998).

Diana Ross or Beyoncé?
Diana Ross.

Sports car or SUV?

I just bought an SUV (my girlfriend has two kids), but I'll say sports car.

Have you ever created a song and due to a technical glitch lost the whole thing?

Yes! I once lost a whole hard drive with I don't know how many GB of files because I was too lazy to create backup files. I also wrote a full book, ready to go to the publisher, called *Life In the Mix*—the craziest stories, 48 chapters long. I never saved it externally and overwrote the document when I had something like 30 windows open—overrode it and then saved it. The publisher wanted to shoot me. To write it again? Impossible!

What tests your patience?

Traffic jams and rude people.

If you weren't in entertainment, what would you be doing today?

That's very hard to imagine. Most likely a lawyer, marine biologist or a chef. I was amazed by Jacques Cousteau when I was younger, and I still love to cook—and think I'm pretty good at it.

D.O.N.S. has rocked the crowds at prestigious venues and festivals around the world, including Amnesia (Miami), Ministry of Sound (London), Pacha (London), Pacha (Buzios/Rio De Janeiro), Pacha (Munich) and Amnesia (Ibiza).

Freemasons
James Wiltshire, Russell Small (DJs, producers, remixers)
"Déjà Vu" (Freemasons Club/Radio Mixes)—
Beyoncé featuring Jay-Z (2006)

"It's human nature I think to love familiarity, but sometimes you do get a true innovator that comes through, and the whole world just sits up and listens…"—Russell Small

"I have no interest in the snobbery that often litters discussions about the change in club culture. At the end of the day, it's actually about the clubbers, and I can see millions of young people having life-changing experiences dancing together in a field in a way that's almost tribal."—James Wiltshire

House music in the twenty-first century has received a tremendous lift from the partnership of two Englishmen, Russell Small and James Wiltshire, producers, remixers and DJs who have gained worldwide fame under the moniker Freemasons. The name has come to be synonymous with music that makes listeners and dancers feel—there's no other way to put it—positively alive. Russell enjoyed a successful production career in dance music beginning in the late '90s as part of Phats & Small (for whom James engineered a few tracks). After Phats & Small disbanded in the early 2000s, James and Russell joined forces to create Freemasons and took their powerful sound to the top of the club and pop charts in the UK, Europe and the U.S.

Among their standout tracks are the riveting retro-disco hit "Love on My Mind" (2005), a Grammy-nominated remix of Faith Evans' 2005 number one U.S. club favorite "Mesmerized," and the Top 20 UK pop smash "Heartbreak"

Russell Small of Freemasons. The duo remixed Beyoncé and Shakira's hit "Beautiful Liar," a number one smash in numerous countries (photograph by Ellis/maxphoto graphic.com).

("Make Me a Dancer"), featuring Sophie Ellis-Bextor, released in 2009. They've remixed for more top names in the dance genre, including Kelly Rowland, Shakira and Kylie. In 2011, the duo took a break from their demanding schedule but returned to the scene a few years ago, reinvigorated to create more uplifting, floor-filling music. Freemasons continue to spin, produce and remix new projects today, including their ongoing compilation series called Shakedown and the 2015 single "True Love Survivor" (featuring Solah).

Gentlemen, please tell me some of the basics about your lives growing up and how you discovered music in your youth.

Russell: I was born in Brighton, England, and raised in a small town just outside it called Newhaven. I have a 30-year-old son named Brett, an older brother Steve and a mum, Carol. My father Mick died a few years ago. Music was always a big thing in our home. Growing up, it was always played in the house or the car. Mum loved Motown and disco, and dad liked whatever mum wanted to hear [*he laughs*]—and a bit of rock and roll. So they heavily influenced my musical taste at a very young age.

My brother and I always bought music with our pocket money. When I was around 12, my brother saved up for some Citronic decks, and we set up a mobile disco, doing anything from school dances to weddings. We had quite a record collection crossing most genres, but my love was always disco and Motown, which still influence my productions to this day.

James: I grew up in Andover, a small town in the south of England once famous for spawning '60s rock legends The Troggs and being the home of Twinings tea. I always knew what I wanted to do [in music], but there was not much of a scene going on. So, after several summers spent begging and borrowing bad samplers and synths at home, I headed off to Manchester. It was right at the mid-point of house music's first explosion, and I was hooked. I got myself a job in a local studio and spent every single minute I could learning the samplers and sequencers that were the house producers' main tools.

After a brief summer in Brighton, I ended up getting a real production gig at DMC—the company that helped propel remix culture to the forefront of the industry. There I worked alongside Brothers In Rhythm (and Dave Seaman), Chad Jackson and ex-rave producer Phil Kelsey (PKA). I even remember editing stuff for John Digweed and completed over 200 remixes and productions. It was a real baptism in how to work quickly and actually get stuff finished on time!

Russell, I'd like to take a look at your breakthrough production duo with Jason Hayward called Phats & Small, which initially utilized the vocal talents of Ben Ofoedu. Would you tell me how you came to form this partnership in the late '90s?

Russell: Phats & Small was formed by myself and Jason, who went under the production name of DJ Phats at the time. So coming up with a name for our band was pretty easy. We used various singers over six years—Ben Ofoedu, Tony Thompson and Carrie Luer. Ben started off just as a front man for our hit song "Turn Around," and we were introduced to him by our record company at the time. Jason and I both took an instant liking to him—he had style and charisma, and ended up becoming the face of the band, writing and performing with us for the next six years.

At the time of "Turn Around," we were just a couple of local DJs who enjoyed clubbing and everything that went with it. We were just having fun. It never entered our heads that our first track together would change our lives forever.

Would you tell me about the step by step process that went into the creation and production of the 1999 house anthem "Turn Around"?

Russell: "Turn Around" was born out of two samples, one by the group Change—"The Glow of Love," which was (and still is) one of my all-time favorite tracks, and Toney Lee's "Reach Up." It originally started as a cut-up of "Glow," but then we found this amazing one-bar loop that you could just listen to over and over for hours (which we did), very reminiscent of Stardust's "Music Sounds Better With You," which was a massive hit the year before. Then we had to find a vocal. Searching through Jason's record collection we found a rare Acapella Anonymous album, and there we found the Toney Lee song. We chopped it up to create an unbelievably catchy verse and chorus—amazing to this day! It took eight hours to make the song on an Atari with about eight tracks of audio. Today, of course, we use so many more.

What was your chemistry like working with Jason—how in sync were you with each other's ideas and inspirations?

Russell: Jason and I had a great liking of all types of music, but we both loved house music. I would say I was slightly more commercial in taste; Jason was a bit more underground. So it was a good combination, and it worked in our productions for a long time.

I'd like to know a little about the inspiration, production and creation of "Sun Comes Out" from 2003. It's a brilliant song, and it was quite successful in the clubs and a hit on numerous Euro-pop charts.

Russell: Writing was always quite organic—someone would throw down some chords, Ben would hum some sort of melody, and we would all throw words and sentences into the hat until it sort of made sense, cleaning it up at the end with the rhyming dictionary. [*Russell laughs.*] I can't remember who had the inspiration for the chorus of the song—this always varied when we were writing, but it's quite obvious what it's about. It has that positive, uplifting vibe that was a trademark of Phats & Small and Freemasons.

You remixed a number of tracks as Phats & Small (and then with Freemasons), including "September" by Earth, Wind & Fire. What inspires you when you hear a vintage song like that and how challenging is it to re-envision it, especially if the original version is so familiar and popular? What elements must be present in the original song for it to work for a contemporary audience?

Russell: Sometimes things can come together quite quickly. Sometimes you are banging your heads against the wall for ages trying to come up with a vibe. It never frightened us taking on well-known songs or artists, however. The better the vocal and song, the better our remixes seemed to become. It was fucking unbelievable to be able to remix some of the greats, more so artists we liked ourselves. If we were lucky enough to get some great [original] elements of the track that we could use, it was a bonus. For us, it was always about the song and the vocal.

The era of Phats & Small represents the last period of significant CD sales as music monetization and technology begin radically changing. Do you remember your reaction at this time to the changes the industry was undergoing?

Russell: I think our thoughts were pretty much what they were a year or so ago—that the world was going to end, so-to-speak, and that the music industry was fucked. It wasn't as bad as we thought then, but it might be now.

What leads to the creation of Freemasons? Was the Freemasons name actually inspired by a pub, as I've often read?

Russell: Basically Jason wanted some time out of the studio, so James Wiltshire and I started working together. James had just moved to Brighton from London via Australia. We had made "Love on My Mind" and found ourselves in the Freemasons Tavern. We were discussing what we should call ourselves—James looked down at the bar menu, and the Freemasons were born!

James and Russell, "Love on My Mind" was an inspired reinvention and melding of the Jackie Moore classic "This Time Baby" and Tina Turner's "When the Heartache Is Over"—quite a way to kick off your partnership in 2004. Would you give me some details about the background of this track?

James: The sample is just one of those moments where many years of patiently looping of things just pays off. No one really knows a sample will repeat and hook until it's looped—and who knew that the first line of a verse would make such a great chorus? The sentiment that sets up the original Jackie Moore record just seemed to strike a chord with clubbing crowds. I remember a friend borrowing a mix-tape from me for a five-hour drive. When his girlfriend heard the basic version of "Love on My Mind," she played it over and over again until the CD started skipping. That's when you know you might have something.

Russell: Vocally, a very similar story to "Turn Around" if I think about it, but no Acapella Anonymous album, just a shed-load of a capellas on a hard drive that we believe came from eBay on DVD. As soon as I heard the Tina Turner chorus, I knew it had to be the one, and we spent a good few hours' time stretching and re-pitching it till it worked. Funny that we basically swapped the Tina chorus into a verse and the Jackie verse into a chorus.

I feel safe assuming you both have a great respect and appreciation for old school disco and heritage vocalists—would I be correct?

Russell: Yes, and we have been so lucky to have been able to work with some greats!

James: We both have an immense love of disco, '80s club and groove, house and basically anything that followed where a great big diva note strides right over a great chord change. I would love to sit here and say how I love pure Chicago acid or that Detroit techno changed my life, and I know I'd look way cooler, but it wouldn't be true. I think melody and harmony are incredibly important (to both of us), which is why we loved making the music we have created.

This might be the right point to ask you about your take on current trends that have the spotlight moving away from the vocalist in contemporary dance and EDM and onto the producer/DJs—who are currently the dance music stars. What brought on this change, and what's your take on it?

James: I think it was a totally natural progression. I remember, many years before the EDM explosion, going to a Sasha gig where stands were set up in a warehouse so everyone was looking at the DJ. These gigs have always placed the DJ center stage, and as they got bigger and the stages turned festival-size, the DJ focal point became even more defined. When it came to records, however, most stayed out of the spotlight and video clips.

For me, the first iconic DJ (visually) was Fatboy Slim—he created the first international DJ persona without it looking cheesy or Euro-trashy. That led the way for Guetta and Calvin Harris. So when they exploded across the U.S., the industry had already gotten used to the fact that the DJ was the new "guitar hero." At this point, all the rock stadiums were being filled with EDM artists—makes perfect sense to push the DJs seen each month by hundreds of thousands of people rather than featured singers that may only be around for one track.

In 2006 you remixed Beyoncé's "Déjà Vu," which earned you a Grammy nomination. Does a Grammy nod significantly improve your work prospects?

Russell: It certainly didn't do us any harm. It was plastered on flyers and posters wherever we went. Everyone always wanted to talk about us being nominated. I'm sure it helped with the gigs—it makes people curious. You still have to have a good body of work though—the Grammys don't totally define your career, but imagine if we'd won!

I'd like to get the background on the single "Heartbreak (Make Me a Dancer)," another top UK smash in 2009 and an inspired collaboration with the accomplished vocalist/songwriter Sophie Ellis-Bextor. Would you tell me how this song came to be and what it was like working with this artist?

James: Lyrically, it was co-written by Sophie and Richard "Biff" Stannard—a pop legend and another Brighton resident. It wasn't going to fit Sophie's album, but she loved it—so it naturally fell into our lap. It has a very interesting little chordal trick to it (not standard in minor-key dance music) that really seems to grab people.

Sophie is not just a very well-respected artist, singer and writer but a lovely warm-hearted human being, and we are very glad to have met her, her husband and her lovely family. To have a hit with it *without* UK Radio 1 backing (they appear to have an age limit for some idiotic reason these days) was the icing on the cake.

In terms of prosperity, does dance music today tend to favor producers who are followers or innovators?

Russell: I certainly find dance music favors followers. It's human nature I think to love familiarity, but sometimes you do get a true innovator that comes through and the whole world just sits up and listens—Deadmau5 being a perfect example.

Today's focus is on very much on DJ/producers (as we mentioned earlier)—who have become the stars of this music genre. Is there pressure today to expand your roles or functions in dance music beyond production, especially since the recorded music itself rarely generates most artists enough money?

Russell: It's more a necessity. The money's gone for most dance recording artists—you either have to do it part-time and fit in a nine-to-five, or try and get out there, DJ, perform live shows, advertising and endorsements. Your revenue has to come from somewhere, and unless you are charting properly it will not come from streaming.

James: The game is finally up with recorded music, but one thing always replaces another. If, as a DJ, you can cement a reputation and secure consistent bookings at large events and clubs, you become the marketers' dream—a personality and brand that has large swathes of the young population looking at you waving your arms about on stage or in the booth. Endorsements and advertising will naturally follow, and that potent combination can create enormous incomes with the right management and handling. If you look at early photos of Calvin Harris and the new and improved 2017 version of him, you will see exactly how precisely he's been molded into the perfect front man for product placement and advertising. Even the über cool are getting involved. I nearly fell off my chair when I first saw Deadmau5 on a Sonos advertisement with his Mau5 head on. But why not?

You never know how long anything in entertainment will last—make hay whilst the sun shines.

Other than monetization, what are some of the major changes in the dance music industry over the past 10 years that you've experienced to be the most challenging?

James: Let's be honest—years ago only a handful of DJs were poster-worthy. Dance's persistent underground nature and counter-culture allowed for the faceless nature of club records and DJs to be generally accepted. That is now all gone, as it's not just about the music anymore. The heavily Photoshopped, styled and quaffed DJs staring out at the clubbers from the billboards littering the roads of dance music's sacred well, Ibiza, are testament to this sea of change.

It is the cult of celebrity mixing perfectly with the sudden influx of tens of millions of new international fans, whose first experience with club music was probably a Black Eyed Peas record. Now I have no interest in the snobbery that often litters discussions about the change in club culture. At the end of the day, it's actually about the clubbers, and I can see millions of young people having life-changing experiences dancing together in a field in a way that's almost tribal. To me, there's really no difference between this and the early '90s rave culture in the UK for the clubbers' experience—just unimaginably better lights and four more lorry loads of pyrotechnics.

My actual concern for the future is that very talented artists may not break through because they don't fit the current accepted DJ look or are not as marketable.

Do shortening human attention spans, increased entertainment distractions and the public's lowering perception of the value of music (in terms at least of paying for downloads, streaming, etc.) affect how you are able to create dance music today?

James: Yes, of course the structure of our use and distribution of music has changed beyond recognition, but this is only one of the modern problems [faced by] producers coming through and those already established.

We have what can only really be considered a crisis of proliferation. I witnessed firsthand the democratization of music technology. The ability to play an instrument is now far from the list of requirements for the modern producer, and the equipment needed to make a fully functioning dance production is now entirely a list of software. All software is cracked, so now every single year hundreds of thousands of potential producers come online and get their music out there.

When I started in dance, there were probably only a few hundred house/club releases a week worldwide—now there are 15,000 releases hitting Beatport and iTunes every single week and probably over 20,000 at peak. For me, this is the first time in music history where great music is getting lost every single day simply due to the sheer amount of material out there. Is it any wonder the public perceives less value to music when there is just so damn much of it?

There is no simple answer or solution to this either; it's all just progress. But for established artists who are used to a certain stream of income, the changes have been extreme and near instant and for younger producers wishing to break through, bloody-minded persistence and just pure luck are now key to making it. Ironically, this will probably mean in the future only the most determined and talented producers will make it through—culture always finds a natural way of creating equilibrium.

Do you believe world events (specifically terrorism) pose (or will pose in the future) a strong and valid threat to the prosperity of dance music and nightlife, since the venues and events are often potential targets?

Russell: It's a possibility that I don't really want to think about. It's happened, but it's not a widespread thing yet.

James: No, absolutely not—isolated and shocking cases of extremist violence happen in all areas of public life, and we should never let fear into any open and diverse culture like clubbing.

The one thing that *has* changed club life in particular is Tinder/Grindr—why bother going out when you can just swipe and wait for the taxi? A UK club promoter I spoke to recently estimated one-third of club [attendance] has dropped since its introduction.

In what ways must dance music progress to keep prospering and growing creatively in the future? Any predictions?

James: Well, we're 30 years into the same beat. Currently we've got a massive tempo drop. Post-Diplo and trap and future bass are all over the underground [as of this point in time]. I see a few years of über cool coming in once the tropical house marimba samples have worn off—then everything will move again.

As to the most important members of clubbing crowds—the girls and the gays get bored of blokey, one-note tech, and they will go searching for some vocals again. After the '90s, I called it the Hed Kandi effect—underground goes way too noisy and production-led and forgets to make music for the punters. Before you know it, you're at a big gig, shoulder-to-shoulder with a load of trainspotter kids complaining that it's not "Detroit" or "Berlin" enough, while next door all the beautiful people have got some brand new cut-up of Chic on at house tempo and are having it right off.

All roads always eventually lead back to disco—it's clubland's classic music and spawned every single thing with a four-four drum beat and a hi-hat or shaker on the offbeat. S-Express, Stardust, Daft Punk, Ronson and Mars, Todd Terry—it's all just disco.

Russell: Dance music seems to work in cycles. I'm hoping that disco house comes back in a big way.

Do you think the dance music of the past 17 years will be remembered in the same way (and with the same "love" shall we say) as classics of the '70s, '80s and '90s?

Russell: Most definitely. The young dance record streaming clubbers of today absolutely love what they are listening to in clubs around the world, even if us over-40s sometimes don't get it, like our mothers and fathers before us. But I think they will look back with the same love.

So, do you ever think of *yourselves* as part of this great five-decade legacy of incredible dance music that goes back to Gloria Gaynor, Donna Summer, Giorgio Moroder, Nile Rodgers and all the earliest disco?

James: Never, really, as we're big proponents of the tried and tested English method of trying to be humble and hoping someone spots it! There are some emails and messages that prove just how happy you've made some people, though, and that fills your heart with pride.

Lastly, what has made dance music so valuable to our culture over the past several decades?
James: The right club crowd will not see the color of someone's skin. They won't care about their sexual orientation. They won't care about their religion or politics. Dance music has bought more people together across more social and political borders than nearly all of the government-led initiatives put together, and long may it continue. People have come together to dance for hundreds of thousands of years—who cares whether it's underground tech or if Guetta's up there pressing the sync button again? That's not the point. It's one world, one people under a groove.

Lightning Round with Freemasons

For or against Brexit?
Russell: Against.
James: Against Brexit—but very much *for* a reformed EU.

Is there a dance track you never tire of hearing?
Russell: Alison Limerick—"Where Love Lives."
James: New Order—"Blue Monday."

Have you ever worked for hours or days on a track and accidentally lost all your work?
James: Yep, it's happened to us a few times in the past. Normally due to Western Digital drives."

Craziest thing you ever saw take place on a dancefloor?
Russell: Never saw it happen, but saw the after-effects—when someone pooed on a dancefloor in Brighton.
James: We just missed it, but someone let off a starting pistol at a Waterside festival in Kazakhstan—it was chaos!

Extended versions or radio edits?
Russell: Extended radio edits.

What do you miss more—vinyl or CDs?
Russell and James in unison: Vinyl!

Biggest lesson you ever learned (so far) in the music business?
Russell: Don't trust *everyone*.
James: No one (and I mean *no one*) really knows what they're doing half the time—it's all just money and luck.

James Wiltshire of Freemasons. The duo has enjoyed numerous Top 20 hits in the UK, including "Love on My Mind" and "Uninvited" (featuring Bailey Tzuke).

First time a stranger recognized you as a star of dance music?

Russell: Can't remember the first time. It doesn't happen very often, but when it does, it certainly makes you feel good!

James: People think I'm [British celebrity chef] Heston Blumenthal more often than a Freemason.

If you weren't in entertainment, what do you think you'd be doing?

Russell: A very long sentence.

James: Motion graphics or video editing—I love it!

Xenia Ghali
(DJ, producer, songwriter)
"Under These Lights" (2016)

"I love experimenting. I don't think anyone will ever be able to say that my tracks all sound similar. My style may be considered uptempo dance and highly melodic in general, but I can't stand the idea of just producing one specific sound."—Xenia Ghali

Xenia Ghali is extraordinary for many enviable reasons. As one of today's top emerging DJ/producers in the crowded world marketplace of EDM music, she is a fascinating figure with a special knack for understanding the inner dynamics of engaging a beat hungry audience. Raised in Greece, Ms. Ghali displayed a powerful connection with music early on. When word of her high-powered talent behind the decks brought her to the attention of the UK's Ministry of Sound club, Xenia's trajectory in dance-floor culture seemed assured—and she exceeded all expectations.

Aside from being one of today's few prominent female *DJs (playing parties, clubs and festivals from Athens to Miami), her ability to deftly produce and remix an electronic dance track to pulsating perfection became crystal clear with the success of her stunning recording debut "Broken," released in 2014. Following collaborations with such prolific stars as Pitbull and Wyclef Jean, Ms. Ghali accomplished something new artists seldom achieve so quickly—a* Billboard *number one dance track, the 2016 smash "Under These Lights."*

Xenia, I'd love to know what life was like for you growing up in Greece, how you came to discover music and what some of your influences were.

Sure! I grew up in Greece, but I was actually born in France, which not a lot of people know. My dad used to work for Disney in France, and both my younger sister and I were born there. My mother's side of the family is all from Greece, and my father is Egyptian, but his family also lives in Greece. My family lived in Los Angeles for a short period of time when I was very young, but my mother and father decided they wanted us to be raised in Greece, so we moved back. I went to an international high school there. That gave me my first formal connection with music. My parents wanted us to be very well versed. I was classically trained on the piano and flute and took my exams at the Royal Academy of Music in the UK.

My dad had introduced me to the sounds of everything from Elvis Presley to Led Zeppelin to Joan Jett. I looked up to Joan Jett a lot. She was a female pioneer of rock music in the industry of that time, so I really looked up to her. I'd say she was one of the most influential women in my life. My mom introduced me to a lot of pop and disco music—The Bee Gees, Michael Jackson, Madonna. And, of course, I went out on my own and explored music.

In my late teens, I went through this whole rock phase. As I mentioned, I had been fully trained in classical piano and flute already, and I learned to play the guitar and drums and formed a high school band. I didn't want to play covers—I really didn't realize that bands played anything but original music—so I started songwriting. I quickly realized that was my passion. I felt that I connected much more with the stuff I was writing and creating rather than stuff I was just playing that already existed. I kind of announced to my parents that this was going to be my direction, and they were very supportive. At the time, I had no idea what producing was all about, and I hadn't even touched DJing. The next step I took was to study film scoring. I found a course of study in England at the University of Surrey called "Creative Music Technology." It was an infusion of film scoring, music production, sound engineering and songwriting—these were the topics covered by this Bachelor's Degree. It was perfect—I would get the best of all worlds.

As I was studying in the UK around 2008—and it sounds funny to say it—I discovered you could make music from a computer! [*Xenia laughs.*] I was kind of old school in my ways. It was a revelation that you could do this—that music didn't have

In the spring of 2017, Xenia Ghali enjoyed her second number one *Billboard* Dance Club chart hit with "Places," featuring Raquel Castro.

to come from organic instruments (which I still, to this day, love). It amazed me how melodic and beautiful music could be, even though it was made completely from electronics. I really got into learning as much as I could about producing and the technology, using Pro Tools, Logic Pro and all the platforms and plug-ins, etc. At the same time I was there in the UK, I was also a bit rebellious and went to a lot of parties—big underground house parties and things like that. The DJs at that time were still largely performing with vinyl and turntables, wanting to be very authentic. I was fascinated by their ability to blend records so seamlessly and accurately, and I wanted to be able to do it myself.

I found an ad somewhere for a guy selling two brand new Technics 1210MK5 turntables, which were manufactured as a special edition. He was selling the pair for £600—which was basically giving them away for free (many people were selling their stuff during the recession at that time). I literally ate cereal and spaghetti for two weeks to get the money for those. I bought them, along with a really basic two channel mixer and about five or six old house records. I set them up in my dorm room and started teaching myself how to spin. With my musical training, I did very well, because that kind of mixing requires a good ear to match up the music and tempo correctly. I used to carry my turntables and my growing vinyl collection of hundreds of records (I hadn't even explored using CDs and U.S.Bs at that time). I'd get my friends to help me carry crates of vinyl—2008 and 2009! People looked at me like I was an idiot. I DJed everywhere I could, whether it was a friend's house party, a local bar or a dingy little club. Not for the money—purely for fun. I honestly loved it, all while finishing my Bachelor's Degree, which took three years to complete in the UK.

So, I'm guessing one of these gigs changed the game for you.
It sure did. I was playing at this tiny club, and this PR guy—a party promoter for Ministry of Sound in London—approached me and asked if I had a manager. I thought that was hilarious—I wasn't taking my DJing to that point; I just did it for the enjoyment. He asked what I was doing—but I didn't understand what his question meant. He asked me if I wanted to try a set at Ministry of Sound. Of course, I knew what Ministry of Sound was and what the venue meant to the house culture, as I was really into that music. Needless to say, I said yes. He said he'd give me a chance, set it up, and I'd play the small room. He seemed to like the idea of a female DJ, too, and he liked my sound. Really, I can say that was the tipping point for me in terms of taking things seriously and making this my career. Being able to have a set there was tremendously significant—beyond anything I could have imagined. With that, I knew I wanted to do this for the rest of my life.

What is it that you brought to the table (I should say tables), that set you apart from so many others at the time who were all looking to make a name for themselves in club music?
I actually don't know for sure. Just the way I don't know how or why a lot of things in my life have happened. Sometimes I think it just—*happens*. It's hard for me to explain. I play what I feel is right, what makes me feel something inside. I guess what makes me feel good, a lot of other people can relate to.

In terms of the work you're doing today as a DJ and producer, you're really in a men's club, so-to-speak. Why aren't there more female DJ/producers?
So, it's very unfortunate what's going on in the scene I'm involved in. If you take singers of any genre, it's generally a 50–50 mix of men and women. For some reason, in the world

of DJing and producing, it's incredible how few women are in it—I can't even give you the statistics. I'm confused by that, and I've thought about it a lot.

I think the answer lies in the fact that, for one thing, as a producer and DJ, it's not always a very glamorous job, in that you're not on stage all the time or having tons of photo shoots. The job that a producer does, it's a very—I guess you would say—solo experience, it's a lot of hours, it's not pretty, and it's not glamorous. You're sitting in front of a computer for hours on end, making tracks, researching the latest technology and trying to raise money for your productions. That's your life. You don't have much of a life, and you're in a room that is often pretty dark.

It's very difficult I think for women to be okay with that or to find that appealing. Many women tend to work with their heart, and being a DJ/producer might not work well if you were planning on also having a social life or family life. There are exceptions, but I think this why we have so few women involved in this side of the business. Men are more easily able to detach from their personal lives and social lives (not that they aren't committed or don't want families). Men just sometimes work differently from women emotionally.

This is also an extremely technical field. There's a lot of women who are incredibly talented in high-tech fields, but it just seems like men tend to be attracted to these areas in their nature more than women. That's just my theory.

Is there a sense of competition—that you have to compete with the men who dominate the DJ/production world of dance music?

I would be lying if I said I didn't have goals I want to reach. But I don't compare myself with whoever is up there on the list. I do try to be aware of what's going on and to up my level to be in the game, if you want to put it that way. But I always stay true to what I feel is right, and I always like to be honest with my work. I wouldn't try to work in areas that I am not comfortable—like hip-hop fused with EDM, for example—that's just not who I am. Although I would love to collaborate with a hip-hop artist. I like learning from other musicians and vice versa. I like bringing my vibe to the collaboration.

Having said that, I think if you know what's going on with others, you get inspired. Right now, in dance music, people are tending to miss hearing organic elements. That may mean incorporating more song-like elements into a dance track or real instruments. It's important to identify that opportunity, because you want to be able to ride the wave where you can tap into what society wants emotionally and also what they want to hear.

I don't feel like I'm competing against anybody. I just want to push myself to be at the same *level* as the people who are making their marks in dance music.

You made a tremendous impression on the dance circuit with your debut single "Broken" featuring Katt Rockell, released on Pitbull's Mr. 305 Records, and the follow-up, "Get Dirty," a collaboration with Grammy winning rapper Wyclef Jean. You recently hit the coveted number one spot on the *Billboard* dance chart with "Under These Lights" in 2016. Would you tell me about your creative process for getting a hit dance song off the ground?

I create in different ways depending upon how I feel in the moment. I may be playing the piano and discover a great chord progression, and then I'll build off that. Other times it may be a drum beat or bass line. I may be just messing around with sounds and discover a really cool one—and a melody will come into my head that can incorporate it.

So, there's no one method of working. My music *does* tend to be melodic as opposed to pure groove.

I'm a huge believer that if you have a great song, no matter what genre it falls into, it's always going to be a great song. "Under These Lights" was like that. I had the song and produced it—and I let the song tell me where to go with it. This song was the most fun I have ever had producing (so far). That's because I didn't care what anybody would think of it. I did things I normally wouldn't do in one of my productions. "Under These Lights" is a cross between a song and an EDM track. So, during the drop you expect to hear a certain type of lead that is expected in an EDM track. But instead of using an EDM lead, I decided to build a lead using a sample of my own voice. I ended up with a Daft Punk type of sound, and I built the whole melody in the drop using it. I fattened it up with a few saw synths—you know, made it bigger sounding in terms of body, but that was it—that was the sound. It sounds sort of familiar, but yet it didn't sound like something you've heard before.

The same applied to the vocals from "Under These Lights." A lot of people ask me who the female singer is on the track, but there isn't one. I actually altered the voice of the *male* singer to make it sound higher pitched in the chorus, but not to the point where it sounded fake—just to the point where you couldn't tell if it was a guy or girl singing. Yeah, the whole song was sung by a male singer. (He's building his own brand, which is a completely different sound, so we didn't draw attention to his name. He's also one of the song's writers.) That manipulation of his vocals was a very interesting approach for me. If a major label had told me in advance they were going to do a big push and promotion for this track, these were all things I probably wouldn't [normally] do in the process of creating it. They don't usually work. But I did it anyway, I loved it, and it ended up doing very well.

I love experimenting. I don't think anyone will ever be able to say that my tracks all sound similar. My style may be considered uptempo dance and highly melodic in general, but I can't stand the idea of producing just one specific sound.

Did going to number one serve as a big game changer for you in terms of professional acceptance?

It definitely was a huge accomplishment for me. I tried to explain that to my parents—they were asking me what happens now. I explained that what happened was, in essence, I won an award by going to number one. That's how I viewed it. It's a very personal achievement, and it did change the way I am viewed in the industry. It created a lot of new opportunities for me. It's incredible. It's a huge honor.

When you see people responding so vigorously, so enthusiastically to your work on a dancefloor, especially when it's one of your own creations like "Under These Lights," what do you feel? What's your personal measure of success?

For me, it's the most magical feeling in the world. To hear someone say they have been moved by one of my tracks, well, it's the most incredible experience. It doesn't compare to anything. When I see thousands of people (or even just 10 people) going crazy over my set, I can genuinely feel the energy they are giving off. That is my measure of success—making that connection and feeling the support of people.

Tell me a little about working with Pitbull.

Oh, he's one of the highest ranking artists in the business; that's for sure. He's amazing. When I first moved to New York after graduating from college, I began studying for a Masters in composition at New York University. While I was there, I began writing and producing, and one of the first things I did was the track "Broken." My manager used to work for Pitbull's management company, and he was completely blown away by the track. He felt we should send it to Pitbull's people—you never know what could happen. So we did, and Pitbull was extremely interested. He offered me a deal with his label as an artist, and we sort of co-released the song through his label, Mr. 305, and my own label, Funky Sheep Records. The second single we released together was "Get Dirty" with Wyclef Jean.

I also did an official remix for Pitbull's single with Chris Brown, "Fun." I had a lot of fun with that song, too. I did the remix in 48 hours. I had a deadline to deliver it to them. I was so, so nervous and will never forget that experience. I had coffee mugs all over my desk—caffeine. My production team from Greece—my director, my stylist, my hairstylist and my make-up artist—were with me in New York at the time because we were also doing the video with Wyclef. So they witnessed me go through this 48-hour deadline to remix Pitbull's song. It was a funny experience.

It was a huge honor that Pitbull believed in me and wanted to sign me. It was a beautiful collaboration and working relationship, and he's truly, truly an incredible person and artist.

In terms of monetary success, the music industry has proven to be a challenging landscape in which to prosper in this century. How do you balance the desire to be a creative artist with the need to make a living from your craft?

It's hard, and it's not. Obviously, sales are not what they once were, and people don't buy music the way they did in the past. Artists today have to just look to other revenue sources and be creative about it. Streaming revenue is improving by the minute, and my shows are doing extremely well thankfully. I'm also involved heavily in the fashion industry, and I am collaborating with a few brands and designers. As a songwriter, publishing creates a revenue stream for me. So, there are ways of moving forward—whether you are in dance music or any other genre. It comes down to creating a brand for yourself and trying to connect with people.

We are living in age where the risk of an act of terrorism at an event or in a club is increasingly real. Do you see this social development impacting nightlife and dance music?

It's a very scary time right now—it's global, not just one country or one region—this whole terrorism/racism phenomenon. So for my generation, I guess we've been thrown into it. I think we've been exposed to it more than past generations. For me, it's something that I not only despise—I find it heartbreaking. I was actually talking to a friend from Greece the other day, and I told her I don't know where you can consider yourself to be safe anymore. It used to be, as a performer, if you were reluctant to be in Europe, you could go to the States. You can't go *anywhere* because [violence] is possible *everywhere*.

I am sure every artist feels that fear, or at least is more aware of the possibility, when doing a show today. I think we have to just keep going and promote thinking that discourages that kind of terrible action. I am very proud of the song "Under These Lights" for that very reason. It promotes love, unity and positive messages that people need to be reminded of as important to humanity. I think music is powerful for doing this.

The world has become really scary—I know I keep saying that. I am just hoping and praying that things will calm down.

On a different subject, how difficult is it for you to maintain a healthy personal life given your increasingly prolific presence in dance music culture and the nature of nightlife?

As far as nightlife goes, that hasn't been a problem. However, the hours I put into creating music and the priority it has in my life—that's what stands in the way of me having a complete balance between my personal life and my career. At this point, it's not an issue for me. I would much rather be in the studio making music than going on a date. I'm not saying I don't have relationships or take care of my personal life in that regard, but if that part doesn't work out, it doesn't work out. You know?

My priority is being able to express everything that's inside me through my music right now. If I want to be in a studio for 12 hours straight, that's what I want. I don't want to have to cut that for something that may be less important to me at this point in my life. So, that's where I'm at. In a few years from now and when (hopefully) I have accomplished certain things in my career, I am sure I will be a lot more balanced with regard to my personal life and my professional life. I would love a family at some point when I'm ready!

I try to always make time for my family and friends, no matter what. They are extremely supportive, and that means the world to me. That's what makes me believe in myself when I have those moments of insecurity—as all of us experience. Self-doubt, fatigue and exhaustion. Or something doesn't work out as you hoped. Those are the people that can pick you back up again. I'm very lucky to have these people, and I try to spend as much time as I can with them. I keep my parents involved with everything I do. Not because they are my parents, but because genuinely they will always be looking out for my best interests. Their advice is always so accurate and on point.

Do you think the dance music of the twenty-first century as it exists so far will be appreciated and revered in the future as much as the classic hits of past decades have been embraced?

Yes! That's the fast answer. I do. I think the music that's being created in the genre now has elements, structure, form and characteristics that definitely will be studied 20 or 30 years from now. I think there will be many people saying things like, "Do you remember that awesome track from 2017 that was so cool?" I definitely think that will happen.

The generation that's launched the twenty-first century discovered new sub-genres in dance. Trap, EDM, future house and so many others. I am sure our grandkids will be hearing our music and thinking it's vintage and cool. I think every generation pioneers a sound. EDM is a phenomenon today.

What do you think has been the underlying appeal of dance music throughout all these generations?

Well, this is something my dad used to tell me when I was very, very young. Music tempos that are around 120–128 beats per minute—he used to have me listen to them and tap on my chest to the beat. He asked if I understood why I liked the beat so much. He told me it was because the music followed the beat of my heart. That four-on-the-floor tempo of dance music basically matches your heart beat—it hits you in your core, your heart. That's my answer.

Owner of the independent label Funky Sheep Records, Xenia Ghali walks the line between mainstream success and underground credibility in the world of dance music.

Lightning Round with Xenia

Favorite dance track you never tire of hearing?
   "I Feel Love" by Donna Summer.

Craziest thing that's happened to you so far in your professional career?
   Oh, that's interesting. A guy came into the DJ booth I was working in, got down on one knee and asked me to marry him. That was pretty crazy!

In today's dance music, is the beat and melody still more important than lyrics?

Well, I think they go hand-in-hand, but, in my opinion, I'd have to give more weight to the beat and music. I guess that's always the way it's been for me. I like to express myself musically, more so than with words.

Favorite thing to eat after a night of clubbing?

Oh gosh, I have to stay away from the junk because I'm always touring and will surely put on weight if I indulge. But if I had to, it would probably be an old-fashioned burger.

What's the single piece of advice you'd give to an aspiring DJ?

I would say that—and I don't mean to offer a cliché here—if you strongly believe in what you do, you feel that incredible passion and are willing to put in all the hours it will take (and you actually wish there were more than 24 hours in a day), there is absolutely no reason why you can't succeed at being a DJ. I truly believe that.

If you weren't a successful DJ/producer, in what area would you have pursued a career?

Probably sports. I waffled between sports and music when I was growing up. My mom was a professional tennis player, and I was playing the game at the same time I was learning classical piano. So I debated what I wanted to do—but clearly music won me over.

Groove Coverage
DJ Novus (Markus Schaffarzyk), Singer Mell (Melanie Münch)
"Moonlight Shadow" (2002)

> "When I was young, there was metal, punk, pop, hip-hop, rave, etc., and so as a youth, you belonged to a specific scene and its music, usually for a number of years. Today, I don't think there is this clear division and affiliation anymore."—DJ Novus

> "We perform together, and we have never had the feeling that just one of us is the leader. At some concerts the audience screams more for the singer, at others for the DJ, but most of the time their demand is for Groove Coverage—as a band."—Singer Mell

While the world of twenty-first dance music is very different from past decades, one characteristic remains the same: many artists and acts can often disappear as fast as they arrive on the scene. Germany's Groove Coverage, fronted by DJ Novus (Markus Schaffarzyk) and singer Mell (Melanie Münch), have defied that leaning and earned a rock solid reputation for making exhilarating, floor-filling dance hits for over 16 years.

The spotlight fell upon the group in 2002, when their heart-pounding remake of the Mike Oldfield evergreen "Moonlight Shadow" and debut album Covergirl captured the clubs, European pop and dance charts, and radio. Since then, they've been delivering electrifying, hard-driving (yet distinctively melodic) Eurodance music that has earned them a powerful worldwide following, even as far away as China. Among their most popular successes have been "Poison" (2003), "7 Years & 50 Days" (2004), "Riot on the Dancefloor" (2012) and "Million Tears" in 2015.

Mell and DJ Novus, would you please tell me a little bit about your youth and how you both discovered music?

Novus: I grew up in a regular household with two siblings in a sleepy backwater town called Rottenburg on the Laaber, near to Landshut. It isn't far from Munich, the main city in Bavaria, Germany. I spent a happy childhood there, and like the other kids back then, I played lots of sports, such as soccer, volleyball and skateboarding and rode a BMX.

I remember just before my 10th birthday, I bought my first record. From the TV I became aware of the German band Trio [Da Da Da Ich Lieb Dich Nicht Du Liebst Mich Nicht Aha Aha Aha (1982)] and, through my uncle, I discovered Elvis. It actually all began

In addition to being Echo award nominees, Groove Coverage (Melanie Münch, left, Markus Schaffarzyk/DJ Novus, right) won the German Dance Award in 2003 and the Sound Music Award in 2008.

for me with Elvis Presley, then later I moved on to Europe and Metallica, followed by various punk rock bands like Bad Religion & NOFX. Then, at some point, the first techno wave hit me. I'm still loyal to bands like Bad Religion, for example, and buy every album and go to as many concerts as possible.

At the age of 14, I earned my own money for the first time as a newspaper delivery boy. When I was 17, I invested these earnings in my first Technics [SL] MK-1210 turntable, which I still have at home today—and I'll never sell it. My first Technics player came from an old sanatorium for seniors, by the way.

Mell: I had my first solo performance at the age of four in a church, and from that moment on, I have been obsessed with music. I have enjoyed listening to all different kinds of genres ever since. I started training my voice at the age of 11 with vocal-coaching in a pop and classical style. I have also always loved singing karaoke, solo and together with friends. I went nearly every weekend to karaoke parties in different bars or clubs in order to sing in front of a small audience.

How did your professional careers get started, and how did Groove Coverage come about? Why was the name "Groove Coverage" chosen?

Novus: At around 16 or 17 years old, I was totally blown away by the first—and back then still illegal—rave parties in Munich. In and around Munich the scene developed rapidly, and suddenly 15,000 people were packed into massive warehouses, dancing to the beat of several DJs. The lights, the sound, the bass in your stomach—I was hooked, fascinated, under the spell. Even today, I get goose pimples when I think back to those long nights and the fantastic memories of the hangars at the old abandoned Munich-Riem airport, which was used as a rave location.

In addition to my Technics [SL] MK-1210 turntable, I also quickly figured out where you could buy good vinyl. I practiced every day in order to get the perfect mix. My dad wasn't too crazy about the "boom-boom" from the basement, which got increasingly louder. I spent all my money on records and got even more new inspiration from the German techno heroes of the early to mid–'90s like RMB, Raver's Nature, Dr. Motte (founder of the Love Parade), etc. After graduating from school and working during my apprenticeship, there was only one other activity for me—secretly spinning the decks in the basement, recording mix tapes and visiting raves all over Germany. My first mix tapes were well-received, and as a result, I was booked for my first open-air party. I didn't even have a proper DJ name, so I had to invent one overnight and DJ Novus was born. The name was inspired by a brand of stapler with which a former colleague had managed to staple into his finger!

A club owner's son happened to be attending the event, and the club offered me my first resident DJ job. After that, things just got better and better. A second club followed, and each week I was getting new offers to perform at various events. This was also the time when I first started arranging my own events. A few months later, friends and fans were following me to my shows in buses. A lot of that I only realized years later, and in moments like this interview I recall it.

Through my (then) girlfriend I got to know DJ Valium (Axel Konrad), who was only known locally at that time. I came across him while looking for an additional techno DJ for my own events. We played bookings together, and we were quickly on the same wavelength—almost 100 percent musically—I was rooted a bit more in the techno scene, Axel was more into the Dutch Eurodance scene. So a great friendship began which has continued to this day—both privately and professionally.

We decided to start a project sometime in the summer of 2001, the name of which was still undecided at that point, because that was only of secondary importance. For the first vocal recording we placed Axel's girlfriend in a closet [as opposed to a sound booth] because we didn't have any idea how to achieve professional results. We really began our work in the basement studio at his parents' apartment in Ingolstadt, Germany. I can remember it like it was yesterday. We sat down and said, "Now we need a name for the act." A CD case was laying on a table with the title "Discovering," and Axel really liked it. I definitely wanted a name consisting of two words and found "groove" very appropriate. "Groove Discovering" sounded weird, so we agreed on Groove Coverage. We didn't realize that the name didn't make any sense in English, but does there always have to be a perfect meaning?

Our first song was quickly rejected by all the labels. Finally, one record company phoned us back. That, at last, made us feel like we were on fire, and in addition to our many bookings as DJs, we were highly motivated to continue producing songs and to live our dream. Our first aim was to appear on VIVA-TV and their show *Clubrotation*, which, at its peak, had several million viewers—and specifically 100 percent of all the ravers. Whoever sat on the couch with presenter Daisy Dee on the program had made it—or so we thought at the time. (In subsequent years, we sat at least 10 times on that couch. The show is now history and doesn't exist anymore, like so many other TV formats that shaped that era.)

[Co-producer] Ole Wierk joined us some time later, as did our singer, Mell. Meanwhile, as DJs, Axel and I were extremely fascinated by the sound of several Dutch artists, such as the Klubbheads. When we played their tracks, we could sense a positive mood in the club. The people reacted differently to these tracks than to the other songs. When we were asked by a magazine about the sound which we represented as DJs, we answered, "Free Trance"—in other words, a mixture of all the previous styles. The people went crazy for this kind of music. Their hands went up as if they'd been struck by lightning. Later, when we were already on the dance and club charts with our first production, VIVA-TV asked us about the sound we produced, and we told them it was "Hands Up Free Trance," and so the "Hands Up" genre came to be born—a style which is still recognized and used today.

Mell: The first time I met the producers, I was singing at a karaoke night at a local bar. They were looking for a new vocalist and after hearing me sing they invited me to their studio. At the time, I was employed at a restaurant and still full of hopes and dreams. That is why I immediately accepted the invitation and thought I might just give it a try. The name Groove Coverage was already established by DJ Novus and Axel Konrad, who founded the band before our first meeting. They had already released two tracks and were now trying to give themselves a more commercial touch with the help of a vocal track.

Speaking for myself, I can only say that I had no idea what to expect after the first recording. I was excited to hear my voice on a CD, and, as I said before, I had all kinds of hopes and dreams. But I would have never thought that they would actually come true. I was married and started family planning with my husband and got pregnant shortly after. You can imagine my surprise when I was told by the producers that we, indeed, had become a *big deal*! I was shocked! We were so grateful for the chance. Immediately, we started working on our first album in order to show the world the variety of our music, and I think that this is a big part of what makes us unique and our sound so recognizable.

Would you tell me a little about the dynamic of working together as a team to keep Groove Coverage moving forward? Few groups have remained together as long as you have.

Novus: Over the many years (2001 through today), each of our tasks in the team have been relatively unstructured and shared in such a way that everyone does what they like doing and what they do best. None of us talk about work because we have far too much fun doing what we do. I would rather say that we all do everything to the best of our ability. After a year on the stage, our group member Verena [Rehm] preferred to return to the background. She composes, writes lyrics, performs the secondary vocals—but she doesn't like long performance nights, little or no sleep, constantly changing hotel rooms, and she doesn't like flying. In contrast, Mell and I still love all of that, even after so many years. Today, the group still meets up together to discuss important decisions, and we spend nights in the studio until we achieve a result that we're 100 percent satisfied with.

Mell: The reason why we still enjoy working together after more than 15 years without fighting is that each one of us has our own important position within the team. As Markus said, this gives us the opportunity to do what we do best and what we feel most comfortable with. Axel and Verena, for example, are the masterminds behind the scenes. They compose, record, mix and handle backing vocals. You can hear their influence in every track. Novus and I are the masters of the public. Besides our work in the studio, we are the ones who carry out the music into the world. We do the touring, get and keep in touch with our fans, and enjoy performing all around the globe.

Respect is the key, and we all equally give and get it. When we are working on new ideas, we all have a voice. Discussions are a part of any functioning relationship, both private and business-related, and even if they get a bit heated from time to time, they are good and healthy fights. At the end we always stand as a team 100 percent behind our work.

The remake of "Moonlight Shadow" (originally by Mike Oldfield) was a big hit (number three on Germany's pop chart) in 2002. Can you remember recording and producing that track? Why was it such a success with the fans, on the radio and in the clubs?

Novus: "At the time, Mell was pregnant with her second child and stood with a big baby bump in the vocal booth. Yes, by this time we actually had one, and so we didn't have to shut her in a closet! [*He laughs.*] We wanted to create something new. Up until that time, any lyrics which were longer than three words were pretty much irrelevant in the techno/rave scene—or however you want to refer to this period. There wasn't the multitude of genres back then. There was either rock, heavy metal, hip-hop, or just "boom-boom"— i.e., techno. Many of the productions contained just a few brief shouts; the vocals were more or less incidental—a trend which currently appears now and again in the EDM scene.

We had initial ideas for cover versions (without actually knowing the term specifically) long before "Moonlight Shadow." We didn't know how to go about tackling such big global hits. We believe it's always important to present such historic hits to a contemporary audience in a danceable way, as we like to call it. Many of the people who bought our single "Moonlight Shadow" thought that the song was written by us because they hadn't ever heard any Mike Oldfield tracks. I think the song is magical, and it made people really happy at the time, even though many of our songs don't have particularly upbeat lyrics. The music took effect—or rather it was about the music and its effect. If there is a secret to our success, then perhaps that's it.

Mell: Our hit "Moonlight Shadow" was something new and fresh at the time. Even though there was a lot of dance music already out there, we managed to stand out because our sound was simply different. The mixing of sad and melancholic lyrics and vocals with the fast pumping beats were a lot darker and more mystical than other tracks that were full of sweet bells and happy vocals. It was also faster and more commercial, which resulted in a new sound. At least that's my impression of it, and I believe it has been reflected by the responses of our fans. Even after all these years, the song still hasn't lost its magic and is still a highlight in every concert.

You chose to cover another song called "Poison" (originally by Alice Cooper) in 2003. Any reflections about this project, which was another big hit for you?

Novus: "Poison" is, so-to-speak, the product of long party nights. After our first big Groove Coverage show, we lay awake in the hotel beds watching television, filled with the euphoria of the crowds, who suddenly wanted pictures and autographs. Back then in Europe, the first ringtone commercials started to appear on TV. I slept with a song in my head ("Poison"), woke up the next day with the song in my head, and it followed me into the studio. We didn't have any doubts. This earworm suited Groove Coverage perfectly, and when permission was granted by the original author (Alice Cooper), we were honored that it was granted for a very unusual remake. Although our rendition is very, very close to the original in many ways, it had been completely transformed for a whole new generation.

Like "Moonlight Shadow," the secret lies in the energy which the song brought to the dancefloor, and even now, 15 years later, it still brings that energy to retro parties worldwide. (Later, several other artists attempted to cover "Moonlight Shadow." However, these versions never reached the status that we achieved.)

Mell: "Poison" is one of our all-time favorites. While we were recording our first album back in 2002, we used to hear Alice Cooper during the breaks and sang along with his song like crazy. There was no escaping it. When we were at home at night and watched TV, it would pop up in commercials for *Best of the 80s* albums. The following day, while driving to the studio, the song would play on the radio. It seemed like it was following us for a long time. We talked about it as a team, and we all loved the idea of maybe covering it one day. We finally did it in 2003, and the response was overwhelming. When asking our fans what they enjoyed the most about our cover, they used to highlight the differences between it and the original, the style, the female vocals, and the beat. We see it as an honorable homage to a great song and a cover version with our own flavor, rather than just a copy.

What's your process for choosing a song to record as Groove Coverage?

Novus: We don't have a formula by which we choose our songs. The song must have a certain magic, immediately blow away most of the team, and the time has to be right to transform the song into a new rendition for a new generation. If all that doesn't happen, the song gets shelved—like many have—and we don't worry about it.

They're often songs which we remember from the past, like "21st Century Digital Girl," for example. The original was from Bad Religion, and now, on reflection several years later, we didn't make a good job of it, and it would have been better to have shelved it. Looking back though, this is the only song which we'd like to erase from our repertoire.

Mell: I guess it is a gut feeling where you either say yes or no. That's it. The song has to reflect our ideas and fit our sound. The key is to make a cover sound like a typical Groove Coverage song without losing the spirit of the original. I want to have that "yes" feeling in my gut while singing it. That might sound a little crazy, I know, but that is just how I am. Sometimes you sing a song, but it just feels like reading lyrics to a random melody. Other times, with other songs, I felt it so much that I nearly cried while recording it. For me, as a singer, this is a very important component.

Has the rise in fame of the DJ/producer, often eclipsing the performer of a dance track, caused any complications in your dynamic in any way?

Novus: I wouldn't say so. Basically, we were always viewed as a duo, sometimes more, sometimes less. It's interesting, for example, how we're perceived in Asia, especially in China. Until Groove Coverage came along, they only knew the super cool DJs (for example, DJ Tiësto), who turned the evening on its head with their mixes and said nothing, and the pop princess Britney Spears, who just sang songs. We offer a healthy balance of both when we perform on stage. In almost every interview we get asked how the combination of DJ and singer on the same stage came about.

Mell: Groove Coverage has always been a band. We perform together, and we have never had the feeling that just one of us is the leader. At some concerts the audience screams more for the singer, at others for the DJ, but most of the time their demand is for Groove

Coverage—as a band. In China, as Markus mentioned, for example, we are special simply because of the fact that we are a duo. They are used to having a DJ *or* a singer perform, and so far we are [one of the very few acts] that is combining both on stage. I would say that it is a good thing to be different, and we always have been.

Would you describe the German market for dance music today and how it differs from the rest of the world?

Novus: Like almost all markets which have open access to the Internet, the German market is strongly influenced by what is currently in or being hyped in the rest of the world. Many things have unfortunately become ubiquitous. On my many worldwide tours, I always discover that, irrespective of whether I'm in Munich, Singapore, Tallinn, or Warsaw, everywhere clubs, labels and DJs are fighting the same problems.

The former "idyllic German world" is no longer an exception. On the contrary, I often find that, compared to other international markets, we have almost no music TV channels and the radio stations only play mainstream music, often to death. I sometimes ask myself where today's generation get their kicks from when the same songs are on the radio, in the clubs, at festivals or are on my iPhone. Separate subcultures, which in Germany often merge into the mainstream, don't exist anymore, or they have become concentrated onto a very small number of Internet stations.

When I was young, there was metal, punk, pop, hip-hop, rave, etc., and so as a youth, you belonged to a specific scene and its music, usually for a number of years. Today, I don't think there is this clear division and affiliation anymore. The demand for music by genre has been declining in recent years. I refuse to say that things were better in the old days—that's definitely not the case, but it was certainly more exciting!

Mell: I think that there are no huge differences when looking at the world music market. In the end, the result is more or less the same everywhere: the audience is longing for dance music all the time, but they are giving it different names. Hands Up, dance, EDM, house, etc.—it is all electronic music, and there will always be a market for it. (As long as you can still call it a market.)

Germany was an important source of creativity in new dance music during the '80s and '90s. Has this dominance declined in the twenty-first century?

Novus: Definitely—*yes*! Why that is I can explain using my own project as an example. Due to the increased pressure from the major labels for chart success and sales, it's easy to simply forget how to assert your own style and ideas in the way in which you would like to. Everything suddenly sounds identical to the music at the top of the charts. Looking back, several labels didn't really believe in what actually worked. While they were surprised by the new success, they drifted from one hit to another without really looking forward into the future. The bigger the success, the less say many artists had in the way the wheels of the music industry turned.

For example, for "Moonlight Shadow" we chose from 15 different video scripts and selected the one we liked. After our eighth single release, the record company just told us how things were going to be done. *Period!* It's difficult to extricate yourself from all of this, and as long as the success keeps coming, you're not particularly conscious of it.

In the '90s and early '00s, it was completely different. The labels wanted whatever was originating from the clubs. Today, it's often the other way around. Club trends are of no interest because they only appeal to the younger generation, and you can only monetize this target group to a limited extent from digital or physical sales. I was thinking as early as the mid-'00s that sometime in the near future it would all be about getting your song as quickly, simply and cost-effectively as possible onto the fans' smartphones, U.S.B sticks or music streams. People laughed at me at the time. In 2016, this has become reality. Not just in Germany. I hate to admit it, but I believe that whatever music isn't available as a download on the top 100 illegal file sharing sites within a week of release won't be a hit!

Mell: It depends on how you define power. When it comes to selling—oh yes, this is a never-ending fall. Dance acts in the '80s, '90s and early 2000s were earning a lot of money, only by selling physical records and CDs. They were often just one-hit wonders sometimes, or weren't around for a long time, but it was still enough for them to get rich.

If you are talking about the power of dance music in terms of connecting people and how it manages to bring hundreds of thousands of people to big festivals and concerts, I would say that it is still very strong. Nothing changed the love for that kind of music, and we still have numerous talented German artists out there.

In view of these limitations, how important is it for you to be successful in other countries (perhaps even in the U.S.A)?

Novus: Global success is a measuring stick for every artist. Our success in certain exotic countries in our portfolio make us particularly proud. We haven't been able to achieve success in the U.S.A, unfortunately. We know, however, that something is lying dormant there, which perhaps just needs a small spark to ignite it. With "Poison" we were already very close to a chart entry in the UK. Those who can remember that period know that this was the time of the Iraq war when the first English and American soldiers were beheaded. Our "Poison" video, which contained swords and scenes which implied a beheading, was taken off the playlists out of respect for the soldiers killed. We were on the way into the Top 10. Who knows what would have happened if it hadn't been for these terrible events?

Mell: Since the start of our career, we have been releasing and touring all over Europe, and we celebrated some of our biggest successes abroad. This is what keeps traveling and touring in general so interesting and fun. We were playing in stadiums all over Asia. We had big concerts in South America and performed at big dance festivals in the U.S., together with many well-known Eurodance artists. We did a tour through South Africa, and this winter we will visit Australia. What a gift! People and music from all over the globe are giving us influences, and we made many new friends.

You bring up a good point. We live in a time when terrorism has had a powerful and detrimental effect on large entertainment events. Do you believe that this trend will become increasingly influential or adversely affect dance music in the future? Do you worry about terrorism on a personal level when you perform?

Novus: I'd be lying if I said that it doesn't affect us. I have been concerned about this personally in recent years, as well as in the past. Back in the early '00s, following a chart entry, we got invited to play large shows in Israel. After some serious consideration, we had to turn these offers down. Terror is everywhere nowadays, even in Germany, and it can reach even the most mundane, everyday occasions, such as a train journey, a shopping trip or, yes, even a music festival.

You have to pay more attention when traveling, especially at the many airports through which we pass. You view the people more skeptically and think twice about traveling to large events. As a father of two children, this question is ever present. This doesn't just affect our tours and concerts, but also our private lives. I think we need to be conscious of the fact that these dangers will be present for longer than we would like. For me personally, the project of [open borders] in Europe has failed—at least in its current form—and it's no longer sustainable. Comparable to a disco franchise which has grown too quickly without paying attention to the back office, Europe has also grown and expanded artificially.

Mell: There is a danger, and we are very aware of it. Every time I sit in a plane I have a strange feeling in my stomach (but I am scared of flying in general). It would be naïve not to think twice about traveling into a dangerous country for a concert. Terrorism is a pressing issue in Europe, which we once always considered safe. I don't want to bring my children into a dangerous situation, but, at the same time, I am not willing to let it influence me too much. I won't stop making music in this fashion because I am too scared to travel. Yes, I want to be safe, but I won't let the threat of terrorism beat me down. This might be a little naïve, as I said, but that is how I feel about it right now.

You've been in this business since 2001. What are some of the biggest changes to it that you've observed, other than those we've discussed?

Novus: Looking back there are many things which have changed. Today, music is worth practically nothing. For many, music is simply a commodity without value. At the beginning of the century, or even back in the '90s when I started out, it was very different. We didn't let ourselves be influenced by these changes because we always saw ourselves as a commodity which would maybe last six months, a year or perhaps five years. We've got both feet firmly on the ground and have other things in the running. We're also qualified in other professions so that we can return to these when the already long musical journey finally comes to an end. I actually wanted to quit at 30, now I'm almost 40, and I'm still having a lot of fun. I think we've reached what I could call—luxury. I view everything that I've experienced since my 30th birthday as a bonus. I think many artists are currently under a lot of pressure, but I don't feel this way at all.

Mell: The business has changed a lot, but this isn't surprising because the music business is constantly changing. When we started, it was already a hard business, and today it is even harder. But we did change. We grew up with it, saw many artists come and go, learned a lot about ourselves, and we learned how to grow with the years, without changing who we are.

In our beginning, there were music television channels like VIVA or MTV and shows like *Top of the Pops*, and so many radio stations that gave you a platform to represent your music. Today, most of those platforms have disappeared, but new ones have emerged. For instance, there is social media and YouTube now. The way you are reaching your audience changed, but we try our best to keep in touch with our fans and adapt to those changes.

Yes, and I would imagine the monetization of music is one of the most dramatic changes with which you've had to cope. Now there's the challenge posed by streaming and digital downloads. Most artists say that it's difficult to make money purely from the music itself. In the last 10 years the number of clubs (and therefore the number of performing opportunities) has also been declining. How have you managed these changes?

Novus: In the late '90s, a moderate chart hit was sufficient to live off without financial difficulties. Today, you need to deliver 10, 20 and often even more good releases in order to be able to earn a living. The gap between global hits, financial stardom and just earning a crust is getting much wider. I think herein partly lies the reason for the constant decline in the quality of the majority of music, not just dance. Anyone can make music, but only a few can do it properly. We're fortunate not to be reliant on one market. If things go quiet for a while in Germany, we have other opportunities elsewhere. We're touring now 10 years after our first chart success in Australia, for example. How and why we don't know ourselves, but we do it gladly. Perhaps there'll even be a new dawn in the U.S. market.

Mell: I definitely agree with your assessment that monetization has changed dramatically, and there are no other words to describe the situation. This issue affects every artist, as music streaming is so strong and illegal downloads are still a big problem. Most of the money you earn now comes from live concerts, and many of the big clubs that we used to play in all the time in the early 2000s are closing. We are very happy to still be very busy and for still having a full schedule, but there is no doubt about it—it is definitely getting harder.

Today's most popular dance genre, EDM, is often described as cold and soulless. Do you agree with that assessment?

Novus: Yes, I agree with that. So far we've never produced a song in less than one to two months. We want to let our songs live and breathe, to provide them with a touch of the here and now, so that the fans can identify themselves with them. I discover again and again at our events that there are many very young people in the audience. It's often said of today's generation that they're no longer interested in music. That's not true of all of them, of course. Those who discover "old" music have a great advantage over their contemporaries; they just don't realize it yet.

Mell: I definitely disagree with that assessment. Anyone can make that argument about any type of music that doesn't suit their personal taste. At a concert when you see the people respond by singing and dancing to the music, it's just impossible to say that it has no soul. Every genre has its own magic and emotion. There is no such thing as "music with no soul or emotion." It always depends on the listener.

I saw people cry at a rock concert, and I saw people tearing up to a DJ set by Armin van Buuren. My mom loves country music, one of my friends got the shivers down her spine from classic hip-hop lyrics—and a few weeks ago some girls were crying at one of our concerts while I was singing "Moonlight Shadow." Emotion is a subjective feeling, and it can be felt everywhere and with every style of music. So, why argue about taste?

With that said, do you think that the dance music from the last 17 years will be considered as unforgettable as the classics from the three decades that came before it?

Novus: The '90s were unbeatable, at least as far as the 30-plus generation is concerned. We experienced such fantastic things, and during this period so many sounds developed like in no other era. I'm sure that other generations have great experiences, and today's youth are experiencing great music to their ears, but these are somewhat different. In my opinion, they definitely are not as enduring and deep-rooted as they were in the '90s and early '00s. Put simply, imagine that today you're at the exit of a club and you ask the clubbers leaving to hum five EDM melodies. Then imagine asking them to do the same thing in 10 years' time. I think that says it all.

Mell: We will see. I don't know if the whole music culture of the 2000s will be remembered one day as an *epic* period, but I am sure that there are tracks that will still be played in 10 years and that will never be forgotten.

On a personal note, how challenging has it been to combine a healthy, balanced lifestyle with the demands of nightlife?

Novus: Well, I don't have a string of failed marriages. I have a fantastic partner whom I've now known for over 20 years and who has given me two wonderful, healthy children. Even after 20 years of nightlife, my health hasn't suffered because I do everything in moderation. I play sports and allow myself time out when my body tells me that I need it. Watching what I eat probably hasn't done me any harm either. Neither has the long and intensive sleep patterns I enjoy. I recharge my batteries quickest when I'm with my family. I support my son with his activities and going to his games is like vacation for me. An intact family life, combined with the music, touring and success is definitely the key to a healthy balanced life.

Mell: Staying healthy is not always easy for me, but it is possible. Working out during the week, eating healthy and balanced and trying to get enough sleep during the week is something that you can and should do. But getting a healthy amount of sleep is tough when you are a full-time mom. It's always a struggle to work out daily, especially when I'm exhausted from my travels. Sometimes I succeed and sometimes (or most of the time) I don't! Eating healthily on tour is sometimes impossible. We try our best, but there are days that we completely spend in planes, cars and clubs, and the only food we eat is some fast food trash. But whenever we do have the time, we gladly enjoy fresh food.

Which achievement in your career paths to date has made you the most proud?

Novus: Truthfully, I've never given much thought to what I've already achieved. I think we must have played over 3,000 concerts and club shows. We were and still are one of the most successful European acts in China and the only one at all from Germany so far, to my knowledge. We performed there for over 580 million people. People write to us almost daily to tell us how they have experienced wonderful things with our music and still look back on it years later. We were there in a time when the Iron Curtain ruled in Russia, and yet, unexpectedly, over 60,000 people were waiting for us there. It's difficult to take such figures in.

It's the same with my bank balance. I don't know what it is exactly, but I know that I'm not in the red, and I live happily and contentedly. I'm really proud when my seven-year-old son asks me about my successes, and I can show him it. These are the moments when I become really conscious of my success.

Mell: There were so many special moments in my career that it is hard for me to come up with a single one. The first time I heard my song on the radio. My first golden vinyl. Our big success in China and a performance in front of millions of people there are surely among them.

What do you think it is that makes dance music affect people so strongly and positively?

Novus: In 1999, I was able to perform as a DJ in front of 1.5 million people at the largest Love Parade in Berlin. Here it was clear what it was all about—letting go of everyday life, experiencing many beautiful emotions. The vibe during this time was simply positive, and that's what dance music is all about.

Mell: There are so many reasons (and this applies to every genre of music). Performing live is perhaps also the best way to explain the power of dance music. It is the combination of the artist, the song, the audience, the lights and the emotions. If you have ever been to a concert, no matter if it was a dance festival or a rock concert, you may have experienced the magic in the air, when 50,000 people raise their hands to the sky, sing, scream or just close their eyes. It is the moment when they are connected to the best of life for a short period of time. People connected with music—there is nothing else like it.

Lightning Round with Groove Coverage

Favorite drink in a nightclub?
Novus: Jägermeister, ice cold!
Mell: Wódka Red Bull

Have you ever forgotten the lyrics to any of your songs?
Novus: No! Never! I never forget anything! *What was the question?*
Mell: I haven't forgotten the words (yet), but sometimes I totally mix up the set list, especially when I am nervous. That drives Novus crazy!

Studio recording or live on stage?
Novus: Live is life! Doesn't matter whether it's a live act show or a DJ set—a set must live and breathe, not be decided beforehand in a studio. Many big festivals unfortunately work this way. There are no fixed playlists for my DJ sets. I don't know which song I will be playing in the next 10 minutes; I act solely on instinct and play with the audience.
Mell: Live!

Craziest thing that's ever happened in a nightclub or during a performance?
Novus: A show in China, back when I was still using vinyl. At the start there were massive fireworks right over the turntables, which hadn't been [properly] arranged beforehand. The sparks came down on the records and burned right through the vinyl—so the show was already over after four seconds. The distraught faces of the Chinese fans and the 2,000 hands raised with camera phones is a graphic memory! Just like my expression when four fans, who after the show had climbed 34 floors up the fire escape on the outside of the hotel in order to knock on my window and ask "Hey Mr. Groove ... where is Mrs. Coverage ... can we take a picture?"
Mell: Half of the club fighting for some reason while I was on stage, and we had to stop the concert. That was weird!

Your all-time favorite dance song?
Novus: Underworld's "Born Slippy" from *Trainspotting*.
Mell: There are too many! One of them is Dash Berlin's "Till the Sky Falls Down."

A personal characteristic which will surprise most people?
Novus: Scrupulously punctual and, due to my star sign (Scorpio), extremely unforgiving. When enough is enough, that's it! I'm done, and there's no going back from there.
Mell: Being in a disgustingly good mood when I wake up and driving everyone crazy

while they are still tired and grumpy.

A piece of advice which you would give to all aspiring artists?

Novus: [*Evoking Ralph Kramden from The Honeymooners.*] Be friendly and courteous to those people who you meet on your way up the career ladder—you'll meet them again on the way down!

Mell: Be who you are, and don't try to be loved by everyone. This is impossible, and you will never be perfect.

Favorite food after a long club night?

Groove Coverage's (Melanie Münch, left, Markus Schaffarzyk/DJ Novus, right) breakthrough hit "Moonlight Shadow" (a remake of the Mike Oldfield '80s staple) reached the Top Three of the German Media Control chart in 2002 and still remains one of their most popular songs.

Novus: Pizza—or potato chips from the minibar, if there's no pizzeria open at five in the morning.

Mell: Usually I fall asleep while thinking about what I could eat!

Extended Versions or Radio Edits?

Novus: I'm all about a good extended remix.

Mell: Radio edit.

If you weren't working in entertainment, what would you be doing?

Novus: Working in my qualified trade, which I always enjoyed and will definitely return to again at some point. There will be a time when Groove Coverage is over. I've always been mindful of that. [*Markus does not reveal what that trade might be.*]

Mell: I guess I would run the streets with my son to catch Pokemon on *Pokemon Go*—it's great to be a mom!

Gryffin
Dan Griffith (DJ, producer, remixer)
"Heading Home" ft. Josef Salvat (2016)

"…not only seeing people dance to ['Heading Home'], but witnessing their reaction at my concerts and reading the messages I get about how much it means to them—I can't describe what that feels like. To have my work have that kind of impact on an audience is the best thing that can possibly happen."—Gryffin

A quick glance at the 2016 U.S. touring schedule of Dan Griffith, better known as Gryffin, shows a whole bunch of sold-out dates, from Los Angeles to Chicago to Washington, D.C. Take a look on recent Beatport, Spotify and iTunes' top selling hit lists, and there he is again. Ask a whole bunch of leading international dance music artists who's the new go-to guy for beautifully constructed and elevating remixes, and you'll quickly hear his name blurted out with the best of them. Gryffin, a soft-spoken young man in his mid–20s, burst upon the dance music scene in a decidedly big way that quickly caught the attention of Interscope Records, and his rise ever since has been described, quite often and accurately, as "meteoric."

Whether serving as a producer, musician or DJ, Gryffin (a classically trained pianist from New York) says he is determined to produce music that, first and foremost, touches his own heart. That focus has led to a string of universally popular hits, including his haunting and magically uplifting ground-breaker "Heading Home" (featuring Josef Salvat), an original track, as well as cutting edge remixes for high profile artists such as Maroon 5 ("Animals"), Years & Years ("King") and Ellie Goulding ("Burn," a mix that helped get him noticed early on). Late in 2016, Gryffin scored another smash with "Whole Heart," a collaboration with Bipolar Sunshine and a top hit on both the Billboard Hot Dance/Electronic Songs chart and Germany's Spotify survey. In an age where electronic saturation has muffled some of dance music's melodic heart and soul, Gryffin is poised to forge a very intimate connection with the genre's core and soar as a leader among dance music's new generation.

You're still a very young man, Dan, but I'd like to know about your early days and how you came into music.

Sure. I started playing the piano when I was seven years old. I was a classically trained pianist, so growing up I had weekly piano lessons and performed at recitals in the summer and at holiday time. I kept progressing to the next level, so I guess you could say I had a very proper education as a classical pianist right through the end of high school. From there, I started expanding my interest in music. My cousin was in a band (he was several years older than me), and they were touring around a lot. They were based in Orange County. I really idolized him. I picked up the guitar and tried to emulate him a bit. I jammed in some bands and played some music on the side, piano and guitar. That was really my introduction to music and how I developed my love for it.

In early 2017, Gryffin collaborated with Illenium for the world hit "Feel Good" (featuring Daya) and remixed Sigrid's "Don't Kill My Vibe."

I studied at a university to become an electrical engineer. I didn't go to school to pursue music. I didn't really make the connection that music might be a career for me in college. I thought of it as more of a hobby. But I really started falling in love with dance music. I remember growing up listening to Fatboy Slim, Daft Punk and Chemical Brothers. I remember the dance music from the late '90s and early 2000s the most from my youth, but I wasn't engulfed by it at that time. Once in college, however, hanging out with friends, I discovered the big room dance tracks—Swedish House Mafia and artists like that. They were approaching mainstream [popularity], but hadn't quite done it yet. I began downloading these tracks and started getting my feet wet in electronic music production. I bought Ableton software, which I still use to this day. When I finally felt my music was decent enough, I slowly began releasing it online through music blogs and whatnot, very unofficially, and it all kind of just grew from there.

There must have been a million guys just like you trying to do the exact same thing, but something about your music caught the ear of the music industry, specifically Interscope Records.

Oh, yeah, I know. I have been very fortunate. I guess I felt like my music was certainly good enough to put it out there and see what would happen. But the reaction I got definitely exceeded my expectations. I think it circles back to my childhood—wanting to be in music, performing and playing. Realizing people actually enjoyed what I created made me realize that maybe this was something I should try to pursue.

Interscope noticed some of the remixes I had put out early on, and they really liked my style. They reached out to me and, maybe a little over a year ago, we had preliminary conversations about seeing whether I'd like to try remixing some Interscope artists. One of my first releases with Interscope was a remix of "Animals" for Maroon 5, then Years & Years and a few others. I guess I was sort of on a trial period. They wanted to see how my music would evolve and, if they liked it, give me an opportunity with their label. It reached the point where they wanted to hear other demos of original music that I was working on. I sent them a few samples, and things started to get more official at that point. They decided they wanted to bring me on.

It's really a testament to your talent that you were able to launch a professional career so quickly. Listening to your hits, there's a distinctive, very identifiable style present, and you seem to have a great appreciation for melody, rather than just the beat. Might this come from your classical training, or does it come from some other source?

I'm not sure if my classical training (or any concepts that I learned from it) is exactly translating over, but I feel like I understand musical theory on a fairly deep level. I have a very good understanding of the technical side of music, and I understand why certain chord progressions work well and how to invert them to make a totally different sound. In that respect, my classical training translates over into my dance music. But I'd say listening to a lot of different music in a lot of genres gave me a good ear for musicality fundamentally.

I think you did hit the nail on the head in that I have a tremendous appreciation for melody—it's what will resonate with me the most. If I love the melody, I'm going to fall in love with the song, regardless of the genre.

Tell me a little bit about what your song creation process is like and how a song like the recent hit "Heading Home" comes about.

Each song kind of happens in different ways. With "Heading Home," I received a very basic demo from Josef Salvat, the vocalist. It was just him singing in almost like a voice-memo style, over a track that was similar to a church organ—very simple sounding. I was able to connect with the lyrics and his way of interpreting them. I asked him to send me the raw recording. That's where I usually start a production, even with my remixes—I have the vocal, and I start with a piano and start messing around with ideas and chord progressions. I try to create a foundation from a melodic standpoint, and that allows me to go somewhere with the song. I sent my ideas back to Josef, and we went back and forth on how to handle the vocals. From my production angle, I just tried to build up from what I originally constructed on the piano. That's how I usually begin—with the piano. By far, that's the instrument I'm most comfortable with.

"Heading Home" was a tremendous success, not only in the U.S., but abroad. The song was a Top 100 hit in Germany on its iTunes bestseller list, for example, right alongside your remix for Troye Sivan's international megahit "Youth." So, you've seen what effect your productions have on people—on a dancefloor—filling them and causing this huge emotional and physical response from your fans. What does something like that do for you as an artist?

Oh wow, it had me almost teary-eyed to see that. It is really special because that song means a lot to me. I was trying to create something uplifting and very emotional at the same time—the lyrics, the message behind the song were important to me. So, not only seeing people dance to it, but witnessing their reaction at my concerts and reading the messages I get about how much it means to them—I can't describe what that feels like. To have my work have that kind of impact on an audience is the best thing that can possibly happen.

Your rise in dance music has been called meteoric by many and, using "Heading Home" once again as an example, you reached number one on Spotify's Global Viral and U.S. Viral charts. You also reportedly accumulated a million plays just one week after its release. I wonder if this kind of breakout success puts a new kind of pressure on you. Is there any second guessing your creative abilities?

If I'm totally honest with you, yes, I feel a little bit of pressure. At the same time, I look at all this as an opportunity to show people there's more to me than this one song and the remix catalog I have put out. I want to push myself to produce the best music possible. Sonically, I do want to maintain that—I have amassed a bit of a following based on my sound, and I don't want to abandon it. But at the same time, I do want to keep evolving and be an innovator without compromising what my music has been about.

So, I think I have to figure out how to maintain the sound that [identifies me with my audience] and keep up with what's going on in music trends. That's where some of the biggest pressure comes from. Music moves so fast now, especially in the electronic world. So, I guess to answer your question, I do feel some pressure to maintain or surpass the success of "Heading Home," but I am actually working on a few records that I feel are really strong and that I am very excited about. As long as I feel emotionally moved by the music I am making, I will be comfortable putting it out, and we'll see what the audience thinks of it.

Is there a difference in the connection you make with a song, the satisfaction you feel with it, when you are remixing someone else's track versus your own original creation?

Creating an original song is definitely the most satisfying and rewarding. These songs are attached exclusively to me and my projects. I do love remixing—I'm not putting that down by any means; that's how I got noticed in the first place. It's very exciting to send a final cut to an artist and hear that they are ecstatic about it. Troye liked his remix [of Youth] so much that he added it to every live show and did an arranged version of it at the *Billboard Music Awards* show on national TV. He messaged me several times telling me how much he loved it. That's really rewarding. But being able to have fans react so positively to music I am creating for myself, that definitely trumps everything.

You are also DJing. Do you aspire to emulate artists like David Guetta and Avicii?

What they have been able to accomplish has been amazing. They are at the forefront of this music movement globally, and there's so much to admire about what they've been able to achieve. I know there's a lot I can draw from them in terms of what a career path might look like. At the same time, I want to pave my own way I guess. I do DJ, but I've been more focused on my live shows, which have been predominantly live over the past year—where I actually played the piano and guitar to my tracks. It's a dance show for sure, but it's live performance. So, there's things like this I want to do as an artist.

As a 27 year old, you pretty much missed the glory days of vinyl and CD sales that were once the bread and butter of the industry. Do you find it a challenge to handle the business side of making music in the twenty-first century?

I definitely understand that the nature of the music industry has shifted dramatically, even within the last five years or so. I have to be aware of the new model, and I think the focus tends to be on performance [revenue] now. But at this point, it's not on my mind that much. To be honest, I'm just so focused on making music and playing live. I guess that is naive, but maybe it's good that I am rolling with the changes in the music industry and not being, well, maybe angry about them. I never experienced what came before—I'm just young and trying to make music.

Do you see yourself as a "dance music artist" today, or do you prefer to see yourself in broader terms?

I do see myself as a dance music artist—definitely. I don't have a problem with that. I don't know if I see myself so much as a "DJ," as opposed to an artist/producer. As I said, I really gravitate to the live performance side of things. I want to show that I am the one creating a lot of this music from organic, true instruments. I understand fundamentally, however, that my music *is* dance; it is electronic. I have no desire to stray from that label, but perhaps I am sort of a hybrid with pop within that world.

One characteristic of our current world as it relates to dance music (that seemed far less threatening in past generations) is the influence of terrorism—attacks in night clubs, at live events—tragic events like those that increasingly make headlines. Do you see this as being the new reality for the dance, night life and entertainment world of your generation?

It's interesting—I'm obviously very aware of what's going on, but I hadn't considered the impact it potentially has on night life and entertainment. It's sad that, as you are pointing out, it can affect everything. Yes, I can see that it would affect people's comfort level and can have a great impact. I don't know—I can only tell you that I believe music has such a powerful, unifying effect. I don't think terrorism will ever completely deter people from wanting to be a part of that experience. It's scary, but I feel the power of music will prevail.

What's been the most unexpected aspect of being a professional music artist that you've encountered so far?

Hmmmm—*really* good question. You are keeping me on my toes. I think it's how fast [the industry] moves, which I mentioned earlier. Music comes out at such a fast pace on so many platforms, like Spotify, Soundcloud, iTunes, Pandora, etc. Trends and styles in dance music are constantly evolving with such incredible speed. It's exciting for the industry, I think, that nothing stays stagnant. It's a challenge for me, as well, because I have to maintain the integrity of my music and keep up with this evolution. Production methods, too, are always changing.

Even among very young people, the biggest classic dance songs from the '70s, '80s and '90s are often very recognizable. Do you think future generations will recognize the dance music created by you and your fellow artists the way the hits from the past have been embraced across the decades?

Yeah, I definitely think so. I admit with the volume of music that is coming out over the past few years, maybe it's harder to identify which are the ones that might last for decades. I'm sure it was the same (proportionally) in the '70s, '80s and '90s—there was a ton of music that came out in each of those periods, but there were those classic tracks that you could cherry pick that ended up standing the test of time. I definitely believe my generation is making music that will be viewed the same way in 20 or 30 years. There's a lot of music being produced today that isn't melodic—let's say it's more directed toward festival experiences. I don't know if that will last that long. But songs that are melodic, fundamentally rich and have the qualities that make a song really exceptional will be remembered.

It's always been sort of a mission for me, the minute I started putting out records. I wanted to create that kind of music you'd remember—that's achieved by making that emotional connection. That's always been on my mission statement when it comes to my music—it has to have soul. If it hasn't moved me, it isn't good enough to put out.

Why do you believe dance music is so popular today?

I think one of the biggest qualities of dance music is really simple—it's fun. It makes you want to move your body and be with other people. It puts you in a different state of mind. Not having a good day? Put on a dance record, and you'll feel better! I think that's what's made it so popular over the past few decades—and so loved.

Lightning Round with Gryffin

Is there a dance track you never tire of hearing?
Oh yeah, Daft Punk's "One More Time."

After a night of clubbing, what's your favorite thing to eat?
Tacos!

Have you ever worked for days and weeks on a track and actually lost the whole thing due to a computer glitch or error?

Oh man—no, but I'm going to knock on wood right now. That's a terrifying thought. I don't always back up my stuff, and my girlfriend is always harping on me to do that. Maybe I have to do that right after we finish talking!

Best time for you to use social media?

Well, now that I live in LA, late morning seems to be the best time for me.

What's your preferred social media outlet?

I use Facebook a lot, as well as Instagram. Snapchat is really starting to grow on me—it's a pretty fun app.

Gryffin's remix of the Troye Sivan smash "Youth" was one of iTunes Germany's most popular dance hits during the summer of 2016.

First time a stranger recognized you as a music star?

That happened in LA. It happened twice in the same day—pretty crazy. I was at a beer festival and someone came up to me, recognized me and asked for a selfie. Later that night, in a different part of town, the same exact thing happened. I have to say it was pretty awesome.

If you weren't a rising music star today, what do you think you'd be?

Easy. I would be an electrical engineer in the San Francisco Bay area. I had a job offer to start working there, but I took a chance on music instead.

Harrison

Harrison Shaw
(DJ, producer, remixer, vocalist)

"Ain't a Party"—David Guetta & Glowinthedark ft. Harrison (2013)

"In dance music, you have a hit and become associated with that one sound. You're often not allowed to change your style until that sound stops selling. As an artist, that's like living in hell."—Harrison

When speaking about his music, Harrison Shaw (known in dance music circles simply as Harrison) has a very confident, genuine tone, and he never mixes words. This rapidly rising young British DJ, songwriter and vocalist (yes, he can spin and sing at the same time) has reason to feel a sense of upbeat confidence. Harrison possesses a remarkably savvy awareness of the realities of the business behind contemporary dance culture for someone only in his early 20s. He also has a deep-rooted appreciation for the integrity of the music at this genre's core and that which bears his name. He's been extremely well-received by fans throughout Europe and the U.S., topping the Beatport chart with hardcore EDM bangers such as "Sit Down" (with Vinai) in 2016.

It all started with his self-penned track, "Take Me Home," a song elevated by the artist's stirring vocals, thoughtful lyrics and an inspiriting EDM beat. It cleared the way for him to be acknowledged by such notables as David Guetta, Avicii, Hardwell and Steve Aoki. His anthem "Ain't a Party" became a hands-in-the air smash in 2013, and subsequent releases, including "The Wave" with Vinai in 2015, have kept the buzz building for Harrison. Though he may be rapidly creating an A-list name for himself in electronic dance music, he says he isn't about to let the genre define him—and he plans to let his creative spirit soar beyond its confines in the years to come.

Please tell me what life was like for you during your youth and how you came into music, Harrison.

I grew up living above a bar, or a pub as we call it here in England. It belonged to my mum. My dad was quite busy working all the time. My earliest memories include going downstairs into the pub at four in the morning and asking my mum if we could please go to bed now. I'd have to head off to school at eight! There was always a DJ playing there on Friday nights. My grandfather was a great musician—he was an amazing saxophonist and a big influence on me. I loved hearing him play, and I would sing Sinatra songs with him—great swing stuff. He definitely introduced me to music and was my hero.

Studio and vocal work with dance superstars that include Steve Aoki and Laidback Luke, as well as releases on industry leader Spinnin' and Armada labels, have kept the Harrison brand firmly in the limelight.

And dance music? It's really your song "Take Me Home" (eventually released by the Armada label with the artist credit Thomas Gold, Harrison & HIIO) that gets things moving for you, correct?

Yes. It's a bit complex, that story. I had a fight with my family, which led to me moving away to the south of London. At that point, I began living with my [natural] dad for the first time in my life. I worked in his hotel—I guess my whole family was really in the service industry. But at 17, I found myself to be quite depressed and dropped out of school. Everything seemed to be going wrong. So, I started writing song lyrics as a way to get things off my chest. All these songs and ideas helped to get this emotional stuff out of me. When I wasn't working in the hotel, I would get work in the London music studios. I started learning how everything works in a studio, how recordings were made and all the techniques. They taught me more and more about the industry.

My grandmother was very sick at the time. She died at one point in her illness, but was resuscitated after something like seven minutes in limbo. That was very unlikely that far into death. She told me that she was in the room observing where it happened and was able to see her body on the exam table—an out-of-the-body experience. There are many cases of this, but medically, they can't explain it. It's a big question, right? What happens when we die? We'd be millionaires if we knew. I was fascinated by this, and as she got better, my grandmother accurately described all the people in the room and things like that. This incident became the foundation of my song "Take Me Home." I developed this progressive melody on the piano thinking about all this and just began writing it through. I knew it was a really special song. I thought I would be able to make this song into a David Guetta–type of track, like "Titanium." Right?

It wasn't the most amazing production I've ever made, looking back now. But it was the start of me working in the dance and crossover scene. I had these other songs, but nobody was paying any attention to them. I literally sent at least a thousand emails to everyone in the music industry, just praying someone would take an interest. This was before everyone was jumping on the EDM bandwagon. One day a man named Sergio (who was in the industry) replied and wanted to hear my tracks. He came by to hear my stuff and said he couldn't really do anything with most of it (too Ed Sheeran-style pop, he said), but he thought "Take Me Home" was really good. He asked if I'd be interested in doing the song with one of his acts. I was like, "Sure!" It was like a lifeline that *anyone* was interested.

I got a phone call that night (actually, two in the morning). It was Sergio, and he connected me with a [Surinamese-Dutch] DJ/producer with a Vegas residency named DJ Chuckie, who has produced some amazing songs for people like 50 Cent, Akon, Kesha and many others. I sang at a rave in Holland for one of his shows—it was crazy! It was the first time I saw a massive LED wall and thousands of people attending this event and going crazy. So between the song "Take Me Home" and working with DJ Chuckie, that's really how I came into dance music.

What do you think it was about you at that time that opened doors for your career to begin?

For me, I just simply was *not* going to work as a night porter or a dish-washer or cut wedding cakes on a Sunday for the rest of my life. That fear of being stuck in that made me determined to find a path to success. I felt like I had nothing—my only purpose at the time was to make sure somebody heard one of my songs. Even if they told me it was shit, I'd go back to the drawing board and listen to whatever advice I could get. I never gave up my dream.

The other thing I think that helped me was my motivation. I wasn't jumping on a bandwagon. I loved the songs I created, and they had my real heart and emotion in them. I wasn't just trying to get a DJ to play it at Tomorrowland. "Take Me Home" was a *real* track that I spent months making, recording with real guitars. I had to really plug in to make this happen—not just throw down a beat. It was a living, breathing song that could have been on the radio without being a dance-style track. And, really, I think I was trying to also make my granddad happy.

The story gets even crazier because after the event with DJ Chuckie, I was incredibly inspired. I told a friend of mine that I had the most amazing party of my life—it was impossible to describe how mad it was. People were acting like they had arrived in Mecca! The only place to be—and the energy was so positive. My friend was like, "Oh, yeah? Well, I had a night in Kingston, and it was amazing." I replied, "Well, whatever you did, it was *not* as good as my night! It's impossible!" He argued, and I responded, "Well, it's not a party without me!" That day I wrote the song "Ain't a Party" (which got picked up by David Guetta).

I played with that line and made the song really hooky. I sent the track to Chuckie, who thought it was amazing. He played it at *Miami Ultra* on the main stage and gave it to all these other DJs, like Afrojack and David Guetta. Suddenly, I was in the midst of all these major DJ stars who wanted to play it, and Guetta signed it two weeks later. The sad part of the story is my grandfather died a week before that happened, so he never got to see that I made it in the music industry.

Were there any challenges for you going from an unknown aspiring singer/songwriter to a hot, rising DJ and performer in dance music so quickly?

"Ain't a Party" was one of those key big drop tracks that came right before EDM exploded. When I performed it, I was talking to the crowd as a raver! I was telling them to put their hands up, and I got a huge reaction. After "Ain't a Party," I started getting attention without having to fight for it. I had no label, though, no manager, no A&R, no people to handle PR, no lawyer. I was just doing it all—*to do it*. And it happened too fast. I had to find all of these people—and it took two years to find good ones that wouldn't screw me and take huge percentages without doing much for them. Even today, I still have problems with people who aren't that great at what they [claim to] do.

The transition to being a performer was hard. I like being a songwriter more than performing. But the reason why I followed the performance road was not for fame, but because I *can't* make a living from Spotify or iTunes. Rave music isn't Justin Bieber crap, where you get paid a million just from the record and radio play. In dance, the only way to earn a living as a DJ or performer, or both, is to get those gigs. If you don't, you'll starve. I needed the money.

So, it seems like very quickly you had three balls in play—your creative musical efforts, your performance work and your role as a businessman. But that doesn't mean there is always a work-reward balance, correct?

That's right. The thing is, I got so dumbed down in 2013. Like I said, I didn't have people behind me. And nobody had seen a guy who could DJ *and* sing at the same time. It was kind of new and different. Normally, the artist you see on a track after the word "featuring" (say, Ellie Goulding or Katy Perry) is just a guest vocalist on the track. But I was the creator of these tracks and being sold as the feature. In this business, DJ/producers can get huge fees, but a featured artist, as I was at this time, didn't.

In this business, it's often guys like me taking our tracks to bigger name DJs, and we get dumbed down on the production side. You don't necessarily make that much money when you sell your track—so what do you end up getting? You have to hope the exposure of being connected with a hotter name boosts your profile, so you can make better deals.

Now that you've been in dance music for a few years, do you subscribe to that philosophy which advises one never meet one's heroes?

Well, it's true, I could tell you stories where *exactly* that has happened. But you know what it comes down to? I am where I am now, and you just have to protect yourself, your art and your work. I am happy to collaborate with other artists, but now I know I won't consider it unless I know my name will be listed first or as "and Harrison"—on equal billing with the other artist(s) involved.

EDM, though still hugely popular, has been criticized by some as lacking depth, emotion and originality. Is this genre becoming too disposable and stunting the growth potential of dance music overall?

I think we have too many people making the same style. Everybody tends to copy everybody—I can't tell the difference between a certain top DJ and the other artists on his label. They are like sheep. If you're going to survive, it's always about creating something fresh and interesting.

Truthfully, I didn't exactly want to make a song like "Ain't a Party" after "Take Me Home," but I felt there was pressure to make a certain sound—otherwise I wouldn't get signed. In dance music, you have a hit and become associated with that one sound. You're often not allowed to change your style until that sound stops selling. As an artist, that's like living in hell. I wouldn't want to go out there as a DJ and play only one track list for the next five years. You know? I imagine many others feel the same way. EDM is coming to a point where they are getting a little bit bored with it and with Tomorrowland. We've been hearing the same type of song for the last three years.

Do you define yourself as an innovator of dance music?

I did three tracks in the style of "Ain't a Party" that became massive after their releases. "Sit Down" was one, and the other was "The Wave" (the most-played song at Tomorrowland in 2015). But the truth is—I'm done. I won't make another song unless it is going to move in an original direction. What's the point of cloning it a third and fourth time? I get it—the songs are fun and energized—but I don't always enjoy screaming at the top of my lungs at a crowd. It can be fun once in a while, but I want to make songs that connect with me and my heart.

I think in order to survive in dance music, you have to have the courage to drop this hard, big room, progressive and deep house style and come up with something new. The shelf-life of these tracks can be as short as two weeks. So what's the point of spending three months making a track that disappears in a week, when you could make a dance or pop track that could actually live for years?

I think I have to find the right label to push that agenda forward, and I believe I have the songs to do that. I can't say they will reach number one, but I feel I have a good track record in songwriting. You know, it's like, "If you liked the other crap, you'll *really* like this new stuff." [*Harrison laughs.*]

Are you able to keep up with the seemingly infinite sub-genres in dance music today?

Most of them. I say that only because it's my job to know them. You get these idiots who invent a lot of these sub-genre names, and often that's all they will listen to. There will always be these niches, though.

Are drugs a big part of the music scene in which you perform?

I can say for myself, I'm clean. But I've seen a lot of DJs this year dropping out of the scene. I think that happens because sometimes they get greedy, doing as much as they possibly can, staying up all night and doing 200 shows a year. I think it can start by taking stuff just to stay awake. It's hard, man. Drugs are a massive part of the dance culture—they always were.

But I will say I see a lot more kids going to festivals just to hear the music, not to take drugs and get high, and they just drink water. I notice age differences in drug use. I find that the people most obviously taking drugs seem to be very young—18 or 19—then you have a gap between 19 and 25 where it's not so much—and then the older crowd who need it to keep going at three in the morning.

I'm interested in hearing your take on the terrorism crisis we face and how you feel it has impacted, or will impact dance music, clubs and festivals.

I'm not a politician—I can't say what the world should or shouldn't do. But how do I feel? Well, for one thing I really don't think everyone saying "Muslims are bad people or horrible extremists" works. Branding a whole group like that because of the actions of some just doesn't make sense. Do we brand all the British because of crazy people in our history like Jack the Ripper? You understand what I mean? The horrible individuals and groups like Isis that do these terrible things are one side. That loner in a small town shooting up a high school dance is another side.

I was in America not long ago, in the South, and people were saying to me that they felt sorry for me living in London because of all the Muslims we have and the so-called risk of that. Shit—that's so naive. So, maybe we have two or three million Muslims—are they all dangerous people? No. Look, I get it—it's a scary time to be alive. I love what Einstein said—he said he wouldn't be around for World War III. But World War IV will be fought with sticks and stones.

As far as dance music is concerned, festivals and such—we know now that nobody is completely safe anymore. There's always going to be the risk of bad people targeting these things. It's no different from someone going into a high school or a cinema anywhere. I don't think dance events are any more a target than, say, the Underground in London. We are all at equal exposure and risk today.

I think the worst thing we can do is live our lives in fear. If we carry on, evolution will knock these forces out. The minority will never overtake the majority.

Do you ever think of yourself as a part of this great lineage that runs through the history of dance music, going back to innovators like Gloria Gaynor, Donna Summer, Giorgio Moroder, Nile Rodgers and the like?

I think anybody that comes up with an answer to that question and says "Yes, I do!" is extremely arrogant and doing their music for the fame. Honestly, I don't care if my name is forgotten two years from now. I'm just making music because it's who I am. I'm pretty sure Donna Summer, Giorgio Moroder, Gloria Gaynor or Stevie Wonder didn't make music in the '70s solely striving to be a really big name that people would remember for the next 50 or 60 years. I'm sure they were doing it for their love of music. They worked their asses off. I think how big you get is fate. Who am I to say I will be remembered as a part of dance music history? I just love what I do!

What makes dance music so valuable and so appealing to so many people around the world?

It just makes you happy. That's it. When I'm at a party or, say a wedding or something, and I hear "Le Freak" or "Oops Upside Your Head," you can feel what great songs these were and are. Dance music can't die—it's been evolving every decade. Who knows what will come next?

Lightning Round with Harrison

Is there a dance track you never get tired of hearing?

No. [*Harrison laughs.*] If anyone says anything else to you, they're lying!

After being out all night, what's your favorite thing to eat?

A pizza or McDonald's. It's not good for me, man. I only do it to absorb the alcohol. I like a lot of bread—I should eat fruit. I guess if I want to live beyond 30, I better think about it.

Best social media platform for promoting dance music?

None of them are that good. My favorite platform to hear new tracks is DemoDrop. Soundcloud, Facebook, Twitter aren't great for uploading tracks. Mixcloud is there, but nobody uses it. The only thing everyone is on is Spotify, and they are terrible about paying an artist—so where are we really at with all this?

First time you were recognized as a dance music star?

I was walking in Italy, in a mall with my mum (I know, with my mum, right?). Someone came up to me and asked if I was Harrison and asked for a picture—they were going to my show that night. It was cool because it was in front of my mom! "Look at me, mum, I'm famous!" [*Harrison lets out a big laugh.*] What's cool about living in the UK is nobody's really into EDM here, so I will never be bothered here—if I continue to make EDM.

In the summer of 2016, Harrison teamed with Kill the Buzz for the hit single "Once Upon a Time."

Were you for or against Brexit?

I liked the idea of unity, but I voted to leave. It happened at a time when I tried to book a doctor's appointment here, and the wait was over three weeks. I wasn't bothered about immigrants coming to the UK, as so many others were, but the fact that I couldn't get a doctor's appointment as a citizen of this country upset me. I just felt like if I was born in this country, I should be able to use this country's services when I need them. So I opted out. Brexit actually makes it tougher for me now because I have to get visas every time I play in Europe. But that problem of getting a doctor's appointment really bugged me on a core level at the time.

If you weren't in entertainment, what would you be doing today?

Probably sweeping roads. [*He laughs.*] Here's what I like to say: "If you do what you love to do, you'll never go to work again." So whatever I'd be doing, it would be something I would enjoy. I just would never allow myself to wake up thinking, "God, I hate my job."

In-Grid
Ingrid Alberini (vocalist, songwriter)
"Tu es foutu" (2001)

> "I had always known I would belong to the magic world of art since I was a child. Singing makes me feel complete."—In-Grid

Italy's beautiful and enchanting singer/songwriter Ingrid Alberini, known throughout the world as In-Grid (sometime spelled In-grid), significantly helped bring her country's penchant for exciting, inventive dance pop music into the twenty-first century. She accomplished this with one of the most original and irresistible songs of its day—"Tu es foutu"—an innovative "screw you" to ex-boyfriends that predated Taylor Swift's trademark message by nearly two decades. The track, sung in French and later released in English as "You Promised Me," was produced by Italian Larry Pignagnoli, no stranger to international success with his massive hit productions by Spagna ("Call Me"), Ann Lee ("2 Times") and Whigfield ("Saturday Night"). "Tu es foutu" reached the Top 10 of the Eurochart Hot 100, *was a smash in numerous countries throughout 2002. It eventually reached the Top 10 of the* Billboard *Club Play, Dance Single Sales and Dance Airplay charts in the U.S.*

In the wake of her tremendous debut success, In-Grid's quirky, captivating performance style and appealing vocal prowess led to a string of popular upbeat releases. The richly romantic "In-Tango" (2003), a homage to film romance and the movie theater environment she grew up within, and the infectious "Mamma Mia" (2004) found great chart success in Germany, Denmark and the Netherlands. The singer helped move the electro-swing genre forward with her invigorating rendition of the stomper "Viva Le Swing" in 2010, and the track's inventive video was one of the most visually ingenious of the year. In-Grid's latest hit, "Chico Gitano," a high-energy affair with a Latin-meets-middle-eastern flair, was unveiled to an enthusiastic reception late in the summer of 2016. The artist remains one of modern dance music's most spirited, cosmopolitan and dependable stars.

To begin Ingrid, would you tell me what makes Italy such a great country in which to live and make music?
I am crazy in love with Italy. I love every single part of it. My country has the power of creating emotions (even though the economic depression here has recently softened some of our enthusiasm). Landscapes are amazing and so different. Food is delicious, as is the music, and the many languages spoken together here blend with our well-known hospitality and history to create an explosive mix. All these aspects obviously affect our creativity.

In-Grid's single, "Tu es foutu," was a mammoth international hit in 2001 that paved the way for a successful album called *Rendez-vous*, which went gold in several countries.

Would you please tell me about your youth, life growing up in Italy and how your interest in music and entertainment evolved?

I grew up surrounded by all kinds of arts. My parents were keen on photography and paintings, but they also kept a huge collection of vinyl records at home. When I was little, they had the idea of opening a movie theater in the center of the town we lived in. I spent the majority of my childhood inside there. Indeed, my environment growing up positively influenced my attitude towards art and movie soundtracks in particular. Each day, I could watch a movie six times in a row and observe and capture different details in the film every time. At that time, I used to sing in a church choir, and I had started taking singing lessons as well. I soon realized that writing lyrics was the best way to express myself—my feelings, my inner moods. The first positive feedback came a few years later—from my audience during my many years working in piano bars and in musical shows.

How did you come to meet Larry Pignagnoli and Marco Soncini, the gentlemen who would go on to produce your smash debut recording "Tu es foutu" in 2001?

I was singing jazz in a piano bar when a gentleman, who was sitting in the audience, invited me for an audition in a recording studio. He was friends with a very famous producer and the owner of this studio—Larry Pignagnoli. I knew about Mr. Pignagnoli's popularity because he had produced several famous '90s dance hits (such as "Saturday Night" with Whigfield and "2 Times" for Ann Lee, just to mention a couple).

Larry, together with guitarist and producer Marco Soncini, provided me with an instrumental dance track enriched by an original French flavor. I wrote some lyrics in the French language for the song. This track really became a huge hit in 2002, licensed in more than 20 countries around the world.

Before we go into this incredible song, would you tell me how the name 'In-Grid' came about?

Well, my real name, as you know, is Ingrid. My father was a great fan of Ingrid Bergman.

It was Larry who suggested I hyphenate the name into two parts. Literally, "grid" means "inside the cage."

Do you recall some of the details behind your lyrical interpretation of "Tu es foutu"? I understand there is a sort of a Taylor Swift-style background to this story.

Yes, my take on the lyrics was born after a broken relationship with a guy I used to be in love with. That love was my "cage." Writing this song (with a touch of irony) was the best way to express my anger. I consider art to be the best therapy. The guy I am referring to was even a DJ—so he had to play the song for that entire summer, and this was my best revenge, indeed! For a long time after I was very popular, but men seemed to be indifferent about a possible relationship with me—probably because they were afraid I could find musical inspiration in their mistakes, and I might reference them in a song. I'm still single! [*In-grid laughs.*]

Do you remember any details of the actual studio recording sessions?

I can remember I followed all my producer's advice because I strongly trusted him. He suggested that I shouldn't rehearse or practice the song before recording it. Larry wanted me to sound self-confident and to sing the song very naturally and spontaneously, just by following my inner instincts. So I did. The result was, perhaps, technically not so perfect, as my pronunciation wasn't always proper, but they didn't mind it. My interpretation reflected the figure of a broken-hearted girl who still believed in real love.

Interestingly enough, (for an Italian production) the song evoked a deeply rich French flavor. Was singing in the French language and evoking the emotions of the song difficult for you, being an Italian performer?

I wrote the lyrics in French because I was staying in the French Riviera at that time. I was so impressed by the colors and the romantic and sensual inflection of their language. Before "Tu es foutu" became a great success, I had always been keen on French songs, and I used to sing popular French tunes during my piano bar days and musical sessions. I have always had a peculiar vibration in my voice, which is difficult to eliminate or even disguise, so I started using it as a point of distinction—and I'm still exploiting it!

I'm curious about how an artist like yourself feels just prior to a song becoming a worldwide sensation. Did you ever anticipate 'Tu es foutu' would be such a huge hit?

No, I didn't! This is what real producers can do! They are able to recognize a genuine hit among hundreds of songs. I was just a young singer. One thing I did recognize, however, was that "Tu es foutu" was one of the first dance songs that had adopted a traditional musical instrument [the accordion—played by Daniele Donadelli], normally reserved for other music genres.

I'd love to know how you felt as you saw the song gain momentum on the charts and as it reached the Top 10 in so many countries.

It was such a great surprise for me, and I still can't believe it! This song earned 14 gold and platinum awards, from Mexico to Australia. The song started life by being played in Greece, and the first time I went there, I couldn't believe what was happening. My song was being played almost everywhere—from TV advertisements to every disco I entered. In Germany, it was among the most played songs—*ever*! It passed through the Netherlands, Spain, Poland, Mexico and right over to Russia. It was amazing when I realized that, as far away as Siberia, I had fans who adored me! My life completely changed. And I have never stopped traveling since then. Even in the U.S., the track was included in the soundtrack for a very popular reality TV show. A brand new experience for a girl who came from a little Italian town. A real dream come true.

What is your favorite memory about this time in your life?

Definitely the emotions I felt when performing in front of thousands and thousands of people, especially during the many music festivals, live dances, TV shows or city celebrations where I sang for even as many as 200,000 people! I should also mention my first autographs or that time in Siberia when a fan of mine, who was a child of about 10, knocked at my hotel room door to offer me a lemon. He told me he was too young to come to my gig so he just wanted to bring me a present before I left. I will never forget that. I also felt really proud when I found out that some French teachers used my song to make students practice with the language.

"Tu es foutu" was released in English a short time after the French version—do you feel alternate languages for this or any song are necessary in a world market, or do they detract from the original style? How about remixes?

The song lyrics were born in French, and trying to record it again in English would have meant losing a bit of the romantic and vintage touch it had. Even though the video was shot in Italy, the place reminded one of the French Riviera. Anyway, it was necessary to record the song in English, and that experience was very nice. By the way, I will say it was a bit difficult to work on the remixes because the original version was the best one, in my opinion. But we did it!

What sort of considerations must come into play in order to successfully perform your style of dance music live for audiences of different nations?

My live concerts are always very interactive. I have always considered my audience as being the real protagonist in my shows. This is the reason why I study the idioms spoken in the countries I visit for my gigs. Understanding the essentials of any language is a primary key to fully getting in touch with people. I have never stopped studying them. I think this is the only way to get my live shows to be unique and to reach the goal of getting my audience to experience *real emotion*. I love jamming and experimenting, playing and having a dialogue with my audience. Most of the time, especially in small, far away countries, I come in contact with people who don't speak English. Among my fans there are also lots of children—I think they may be fond of me because I'm often quirky and funny on stage. I have studied psychology and philosophy for a long time, and I think I'm particularly able to understand what people want.

You are now an important part of Italy's phenomenal dance music heritage, made famous in the '80s with Italo-disco (Sabrina, Spagna, etc.) and the '90s with Italo-dance (Whigfield, Black Box, etc.). What are your observations about your homeland's contribution to energized dance music?

I still remember the '90s and Italo-dance music and the pleasure it provided with its great attention to melodies and its surprising positivity and powerful rhythms. Even though all the lyrics were usually recorded in English, Italian producers were, without a doubt, the masters of this genre. It's definitely impossible to forget songs like "Blue" (Eiffel 65), "L'Amour Toujours" (Gigi D'Agostino) and "The Rhythm of the Night" (Corona), just to name a few key tracks.

After having such enormous success, how did your personal and professional life change? Did the positive changes and gains outweigh any negatives?

I had always known I would belong to the magic world of the arts since I was a child. Singing makes me feel complete. Furthermore, I have been traveling a lot since 2002. I can't stop in any one place for more than three days. I'm completely in love with traveling. It's the most fascinating experience a person can have for many different reasons. I experienced no negative changes in my life at all as a result of my success.

"In-Tango" was a brilliant follow-up single in 2003. Can you tell me how you and your production team developed this song after the success of "Tu es foutu"?

"In-Tango" was chosen because of its touch of sensuality. It was another attempt to merge different sounds and styles—in other words, a new dance tango! In Eastern European countries, the song enjoyed even more success than "Tu es foutu," thanks to its melancholic wave that people loved. Perhaps the same wave can be found in my soul.

I'd like to talk a bit about the very distinctive video for "In-Tango," portions of which take place in a movie theater. Can you tell me how this production was developed?

I find this video brilliant! The video of "Tu es foutu" was inspired by the 1955 movie *Caccia al Ladro* [*To Catch a Thief*] by Alfred Hitchcock, starring Cary Grant and Grace Kelly. The "In-Tango" video celebrated the wonderful 1985 movie *La rosa purpurea del Cairo* [*The Purple Rose of Cairo*] by Woody Allen, where a character comes out from a cinema screen to woo a young woman. As you'll notice, I never abandoned the world of cinema. My graduation thesis was exactly about this topic: the relationship between the beneficiary of a representational work of art (in cinema, painting and literature) and the work itself.

Was there a great deal of pressure for "In-Tango" to measure up to the success of "Tu es foutu"?

I can't say I felt any negative pressure at all. On the contrary, I lived [the experience of working on a follow-up single] with a great deal of passion, devotion, energy and adrenaline! Sometimes I just felt a bit tired because of the many journeys I had at the time, but I never felt so fatigued that I wanted to stop.

Over time, there developed what one might call an "In-Grid sound"—music that wasn't too distant from the flavor of your original hits. Is it challenging to go in a new direction with your music—or do fans tend to want the same type of material? As a creative artist, how do you approach that?

It's absolutely true that fans expect you to make something which can recreate the same feelings and emotions, the same touch, they fell in love with the first time they heard your big hits. I think this can bring great satisfaction for an artist. On the other hand, it can also become a big problem because things change, music changes, the artist changes, and it's not always so easy to stay with your original stylistic choices and stay up-to-date with new trends at the same time. Not easy and challenging, indeed!

The *Lounge Musique* album from 2010 (featuring your brilliant take on Caroline Loeb's classic French '80s hit, "C'est la ouate") had a very different sound and was an unexpected departure for you from pure dance music.

Yes, my dance albums include *Voilà!* (2005) and *Passion* (2009). Definitely energetic. My two lounge albums are *La Vie en Rose* (2004) and *Lounge Musique*. You can easily find the *real* In-Grid in the last two, as in those projects I was able to personally choose among famous past hits (mostly French) and re-edit them in a lounge/chill/jazz/swing key. An electrifying challenge! I've always been keen on Edith Piaf.

Tell me your impressions of the dance and pop music industry? Since you began working in the industry, how has your attitude about it changed?

The music industry has deeply changed its identity. In the past, producers got in touch with talented singers or musicians and offered them good contracts. Today, everyone can make music from their homes. This has inevitably affected the work that's out there.

The music sales environment has always been challenging. Once, an artist usually had an opportunity to earn money once he or she had signed a contract with a label. But this happened to a lucky one percent of entertainers. Today's open market for creating music is providing the opportunity for an artist to rise, even without a contract. But making a living from recorded music directly remains very difficult. Personally, I still think working with a good label and production team [is the best way to] work in this field.

As far as I'm concerned, my experience working with recording labels has been, luckily, positive. I have always worked with people who strongly believed in respect, which is fundamental in life. And I think I've always been respectful towards my mates. I am a hard worker, and this is my greatest passion and mission in life.

As a woman, specifically, has your gender created challenges for you in the music business?

Physically, I am a woman—I am sweet and tender, and my curves don't lie. But my approach to work is that of a man in many respects. I have always had a masculine attitude in that area. This is probably the reason why I've never found myself in strange or ambiguous situations. I can make a person feel uncomfortable sometimes, and I can give the impression of being very tough. As a result, I've hardly ever been in situations where people would consider offering me—well, let's say weird proposals!

Are you pleased with your life and with the progression of your career at this point in time?

I'm thankful and satisfied with all of it. I feel proud of myself and happy. I wouldn't stop, even if I could, as this kind of life is something you get fond of very quickly. I'm not just referring to the emotions felt on stage, the autographs, the pictures fans take, or hearing your voice on the radio. I'm also speaking of all the roads you hit, all the airports, hotels, countries and people you get in touch with. I wouldn't be happy without all of this. I never want to lose my curiosity for life. I always look forward to creating new songs and working in new collaborations. You'll always find me working hard to get them. I recently released a new single called "Chico Gitano"—it is my newborn!

In the current culture of DJ/producers dominating the dance genre, do you feel the music is moving in a positive direction?

DJs became real producers, and they seem to know exactly what people want today. But it's no mystery that today they are placing less attention on lyrics and melodies to concentrate on more global sonorities.

There are trends [in every genre of] music. I just think that the "emperor DJs" is one such trend. They couldn't do without singers. The only instruments they cannot really substitute with electronics are human voices. I mean, they tried, but their attempt totally failed. The human voice is irreplaceable.

We now live in a world where terrorism is very real and large events like dance festivals and concerts are the targets of violence. Do you feel anxiety because of this? Do you feel this trend will damage nightlife and people's sense of security when going out to dance and enjoy a concert or event?

The world is experiencing a real nightmare. Terrorism is attacking our values, our idea of respect and peace—I even think giving birth to new lives is becoming less appealing. I can't hide the fact that I'm sometimes afraid of getting in an airplane or staying in a crowded place for a long time. I feel completely helpless towards what's going on. We're destroying the world we built and we trusted in. I hope something will change in the future and all human beings will find the way to live in peace in a new globalized world. What is happening is awful.

Do you believe the dance music of today has the quality and power of dance music from the '70s, '80s and '90s—and that it will be remembered and embraced 20 or 30 years from now as past classics have been?

I'm really keen on dance music, the kind that favors the power of melodies. It seemed like it reached the highest level of quality in those years you mentioned through the '90s. Then everything turned into meaningless genres, lacking in melody, almost instrumental—*sounds without music,* I would say. These new tunes did not allow the people to sing while dancing, which I think is something fundamental if you are really going to have fun. Anyway, the dancefloor never lies, so look at the many people dancing during a revival disco and '80s/'90s parties that are so popular, and you will get your answer!

Can you tell me what you think is the power behind dance music—why do people enjoy it so much, decade after decade?

I believe the origins of European dance pop music [were reflected in] the culture and music of "The Beat Generation" from America. The term *beat* was coined to refer to a new generation of people who were beaten (knocked out by the loss of real values) and "beatus" (free from the "sin" of being part of a system and strictly connected to the idea of sound), as the word suggests (beat—as in noise).

In Europe, the Beatles turned their gigs into a real revolution. Women started dancing on their own (they couldn't dance alone in front of an orchestra before) and progressively distanced themselves from their role of being the "property of a man." The mini-skirt did the rest. Dancing was part of this cultural revolution, and the increasing tempo of the beat was evidence of a world moving at a very high speed. I see dance music as society's attempt to further evolve and break free.

Let's look again at a point in time in the distant future—what do you want people to say about In-Grid's place in pop culture and music history?

I can't answer that question. That's the job of future generations, if they should hear my music. I'm just happy to know that I made someone smile and dance.

Lightning Round with In-Grid

Diana Ross or Beyoncé?
Diana Ross—I'm a retro girl!

Saturday night or Sunday morning?
Sunday morning. (Sorry Whigfield!)

Favorite cocktail or drink?
Wine.

Extended versions or radio edits?
Radio edits.

Where have you experienced audiences with the most passionate reaction to your music?
I'd have to say Siberia!

Spender or saver?
I'm a saver, so I can spend later.

A weekend in Mallorca or in the Alps?
Better at the seaside. I am sea-addicted!

Favorite song you wish you had recorded?
"The Power of Love" by Frankie Goes to Hollywood.

In-Grid has a cum laude degree in philosophy and continues to tour worldwide, releasing popular tracks in the dance, electro-swing, jazz and lounge genres from her home base in Italy.

Kimberley Locke
(vocalist, songwriter)
"8th World Wonder" (2004)

"I feel like it was almost as if God cleared a little pathway for me for like three or four years to excel in the dance lane, and it was great for me."—Kimberley Locke

Few television entertainment programs helped define pop culture during the first and second decades of the twenty-first century as did Fox TV's American Idol. *This remarkable breakthrough pop music program smartly combined the public's unstoppable attraction to and passion for new and exciting young singers with the appeal of a reality TV show contest. It quickly became one of the most memorable ongoing entertainment experiences of its time, eventually racking up an astonishing 15 seasons. A nail-biting competition viewed by millions, AI launched the careers of a new generation of pop singers, including Kelly Clarkson, Clay Aiken, Taylor Hicks, Carrie Underwood, Fantasia Barrino—and Kimberley Locke.*

Ultimately placing third at the finale of the 2003 season, Ms. Locke quickly became one of the show's most prolific alumni, establishing a formidable presence on the dance music scene. Though she scored hit singles and albums that tapped into several musical genres, clubland was among her most enthusiastic supporters. Scoring multiple number one hits on the Billboard *dance chart, including the infectiously uplifting "8th World Wonder" (also a Top 50 pop hit), "Change," "Fall" and her sizzling remake*

Following her success on *American Idol*, Kimberley Locke was signed to Curb Records where she enjoyed a very successful career as a recording artist, releasing three albums with the label and enjoying numerous club hits.

of the Freda Payne nugget "Band of Gold," Kimberley was quickly acknowledged as one of the new century's most appealing and popular dance music artists.

Kimberley continued to expand the scope of her career in the years that followed her auspicious debut. After scoring yet another top dance hit in 2010 ("Strobelight"—a project created with AI judge, renowned bass player and producer Randy Jackson), she formed her own consulting company (I AM Entertainment), appeared on numerous television shows (such as The View), *and championed many charities, raising awareness of HIV/AIDS and breast cancer. Kimberley Locke released a new single in early 2017, "Dangerous Woman" (featuring Bond Villain) on her private label.*

Kimberley, would you tell me about your youth, growing up in Tennessee and how you came into music?

That's a very good question, because I don't come from a musical family. When I was a little girl, the extent of my music exposure was me listening to records in my room. My family wasn't really into music, and I was kind of left to my own devices to figure it out. Maybe that's not the best way to put that—because I don't want to say I knew when I was young that I had a voice or passion for music. I didn't.

I had several cousins, and somehow they were all in the marching band at school. My cousins and I would mime to the music we heard on records. We would put on little shows for my aunts and uncles at my grandmother's house. I was probably six, seven or eight. My parents got divorced when I was about eight, and we moved to the next town over. I started going to a new school, and I was in my first talent show when I was in the fifth grade. From that talent show I got connected with some other girls who were really great singers. That was kind of the beginning of everything. We started a little group (called Shadz of U), and that became our lives, right up to my junior year in high school. We were an a cappella group who sang mostly at church. Although we had no formal training, we had a lot of help from Vera Warwick, who taught us how to become better singers as a group and how to blend and sound like one. This was in addition to [the valuable instruction I received] from my high school teacher, James Story. Singing with those girls, I really learned a lot and started to grow. I realized I really loved singing and that this was my thing.

It sounds like you discovered your voice through a natural process, without the aid of any formal training. Were your parents very supportive of your growing passion for music?

Yes, it was very natural, but I don't think my parents really knew what to do with my interest in music and in my voice. [*Kimberley laughs.*] They didn't quite understand it. They didn't try to steer me in any direction one way or the other. They probably knew I had talent, but they didn't really know what to do with that.

What led to your participation in the second season of *American Idol* **in 2003? Would you share some of the details of this extraordinary experience?**

Gosh, let me tell you, it was shocking and a whirlwind! It was one of those situations that you dream about and think you know what you're going into, *but you don't have a clue.* With every turn there was a surprise. I auditioned for *AI* on October 30, 2002, in Nashville.

At that point in my singing career, I had pretty much tabled it. I'm the kind of person that if I can't do something a certain way, I don't want to do it at all. I knew I didn't want to sing at wedding parties for the rest of my life. I had gotten to the point where I was going to shift gears, focus on my education, stop singing and go to law school. I kind of really put my singing career on the shelf. But, as they say, you have a plan—but God's plan is always bigger.

American Idol was coming to Nashville, and some of my friends and family had heard about it. They encouraged me to watch the show and said that I needed to audition. I wasn't very keen on it at that time because I had been accepted into law school and thought, "Oh, no. I have my plan, and I'm not changing lanes now." I literally got up that morning and went to the audition thinking if I did, I can at least say I went to it, and the worst that can happen is I wouldn't make it. I'd already been on a thousand auditions. So, as it turned out, that was the audition that changed my life. I made the cut.

We went out to California in January of 2003 to start filming the show. Every step was thrilling, exhilarating and exciting. It was literally like entering a whole other universe. You went from complete anonymity to everyone knowing your name. I suddenly felt like everything I had done up until that point was in preparation for that moment. I was very prepared, and I was living the dream. It was the best experience that I could have asked for. I learned so much. For nine months I was consumed by it. I wouldn't have missed it for the world, and I wouldn't change anything about it. It was fantastic.

What would you say was one of the more unexpected aspects of doing the show that most people—the TV viewing audience—probably had no clue about at the time?

I think people would be surprised to know that we didn't rehearse very much. That show is *not* about practicing and singing your song. We would get up at five in the morning and start doing press, photo shoots and video shoots. You want to practice your songs? Practice in your sleep. That was kind of how it was. *AI* was such a brand and such a machine, especially at that time, and we didn't get a lot of down time. We had to *beg* for down time.

I think people would be surprised by that, but it was a testament to all of us competing on that show—to our talent and professionalism. No, we didn't get to practice an hour or two a day. We were lucky if we got a half hour. When people saw the show on TV, it seemed to be all about the singing. But we did a hundred things before we ever got to that aspect of the program.

You were up against Ruben Studdard and Clay Aiken, who were vying to win, just like you. How much pressure did you feel to separate yourself from this formidable pack?

Sure. We all had to figure out how to set ourselves apart. That's what it was really about. Not only did we not know how to do that, we were singing cover songs—someone else's music. That made it even more difficult. You weren't being identified by your own sound; you were being judged based on someone else's music. It put you in a very precarious position from an artist's standpoint. When you think about what it means to be an artist, it is all about self-expression and creating your own persona. But here we are on this TV show—a brand that is bigger than all of us put together—and we don't even understand this brand at the time. It was just becoming so huge. Now you throw into the mix the dilemma of standing out from the *American Idol* brand and all these cover songs. It was a tough thing to do, finding your own voice and making it stand out.

When we were on the show, we were singing Billy Joel, Smokey Robinson, Gladys Knight—iconic musicians and singers. And us little no-name kids from Podunk, wherever, were supposed to do these classic songs and make them our own. *Really?* [*Kimberley laughs heartily.*] It's a lot of pressure! Of all the barriers on the show that you had to break through, that was certainly one of the biggest.

What were your impressions of the judging panel?
I think we had the best panel of judges ever from the show. We had the original line-up: Paula Abdul, Randy Jackson and Simon Cowell. I think that panel *was American Idol*. I don't think you could find a better dynamic. It was the perfect fit and balance. I'm just really glad I got to work with the original judges.

You ranked third at the end of the season. Did you feel a sense of pressure to keep the momentum going, despite the lack of an actual win?
Absolutely! The one thing I knew coming off the show was that *American Idol* had first right of refusal [for a recording contract] with all of the Top 10 contestants, not just the winner. From the date of the finale, they had 90 days to make that decision. I was calling them every week asking if they were going to sign me. I knew that every day I went without being signed, I felt like the window was closing for me. Though they eventually said no, I already had my troops on the ground, so to speak, to help me find me a record deal. That's how I came to sign with Curb. I was very happy when I did. Sure, I was probably a little disappointed I didn't get signed to the *American Idol* label, but I didn't dwell on it or allow it to stop me. I just spent nine months on international television—*someone was gonna sign me*!

Of all the labels we talked to, Curb literally came to the table with an actual contract. It wasn't a hard sell. The funny thing was I went to Belmont University in Nashville, and Mike Curb's music business was part of Belmont University. The record label is literally a stone's throw away from the university, but I went all the way to California to get that deal.

I have to give credit to Bryan Stewart, the head of A&R at Curb Records, and Jerry Sharell, my first manager, for launching me into the dance world. Bryan played a major role in exposing me to the genre. I think he got the ball rolling, and Jerry was a huge advocate and worked it. If it had not been for Bryan, who was head of A&R at Curb, I would never have gotten my opportunity to move into the dance music world.

Let's talk about that. Your first and second albums for Curb, *One Love (2004)* and *Based on a True Story (2007)*, were very pop-oriented collections. Yet Curb took a number of singles off these sets and extensively remixed them, effectively turning these songs into major number one anthems on the *Billboard* dance chart—and you into a celebrated dance diva. They included the hits "8th World Wonder," the electrifying remake of Freda Payne's "Band of Gold" and "Change"—these were among your biggest successes. Was the plan to create a duality in your career between pop and dance, and did you have an appreciation for your high ranking in the dance genre?
What was happening at that time was I was the only artist on their roster that was charting on multiple formats—pop, Adult Contemporary and dance. Curb Records was a major player, but an indie label. So for them, to have an artist (that was not country) successfully crossing into a number of genres was a very big deal. They really wanted to get me out there, and it worked. It definitely worked.

Specifically, in regard to dance music, I'll be honest with you—I didn't really know what was happening. That's why I give Bryan the credit for that. I remember going to the label one day (I was at their offices often), and Bryan and I had lunch. He said he had just gotten 15 dance remixes of "8th World Wonder." I didn't even really know what that meant—I had no idea. Bryan was very successful with "8th World Wonder," which went to number one on the dance chart, and after that, he did it with every song I released as a single.

Listen, I was so fortunate and blessed because, at that time, the dance chart was wide open. Dance was just starting to resurge again, and I got in on it before [major pop stars] starting remixing all of their songs for the dance market. Usher, Chris Brown—artists like these weren't fully capitalizing on dance mixes yet. I wasn't competing with them. I feel like it was almost as if God cleared a little pathway for me for like three or four years to excel in the dance lane, and it was great for me.

So, you were not directly involved with the remix process?

No, not while I was with Curb. By the time of my second album, I had become familiar with the remixers and knew who they were and had my favorites. But I trusted Bryan's knack for knowing what would work best. But I really loved how my voice translated to dance music, and I think that he knew my voice would resonate in the genre and on the dancefloor, and he made it happen.

How did you react to the success you enjoyed in the clubs and on the dance charts—knowing your music was filling dancefloors and exciting so many people?

Oh my gosh—still, to this day, it is incredible to me! I had a friend in Sydney, Australia. One or two years ago, he sent me a video of one of the biggest clubs in Sydney and everyone dancing and going crazy to my latest single at the time, "Feel the Love." Watching the video—well, it was just one of the best things that can happen to an artist. There are two things—watching people dance to your song and being on stage and hearing the people singing your song back to you! That is just—wow. Unbelievable! When that happened to me the first time, I actually stopped singing and just absorbed the moment on stage because I couldn't believe it. It's a huge rush.

Randy Jackson reconnected with you in 2010 for a wonderful retro-dance single called "Strobelight." How did that project come about and what was Jackson like to work with as a producer?

It was a one-off single project. I was living in California at the time, and my manager, Jay Schwartz, had a relationship with Randy, as did I. Jay felt it would be a great fit. I really enjoyed working with Randy. It was seven years after I had been on *American Idol*, so that made me feel very good—that I had done well enough in my career that Randy saw value in making a record with me years later. I felt very fortunate and blessed.

And let's be realistic—Randy is brilliant. I have a lot of admiration and respect for him and how he has successfully worked in so many aspects of the business. So to have Randy on my résumé is really something. I think the record went to number five on the dance chart, so I was very proud of that experience. Randy had the ability to push me outside of my comfort zone, and that's what he did on "Strobelight" and why the sound was a bit different.

You also worked with the prolific production and remix team Cahill for a UK project that you mentioned earlier, "Feel the Love," a song you also co-wrote with Damon Sharpe. I understand this was a somewhat different experience?

I have to be honest with you. On this project, I didn't work with Cahill directly at all. It was a record in which I was completely hands off. The song was my baby, however.

I sat on the song for three or four years after writing it with Damon Sharpe (who had worked with me on my albums and with whom I had a great relationship). I held this song close to my vest. It was inspired by a lesbian couple who had been together for 10 years and lived in Vermont. One of the ladies was American, and the other was Japanese. They were being forced to separate because same sex marriage was not possible at the time, and the Japanese woman was going to be deported. It was so awful to me that two people couldn't be together because of politics and propaganda. I called up Damon and told him I wanted to write a song [with this theme in mind]. We put that song down within 45 minutes. I give Damon credit for that.

Unfortunately, this record got caught up in some politics and complications with the handling of the business, if you will. The video was shot without me, and that was disappointing. I felt the video failed to capture the real essence of the song. But that said, I don't want to dwell on the negative things. It's better to stay positive. I can say to you that "Feel the Love" is, in my opinion, one of the best songs that I ever recorded.

Please tell me about the creation of your music consulting company and recording label, I Am Entertainment.

One of the reasons I started I Am Entertainment was to release my own music, be independent and maintain more control. My first release was "Finally Free." (I partnered with Cahill after that release.) After these experiences, I realized that artists need an advocate. That became my company's stance—a company for artists, by artists. In whatever capacity I work with other artists, they can be confident that I am their advocate to help them navigate the industry and avoid some of its pitfalls.

You recently recorded and released a new spin on Gloria Gaynor's disco classic "I Will Survive," incorporating the 1996 Chantay Savage arrangement.

Chantay Savage did a brilliant cover of this song (which came out the year I graduated from high school). It was one of those songs that flew under the radar, but I loved it. I wanted to do the song because when you turn that song into a ballad, it takes on a whole different life. That's kind of where I am at now. When I release music going forward, it's gonna be music that I love and that has a purpose, a reason for it. When I recorded the song, I remember thinking, well, I've survived. I survived—whether in my personal life, business life or career—I have survived. So I felt a connection with the message of this song.

How are you dealing with the challenges of monetization in the music industry today?

The industry has changed tremendously over the 13 or 14 years I've been in it. Social media and the way you promote a record has changed completely, as well as the way you make a living from it. I always tell artists the business is now the wild, wild west—which can be a good thing and a bad thing. Until you can start to figure it out, an artist can lose money left and right. But the beautiful thing is, if the artist can really understand their business, the intricacies and subtleties of it, they *can* do really well. This is a time where artists can have ownership of their music and careers—they don't have to give that away. I think that's the beauty of what's happening now.

Have you experienced any challenges in this business being a woman or, more precisely, a woman of color?

You know what? In my experience, no. Issues like that haven't even registered in my brain. A big part of what I'm doing now is consulting on the projects of other artists. The fact that I am getting many clients, I feel, is a testament to my track record, what I've accomplished in my own career. The issues you mentioned—I don't think I would have been able to validate my career had they been big problems. I don't think I have encountered much resistance in this way—or if I have, maybe I am oblivious to it. [*Kimberley laughs.*] I think I would have noticed it, though.

Before we began our interview, we were discussing the terrible tragedy that occurred in Orlando, Florida, in which a gunman went on a brutal killing rampage at Pulse, a nightclub popular with the LGBT community. Such horrific events seem to be on the rise. How do you see entertainers and dance culture addressing fears of violence and terrorism like this?

[*Kimberley sighs and pauses momentarily.*] Unfortunately, there's always going to be bad people out there. But we can't live in fear. I see horrible things like what happened with the young singer from *The Voice*, Christina Grimmie, too. As artists, we have to pay attention. Social media sometimes gives us some warning, and I think artists have to do their due diligence on there to protect ourselves and our fans.

In live performances, everyone is exposed. We can't stop doing that—it's our craft and our livelihood. So, I think we have to try to become more aware and look for warning signs. We need to put fellow artists on high alert when we see something that doesn't look (or read right) on social media, and our friends need to do the same for us.

This stuff is real. It can happen, and it can happen anywhere. Anyone who went to the [Pulse] club in Orlando that night had no idea that such a horrible thing could happen—I'm sure they were never thinking that such violence and death was a possibility. We have so many potential targets in our country, whether it's a church, a club or a theater. But we all have to start paying attention to the people around us. I think this is going to become a new way of life. If you see something, say something—*and do something*. Because sometimes there's not a lot of time between seeing something and something happening.

As a singer, an artist who is an easy target on that stage, I just can't live my life in fear. I just can't. If artists succumb to that fear, we'll all be behind locked doors and peeking through windows, and we'll never enjoy the sunshine again.

In your personal life, how are you staying grounded, healthy and focused?

It's really important that I continue to grow as an artist and person. I am learning what real peace is all about. I do believe in a higher power. I am a spiritual person, and I try to stay connected to that. That's what keeps me grounded, especially in our business, which can be very volatile, with big highs and big lows. I eat well most of the time, go to the gym and try to focus on the positive as much as possible. I wake up each morning and look at each day as a gift. I try to remember that whatever is happening in my life is small beans compared to the bigger picture. There's nothing going in one's life that we can't handle—we just have to believe that.

Where do you see your career going in the future?

My focus is to grow my company, and I just signed my first artist. I'm looking forward to making great music for myself and other artists. And you know what else? I'd like to explore being a talk show host. I shot a pilot not long ago, and it's been well-received, so we'll see where that goes.

We have those amazing dance music classics from the '70s, '80s and '90s that everyone seems to remember and love. Do you think dance music from the first 17 years or so of the twenty-first century will be remembered in the same way?

Oooh, that's a big question. I'm gonna broad-stroke it and say no, unfortunately. I think dance music from the previous decades you mentioned was more of an actual movement. A social movement. A powerful movement. Just think of house music. I think now—how do I say this—dance is, more simply, just another genre. Today, you have some glimpses of that power it once had, but I tend to think it is simpler now—really just another music genre that's out there.

Dance music is everywhere today and some have proposed it is the pop music of this century, at least so far. Regardless of the era, what do you think is the quality dance music possesses that draws so many people to it?

I'd say it's the way it brings people together. You can say that about music in general, but people just love that rhythm, that pounding beat of dance. When you're in a club, it can be 110 degrees and nobody cares because the music has taken over. Dance music has always been about anthems—it unites people in a positive, uplifting way. And that's no matter what subject you are singing about—even heartache.

Lightning Round with Kimberley

Have you ever forgotten lyrics to one of your songs while performing?

Oh, yes. You either repeat the first verse or mumble your way through it. Or, better yet, it's the perfect time to flip the microphone to your audience!

Social media preference: Facebook, Twitter, Instagram or Snapchat?

Facebook. It's the easiest.

Single biggest advantage of being a dance pop star?

All the free stuff and traveling the world on someone else's dime. It's seriously awesome!

Extended versions or radio edits?

Extended versions. There's always a breakdown in the song, and I love to hear the bass—that incredible beat!

Saturday night or Sunday morning?

Oh my gosh—I'm gonna say Sunday morning.

If you could be eternally stuck in one year of your career, which would it be?

2007. It was great! I was living in New York City. I opened a restaurant, I was on the road, and I was loving life!

Milk & Sugar

Michael K (Mike Milk), Steven Harding (Steven Sugar) (DJs, producers, remixers)
"Let the Sun Shine" (2003)

> "It was great in the beginning to not have any pressure or people on your back. We were doing music more for ourselves, and if something great came out of our work in the studio, fine. If not, that was also fine."—Michael K

> "I think some of our success is measured by our ability to reach all the different channels with a record. Maybe no one single chart is a [deal-breaker], but it is important to get that wide exposure. For example, our recent record with Barbara Tucker didn't make one of the key charts, but it was still huge in the clubs. So, I must admit, I wonder how the system really works at times."—Steven Harding

Among Germany's most prolific DJ/producer/record label owners is the team of Michael K (aka Mike Milk) and Steven Harding (aka Steven Sugar). Known the world over as Milk & Sugar, these gentlemen have a knack for delivering what many consider to be perfect club mixes, songs bursting with the power to tear the roof off any venue. One of their biggest hits, "Let the Sun Shine" (a remake of the 5th Dimension evergreen from 1969), has been a career milestone, vaulting in 2003 straight from the Ibiza clubs to number one on the Billboard *dance chart and the Top 20 of the UK pop charts.*

Since that monumental event, Milk & Sugar have unleashed a steady stream of dance hits that cover a wide spectrum of dance sounds, from house to deep house to electro-swing. Among their most popular hits have been "Hey (Nah Neh Nah)" (Milk & Sugar vs. Vaya Con Dios, 2010), "Stay Around (For This)" featuring Ayak (2012), "Canto Del Pilón" (Milk & Sugar featuring Maria Marquez, 2013), as well as some hugely popular remixes of their classic sun-shine smash. Over the past several years, the duo has put together popular compilation albums, including the House Nation *and seasonal* Sessions *series on their Milk & Sugar Recordings label. In 2016, they released the single "My Lovin" featuring Barbara Tucker (of "Beautiful People" and "I Get Lifted" fame).*

Gentlemen, please tell me a little about your youth and how you came to connect with each other.

Steven: I grew up in a small city in the middle of Germany. I was always surrounded by music. I don't come from a musical family, but my grandmother played a few instruments and had a great deal of influence upon me. I learned piano and guitar at a very early age.

As DJs, producers and label owners, Milk & Sugar (Michael Milk, left, Steven Sugar, right) have won several awards (such as the German and Italian DJ Award) and received numerous gold records.

Music quickly became a passion for me. I was very enthusiastic about learning more and was in the school choir. We had a great conductor (he had a broad cultural and musical background), who was an excellent mentor for me. I then started DJing at school parties and for friends. Somewhere between 14 and 17 years of age, I had two Technics turntables and some good equipment. I eventually moved to another city in Germany to continue my studies, and there I had my first resident DJ job in a club. I also worked at a radio station and learned more about production, creating commercials and things like that.

From there, I moved to Munich in the early '90s, where I met Michael. He was a DJ as well. We decided to start working together on projects, and we began creating our first tracks.

Michael: I grew up in Munich, and my dad played the accordion, keyboards and drums. I think that's basically how I was introduced to music. I was obsessed with vinyl and built a huge record collection. By the time I was in the fifth grade, I was buying records—not just dance records (going back to Salsoul and disco), but Bowie, Pixies, Iggy Pop and many more. I always had a dual personality when it came to music—on the one side rock and the other side dance.

When I was 17, my dad bought me some turntables and I started throwing parties in our cellar. By the time I was 18, I had earned a DJ residency in a Munich club and was throwing parties everywhere—warehouses, empty swimming pools—you name it. A friend of mine introduced me to Steven at one of these parties, and we began working together.

How did Milk & Sugar become a reality?

Michael: We were doing some work together for a few years without a real name. My former girlfriend was living in London, and I'd visit there every other weekend. I was really obsessed with Ministry of Sound, listening to Erick Morillo ["I Like to Move It"] and listening to this London house vibe that was so popular. I came back and said to Steven we needed to create music like that. We had been creating a lot of German techno and trance stuff, and we decided to move into this new musical territory. That's when we decided we needed a name for ourselves—and we just came up with Milk & Sugar.

Tell me about the track that first broke you onto the dance scene.

Steven: It was a record we did called *Higher & Higher* in 2000, which DJ David Morales discovered. He also remixed it. When he started playing it late in 1999, everybody started focusing on this track. We ended up making a big deal with Universal for it, we did a video, and it ended up being our international breakthrough hit. Thanks to this record, we started playing everywhere. I must also say that DJ Robbie Rivera also contributed greatly to our initial success. We signed an instrumental track from him called "Bang" (Robbie Rivera presents Rhythm Bangers), we put some vocals on top, and it too became a big hit.

Would you describe how you came together in those days to create tracks? What was your process like?

Steven: When we were just beginning in our careers, it was just as if we were throwing a party in the studio, inviting our friends and creating music!

Michael: It was great! We'd come to the studio at really crazy times (like four in the morning, after a party). We couldn't get a lot of studio time during the day because it was always booked. We'd work in the evening—sometimes go in with some girls [*he laughs*] and ask them if they were able to sing something. It was very casual—not very professional or planned in those days.

Steven: Yeah, it was more like "go with the flow." Old friends who know us from those days tell us they like our records more from back then. They liked the party atmosphere. Now they're not even allowed to smoke in our studio!

Michael: We weren't under any pressure in those days. It was another time and another scenario.

Steven: Yes, exactly. I think of one of our more recent successes—"Hey (Nah Neh Nah)" (Milk & Sugar vs. Vaya Con Dios). It was a big hit, but you'd have the label on the phone telling us, "Don't lose the momentum!" It was great in the beginning to not have any pressure or people on your back. We were doing music more for ourselves, and if something great came out of our work in the studio, fine. If not, that was also fine.

Michael: I have to jump in and add that it *did* become a more structured process for us, eventually. We went to our record dealer in Munich, who had an amazing collection of rare grooves, disco originals, test pressings and such, and we started collecting music to create loops for our early productions. From that point, we really started to develop our own style, step by step.

There was a freedom back then I imagine you don't feel quite as much today.

Steven: Yes. Today, I think we are very keen to watch our competitors and to see how records are structured and how they seem to be targeted to the audience we want to reach. So we must be very aware of what people's preferences are at any given time—how a record must be put together, its build-up, how they must work on the dancefloor, etc. In our early days, *anything* was possible. I think our track "Higher & Higher" was something like eight and half minutes long, with a two minute saxophone solo. Totally crazy!

[*Michael nods in agreement.*]

Michael: The day we recorded "Higher & Higher," we had this crazy musician from Los Angeles doing a big saxophone solo, and I had just watched a documentary about George Michael's hit, "Careless Whisper." They mentioned that his song had the world's longest saxophone solo in it. So I came into the studio saying we have to make *our* saxophone solo the longest!

How challenging is it for you to be innovators of sounds and styles, as opposed to followers of trends in dance music today?

Michael: I don't really think it's that challenging. We aren't trying to follow what others do—we try to identify our target audience, where are we playing, what the clubs are like, what our audiences want to hear. Everything has a name now—deep house, tech house, etc.—and all these genres are very separate. We have to think about which categories we want to move in and take part in.

Steven: Things are changing and evolving in dance music rapidly. Many artists stop their development at a certain point and just copy themselves. We play in a lot of different countries, and we always try to observe where people are moving in terms of their [musical tastes]. We don't want to lose that momentum or come into sounds too late. Getting in as early as possible will give us a stronger evolution in our music, and it will take us further.

Michael: The other side of this is that it's also important not to lose your roots. We come from funk and disco. At this moment, funk, disco and house are huge in Europe, more so than in America. That's a change from even just last year. Vocals are back. I think that made one of our recent records, "My Lovin" with Barbara Tucker in 2016, huge.

I'd like to take a moment to talk about vocalists. You've worked with many, some of whom go back to the old school days. What do you consider when working with a singer? How do you feel about the shift in attention from the singer to the DJ/producer in dance music?

Michael: It's a very individual thing—and that applies to songwriters, as well. If we are looking for a very strong voice, a soulful vocal or a shout-out diva, we try to connect with those who have a solid history in this area—someone like Barbara Tucker or Ayak [Thiik]. There's the new side of dance music that has a moodier sound, so we need to connect with contemporary songwriters and singers who can produce that type of material too. We have to know what we want to achieve.

Steven: I think the changing [stature] in the role of the singer is largely because of the Internet and the way people work with each other all over the world in music today. I can be in a small village in the countryside and connect with a singer in a major city, and we can make music together. That gives DJ/producers a lot of options to work with different people—a way of working that didn't exist before. Going back in time, we needed vocalists in the studio. That might mean we had to go to London if we wanted a British singer, or we'd have to fly them here. The network back then was smaller because connection was more challenging. In the past, if you built a good team, that team would stick together for a longer period of time—same singers, same bands, repeatedly making tracks together.

Now, in electronic music, a track is made, the DJ/producer signs it to a publisher, and they get a singer's vocals recorded from anywhere. That's how it works. In many ways, I think it's a natural evolution, the result of technology.

Michael: I think a singer's management plays a role as well. I think if they have strong management, they are more careful about how they are billed as a featured artist. If they don't have good management, and are feeling the competition, they accept agreements that they normally might not go for. I think this is a big reason why you have so many DJs "featuring" unknown singers, or those with just one name.

Do you believe the way we produce dance music in the twenty-first century has made the genre less personal or reduced the amount of heart and soul conveyed in the music?

Steven: It's true that in many productions today, you don't meet the people involved, one-to-one. You send the song to someone, and they send the recording back. What's missing is the work together in the studio. You lose some of that spontaneity that used to occur—nothing unexpected happens anymore. You can't say at the moment of laying down the vocals that it was great. "Good job! Can you repeat it with just this slight change?" The creative process is very predictably structured now if you are bouncing tracks between countries.

Michael: You have less influence over the track—and, of course, that is based in money. Nowadays, you have so many productions because everybody is exchanging through the Internet. It would be tremendously more expensive to fly in singers, put them in a hotel, pay for dinners and not know if the project is going to come out well. Young producers either don't have the money or don't want to invest in such a process, so they send the track out and get a result. But they have no influence upon it. I will say that it is nice to hang out with the singer and get to know each other better. That is a much closer relationship and connection.

Take our song "Stay Around," featuring Ayak. We have worked together with Ayak for nearly 10 years and have become very close friends. It isn't possible for us to exchange tracks with her—no, we fly her in and what we achieve as a result is very special.

Steven: It's true, perhaps you have a better chance of creating something spectacular with that personal interconnection, but sometimes it still happens even without socializing.

You've had some tremendous success with your music by any standard. But how do you personally measure that success?

Michael: I always think getting great DJ feedback from those we like and respect is the most important thing. Personally, that means more to me than going to number one or two on Beatport or whatever. It's always nice to earn money and be able to pay your rent, but at the end of the day, music is passion. I am always more excited by news that people are playing our records, rather than reaching a certain number on the charts.

Steven: I would add that today I think there is a necessity to have our tracks perform well on Beatport, Spotify, YouTube, Soundcloud, the important blogs and DJ charts. I think some of our success is measured by our ability to reach all the different channels with a record. Maybe no one single chart is a [deal-breaker], but it is important to get that wide exposure. For example, our recent record with Barbara Tucker didn't make one of the key charts, but it was still huge in the clubs. So, I must admit, I wonder how the system really works at times.

Let's talk about some of your biggest successes—starting with an early one, "Love Is in the Air," your 2001 version of the disco classic featuring John Paul Young. It was a major pop hit in Germany, Spain and the UK. What's the story behind it?

Michael: At that time, we were making some music with a good friend of ours, Angie Brown (vocalist of some of Bizarre Inc's '90s hits, like "I'm Gonna Get You"). Angie knew the master owners were looking to do a new version of "Love Is in the Air" and recommended us. When the record was done and we had to sell and promote it, it turned into a big pain. The real owners of the song were the guys from AC/DC. Believe it or not, they wrote the song. John Paul Young, the singer, had nothing to do with the song; he was the artist they hired to sing it. But, boy, that management outfit was really tight and tough. It would take them ages to make any decisions about the record. But finally that summer it was played, and it was a very big hit.

Unfortunately, it ended up being a record I often want to forget about. We then had 9/11, and we had this video with a small plane in it skywriting "Love Is in the Air." Well, after the tragedy, there was no love for airplanes, and all the radio stations and video programs dropped the track. We postponed the release of the single in Germany for about two months because of all these problems. Then there was another terrible plane crash in Brooklyn and another one in Zurich I believe (in which singer Melanie Thornton was killed). The record peaked in the Top 30 in Germany and the UK as I recall, but because of all these awful events, we felt it just was cursed.

Steven: Going back to the production of the track, I have another bad story from the technical side to share. We received the original 24-track on a ProTools session, which was cool. But a complication occurred, and the audio wasn't elastic, so we had few options how to fix the problem we were experiencing with the track. We ended up cutting it into 24 slices, each with four bars and a consistent tempo, then matched those bars individually to the design tempo, then put them back together again. All that work took many days to complete! Then we found out the groove somehow disappeared from the track. So, I ended up sampling every single bass note, in order, cutting out the kick drum, putting these elements in the sampler—oh wow, it was so hard to do. Today it would be easy, but back then it was a nightmare! After doing all that, I realized I chose the wrong sample rate, and the pitch and tempo were all wrong—so I had to start all over yet again!

That sounds unbelievably frustrating. I hope the original "Let the Sun Shine" from 2003 (which many consider your signature classic) was a better experience.

Steven: Sadly, this track also gave us a few headaches. There was a clash of problems of major and minor scales all over this song. For example, dance music is usually a four, eight or 16-bar measurement—and the chorus of this track was a six-bar. To solve the harmonic structure issue was very, very hard work, but we figured it out and were finally able to make the record sound logical.

For the vocal recording, we had 10 of the best professional studio singers here in Munich—some from the old disco era who worked with Harold Faltermeyer. We also had musicians like Mats Björklund (he was our secret weapon in terms of funky guitar work on some of our early recordings—he played for Donna Summer, Boney M., Milli Vanilli, Silver Convention, etc.).

We did the recording at a major studio with top-of-the-line equipment. I'm very proud of the choir recording—it's so special. I don't think anybody who ever did a recording of this song has a better one than we do.

What makes you feel the time is right to revisit one of your hit songs, as you did in 2009 with your very successful remix version of "Let the Sun Shine"?

Michael: I believe in 2009 it was because we had some business partners who suggested remixing the song again for a specific territory. I don't like the idea of giving a track up to someone and saying goodbye and good luck. We want to have control. So we organized the remix and found the people to work on it. It turned out people liked it, and it went to number one again in a few places. We are thinking of trying it again for our track's 20th anniversary. Our interest isn't so much commercial—it's more for ourselves. We play this record in every set of every show we do—people ask for it every single time, in every city. To be honest, I can't hear it or play it again—so we definitely need a new version. [*He laughs.*] Desperately! So, we're talking to some people now.

Steven: I'd like to add that if we do it again, we might break our old record. I think we are the only artists to have been number one three times with the same song in the UK on the DMC Buzz chart—2003, 2009 and 2012. It would be quite remarkable if we were able to do it a fourth time.

You run your own music label/production company (Milk & Sugar Recordings)—is it challenging to be creative individuals and savvy businessmen at the same time?

Michael: I would say as an artist today, you must try to juggle all these things because otherwise you won't understand how reaching people, touching people with music, works.

Steven: I just strive to be the best I can be—whether it is about the quality of music we are producing or getting it to the people.

Michael: There is no question it is a big challenge to run the label and be thinking of new tracks and being creative. Because you are doing both, it's easy to get interrupted. The older I get, the more I get pissed off by this. If you have a creative idea, you want to follow it. Then an issue with Spotify or something comes up and brings you out of that mode. You lose your momentum or forget your idea.

How about being producers vs. being live performers?

Steven: I think we are very lucky that we don't have to wear funny outfits to be noticed in the DJ booth. We come from an era when it was about the music and not so much the style of the DJ. I think we are very much respected for the music we play and produce, and it's very good that we aren't in the situation where we have to be so focused on one's social media profile.

Michael: Yeah, I was DJing before I was a producer, when it was about entertaining with music and records. What I don't like today is seeing DJs open their computer, hit the sync button, play some tracks and have a cigarette and two drinks in between, push the button, and do it again. Then they grab the mic and scream, "Put your fucking hands up in the air!" To me, this has nothing to do with entertaining.

There's little doubt now that the threat of terrorism is potentially very damaging to nightlife. Since many artists are increasingly dependent on live performance gigs to make money, do you see this situation becoming a crisis for the dance music industry?

Michael: Definitely. We play in many of the countries recently affected by these acts of terrorism. Two weeks ago we had a gig in Tunisia, and it was only half full. It was a holiday resort—an open air festival. Two years ago we played the same gig for the promoter, and it was huge—four or five thousand people. This time, the tourists were very scared to go out. This party was sponsored by the government to help bolster the area's image and to get people going out. Despite a big campaign and the fact that we had a big hit there at the time—it was a good party, but far less of a crowd than was planned for. The whole resort was fully booked, but people didn't go out. We were also scheduled to play in Turkey, the same week as their recent coup attempt. Everything was cancelled. So, yes, we have already been affected by this.

Steven: What we are noticing in Europe now is that people are starting to avoid traditional holiday regions. But there are still destinations, like Spain, where people are visiting and going out. Promoters are increasing security—which is a very good thing. We played in many countries in the past where security was a challenge, Russia and El Salvador for example, so I think we have grown used to this rise in security. The fact that Europe and Germany are taking security more seriously now is not a bad thing.

Michael: I think it's affecting us a lot here in Germany. Oktoberfest is held right near our offices, and visitor attendance dropped by 50 percent during the first weekend compared to the year before. People are passing on it because of the fear of terrorism. People are scared. If governments can't get a handle on it, I think you will see the dance music industry affected in a very dramatic way.

Do you think dance music and the genre's artists of the twenty-first century will have the same impact and staying power over the long haul as those of the '70s, '80s and '90s?

Steven: I'm sure some of them will. We can't say now, but fast forward 10 or 20 years, I think you'll see who stood the test of time. We may have produced some great records over the past 19 years, but nobody knows for sure which ones will stay in the public's memory. If I look back at the eras you mentioned and look at all the stuff that came out—I have to say to you, I'm sorry, there was a lot of rubbish. There is a tendency to say music from the '70s and '80s was great—well, not *everything* was that good. I'd say the majority was *not* good. But there will always be a few songs that will make it and be viewed as great, whatever era they came from. That's part of the fun—wondering what will become big and survive.

We can say that one of the most important songs from all these eras was Robin S' "Show Me Love." This is one absolutely outstanding song that has been a part of electronic music history for almost three decades—and it's still a great song today. Every year a new version comes out! It's unbelievable.

Michael: Wow—I booked her at one of my parties back in 1993!

Lightning Round with Milk & Sugar

Is there one dance song you never tire of hearing (aside from Robin S and "Show Me Love")?

Steven: Well, Robin is it for me.

Michael: There is a song, and I don't care whether other people like it or not when I play it—David Bowie's "Let's Dance" (the original version).

Craziest thing you ever saw take place on a dancefloor?

Steven: We played at club in Frankfurt, unaware it was kind of a "gay night." A guy came by the DJ booth and asked if he could put his clothes down. We thought okay—assuming he meant his coat. He took off everything—*everything*!

Michael: Except for his S&M leather mask.

Steven: It was a great night, though we saw more than we probably needed to.

Favorite thing to eat after a night of clubbing?

Michael: The best thing is *not* to eat—better for your health. I remember I had a few too many drinks at a club in Hamburg one night and ate some kind of junk at a small store nearby. I got seriously bad food poisoning. I couldn't leave my hotel for 24 hours. After that, I lost my appetite for eating after gigs.

Steven: When I started DJing, there was only one place you could have proper food late at night—well, not exactly proper—McDonald's. There was no other place—so that's where the party always moved to after the club closed.

Personal characteristic about you that might surprise people?

Steven: I think just that fact that I'm a DJ. People are always surprised by that, saying I seem so "normal!"

Michael: I have no idea!

Steven: Michael loves fishing, and I doubt anyone would suspect that about him.

Michael: That's true! I just caught a huge pike last week!

If you weren't in entertainment, what would you be doing?

Michael: That's why I'm in entertainment—I tried all that other stuff, and it definitely didn't work. I started out as a bank clerk, as my parents wanted, but it was just no good for me.

Steven: I was creative all my life, so I never thought about many other options. Sometimes I think it might be easier to have an office job, to end your day and come home. Though this job never ends, it's never boring.

Milk & Sugar's (Michael Milk, left, Steven Sugar, right) epic tracks "Higher & Higher" and their all-time Ibiza classic "Let the Sun Shine" remain landmark dance recordings of the twenty-first century.

Sak Noel

Isaac Noell (DJ, producer, remixer)
"Loca People" (2011)

> "If you are trying to be an innovator, it's very tricky. The pressure you are putting on yourself blocks you from thinking clearly. The only thing you can do is try to have fun with what you are doing."—Sak Noel

Isaac Noell, better known as Sak Noel, gained the world's attention in 2011 when he released an unstoppable party anthem called "Loca People," a high-energy floor-filler that swept Europe and debuted at the top of the BBC pop singles chart. Since then, he has released a series of hit dance tracks that have uniquely combined house, Latin, trip, hip-hop and EDM styles and which tap into the very core of what makes today's club music so electrifying. This articulate, observant and unpretentious artist has gained a substantial global following since his stellar arrival on the scene, and he now collaborates with the likes of Pitbull, Sean Paul, Da Beat Freakz and other A-list hitmakers. In 2015, he released his first album, Born to Party, *and most recently the single "Trumpets," a top European crossover hit in the fall of 2016.*

Isaac, please tell me what it was like growing up in northern Spain and how you first connected to dance music.

I was born here in Barcelona, Catalonia. When I was younger, trance music and northern European and German dance music were very popular. Eurodance was really kicking in, and I was very inspired by that. However, here in Barcelona there was no real culture for this music. It was very underground at the time—both the music and the good Spanish dance clubs. You had to go through other channels to get the music—before the Internet really kicked in. You had to go through France or to very specialized shops. I decided to try making this kind of music just for fun in the mid-'90s—obviously I had no luck taking it further. I had no real skills when I was a teenager and no real way to run with it, simply because there wasn't anyone really doing it in Spain.

I finished high school and studied journalism in college for a while. When Eurodance music finally started catching on big here in Spain, around 2003, I saw the opportunity to grow my passion. So I then decided to really focus on a music career.

In that year I believe you started your own entertainment company called Moguda. You were very young to be an entrepreneur—what did you want to accomplish with this business?

It was a way for me to put everything I wanted to do in one company. I started doing parties and had people cover the parties with cameras, making videos for YouTube and other media channels. I wanted to create a whole media package for clubs in Spain. With the passage of time and after taking on more and more, it became difficult to focus on Moguda if I was going to create my own personal path to grow. I closed it and moved into my music career.

In 2011, you released the single "Loca People," a massive worldwide hit performed by vocalist Esthera Sarita. It reached the top of the charts in the UK, Denmark, Israel, Austria and a few other territories—extremely impressive for a debut track. Can you tell me about the making of this song and the inspiration behind it?

When you are making music, you never know what will happen—it's a white canvas. I started with this little bit of an idea, and from that I was able to grow it into something bigger. Very close to where I live, there is this huge party on the coast line where all the people from northern Europe come to party in the summer. I'd been watching people come to this place for ages. I always wanted to make a song about this phenomena. I got this idea of telling the story of a girl who visits Barcelona, but instead of visiting the regular tourist attractions, she goes to the party scene. That was the basis of "Loca People."

Sak Noel's "Loca People" became an international sensation in more than 15 countries around the globe in 2011. He was the first Catalan artist to be number one on the BBC Official Singles Chart in the UK.

It was a tremendous international success. Did its popularity catch you by surprise and why do you think the song was, in fact, so popular?

Well, it *definitely* caught me by surprise. Otherwise I would have planned something bigger around my life for it! [*Isaac laughs.*] It just blew up. Actually, I have many theories about why it was so popular. It was probably a combination of many things—like when you have an accident, they say it is a combination of many factors. It was the same for "Loca People," but in a positive way.

It was the right time, the right beat and the right story. The storyline was very universal—everybody, pretty much regardless of culture, can relate to going on a trip and discovering the party zone. It was kind of a new style at the time because the majority of songs at the time were about love—the usual thing—and this song was *not* about love. The song was also spoken, not sung. I felt maybe I could create a new type of lyric on the subject of partying if you didn't have to sing it. Having just a girl talking, I could literally write whatever I wanted.

I notice in many of your tracks you utilize spoken word over a beat rather than traditional singing—and it is a very effective means of planting the track into the brain. Is that sort of a signature sound you are trying to create for yourself?

Definitely. For me, as a student of journalism and someone who likes to write a lot, there was one rule I learned. If you can explain something in one word rather than two, it's better. That's what I try to do in my songs. But in order to effectively do that in a song, the lyrics have to be spoken, not sung. The way I record the songs, we don't even use the beat or melody when recording the vocal. I want the vocalist to be natural—as if she is explaining something simply—not trying to say it while matching a beat. I first give the vocalist the story and record her words, which are spoken naturally, and then match them to the beat.

In "Paso," for example, there was nothing planned. I simply told the vocalist to say the words, and then I'd choose the right ones to fit the rhythm.

"Paso (The Nini Anthem)" was an amazing follow-up hit, and personally I could not stop playing that song. Can you tell me about the track and how you created a follow-up to something as big as "Loca People"? Is there a temptation to coast on the fumes of a previous hit when formulating a second release?

When I made "Paso," I really didn't think about the previous hit. Normally, there is sort of an unspoken rule that when you have a big hit, you can actually do a second one that is somewhat similar. Nobody will say anything because you're exploring the heat of the moment. But after the second hit, that's when the pressure comes. You can't do it again for the third time. You have to do something different, evolve or change your style. After "Paso," I definitely had to bring something new to the table. So I created a new track called "Where (I Lost My Underwear)." It had the same energy and fun feeling, but I changed the beat and used a computerized voice instead of a human voice.

The real change for me was the (2014) song "No Boyfriend (No Problem)." It was very successful and brought me again to the real music market and was a solid evolution from "Loca People" and "Paso." It is very difficult sometimes to create something and achieve your personal goals at the same time. When an artist creates something, really his goal is to achieve *nothing*. The goal is simply to create. When another goal is added into the mix, it becomes more challenging.

The Latin influence in your songs is very powerful and your blending of the Spanish language with English works so well.

Obviously my first language is Spanish or Catalan, not English. When I write in English, there's one good thing and one bad. The bad thing is I cannot write [as eloquently as someone for whom English is a first language]. That gives me a bit of a handicap. But the English I do know is understood by 90 percent of the population around the world. More or less, my lyrics can be understood by anyone that speaks even just a little English. That's good because it opens me up to the Asian markets, people who don't use a lot of English but can still relate to the song.

If you view the online reviews of your songs or critiques on iTunes, etc., people often refer to them as dancefloor "anthems." What does that word mean to you, and is it usually your ambition to create anthems?

Yes. For me an anthem—again in relation to the journalism thing—is like a headline. Anthem means it's memorable. It has to be something really powerful. People will only remember something that impacts them, something that's really interesting. Even if they don't remember the name of the song, they will remember the lyrics—and that's the sign of a good anthem to me.

You gained the interest of many major labels with your success, including music companies like Sony. How do partnerships with major labels affect your freedom to be creative?

In my case, they have had no effect at all. It depends on what kind of a contract you sign with a record company. I wouldn't sign a contract where I pass all my power over to a label. Actually, in my arrangement, I bring them my songs, and they don't ever tell me to change a single beat. I deliver it the way I want because my contract doesn't mean I belong to them. But that's only in my case. If you sign a contract where the label funds your videos and puts money into your career, obviously they have something to say. But if you are funding yourself and delivering the songs to them, they have nothing to say. They just work the music and try to get it out there.

You've also collaborated with some of the most popular artists in the business, including Pitbull. Does a collaboration such as this change the dynamic of making music?

When you collaborate with new people, they can bring great things to the table. Honestly, I can say my music really evolved when I started working with other artists. The first three songs I made by myself, and they had a similar flavor. I was having difficulty seeing a way to evolve my style because it was all about myself. But when you start working with others, talking to new people and creating in new environments, everything—your music—changes. The artists working with you never overlap or overshadow you—they just bring something new. Like when I worked with Sean Paul on "Trumpets." He brought something new, and that combination worked out so well. From time to time, yes, I may want to work alone, but I really enjoy collaborating now.

You've begun to make your mark in the U.S. and not long ago you hit the *Billboard* dance chart with the song "My Boyfriend." How important is the U.S. market in your vision?

For me, the American market is the most important one in the world. It's where everything happens. That's not meant to be disrespectful to the European market, which has so many countries and opportunities. The cultural differences can be good, but they can also be difficult in relation to getting your music heard by different people. In the U.S., everyone pretty much speaks the same language and shares the same media and channels, even though there are many cultures. It is easier to have your music be heard. On the other hand, the U.S. market is also difficult because there is so much competition. Also, overall, Americans are more [selective], and they won't listen to things that aren't really good. Being heard and respected in America as an artist from another country—it's a big deal.

Styles and trends generally come and go quickly in dance music. Is it challenging to be an innovator of these styles, as opposed to a follower?

Innovation is a great thing, but at the end of the day you can never be sure you are going to succeed [in that quest]. We are speaking about creativity, and sometimes you have to do something to spark that. This is the music business, don't forget, and you have to feed the people with something new and exciting. But for me, creating music is like creating art. Music *is* art. When you are creating art—let me say Picasso probably didn't intend to create a style or trend. He just created what he felt. If it happens to be something nobody else has done before, people decide if it is brought to a higher level. If you are trying to be an innovator, it's very tricky. The pressure you are putting on yourself blocks you from thinking clearly. The only thing you can do is try to have fun with what you are doing. If it happens to be something new and is accepted—jackpot!

How are you handling the challenge of the monetization of music as an artist and businessman?

I'm 100 percent independent, so I can control all the monetization of my music. I'm definitely not a millionaire, though. If you are asking if I make millions with my music, I'd definitely say no. Can I make a living? Yes. It depends how "big" you want to live. To live the high life, you need to be doing concerts and a lot of other things. If you're independent, you can always give your music away for free and ask people to make donations. It's true. You'd be surprised how much people will give simply because they love your music. But I want to say this—if music is your art, you need to share it. But you shouldn't think of music as a way to make money. It may not happen.

When you see people responding so positively to your music, what does that do for you as an artist?

Well, I think that the person is drunk. I'm just kidding. It's really a rewarding feeling that I get—just very satisfying. I haven't had a child, but I guess it's like when you see your child do something good that affects others.

Well, speaking of drinking, let's talk a little about alcohol and drug use as it is connected with clubs and dance music. Is it something that just goes with the territory?

Obviously, if you drink or smoke too much it's a bad situation. I mean, if you smoke at all it's a bad thing. If I go to a club, I'm not saying I don't have a drink. I have a personal opinion about drugs, and I don't do them. I don't judge people who do them—they can do whatever they like if they don't affect other people's lives.

We live in an increasingly dangerous world where nightclubs and large events are the targets of terrorism. Does this cause any anxiety for you? Have you seen these influences affect the popularity of clubs?

Not in my case; not yet. But I suppose if you are close to where some kind of terrorist attack takes place, you would have a different viewpoint. In my case, I haven't been close to such an event. I've felt safe for the most part. I can play a club date, and I don't usually even think that something could happen to the people attending or myself. But you're right—it's a dangerous world. It's a lottery. But I think you have to be careful also about thinking too much about it. You can become paranoid, and it can start messing with your head. I think, ultimately, it's best to focus on your job and do the best you can.

Do you think the dance music hits of the past 17 years will be viewed as warmly as are some of the classics of previous decades?

I'd love it if the people in the future still remember my songs. I don't know if that will happen. There will always be classics, but it's impossible to know what will be considered one over time. It will be about the feeling of the song; that is for certain. Technology is always going to change, but it will always be about the feeling the song creates in people. "Loca People" was a huge hit, but it was made with a minimum of equipment. The music I do now compared to how I made "Loca"—I don't know, it's like driving a Ferrari vs a Volkswagen. The small car actually took me further than because of the feeling of the music. We will have to see what happens

How difficult is it to maintain a healthy personal life and relationships with the demands of nightlife and running a business?

It was difficult in the beginning when success came on very quickly and I had to handle it with no experience. Now, after four or five years in the business, I can balance things more, and I can have my personal and professional life on the same page. I will never do things the way I did at the beginning—like five gigs back-to-back in five countries. That's insane. You can do it at the beginning, but constantly? It's not good for your health, and it's not good for you as a businessman. You stop thinking, and it affects your creation skills. It's impossible to create when you can't even stay awake. You need a system, to organize yourself, and then it's like any other job.

What's been your best moment at this point in your career and life? What do you want to still accomplish?

I would say the highlight of my professional career is—life—right now, happening as we speak. At the time of "Loca People," I didn't even know what I was doing. I was having fun, but I didn't plan and didn't properly dedicate myself into the music business. But now I've designed a plan, and it's more or less happening as I'd like. The lessons I've learned have led me on to a very promising path. And I'm *feeling* it. In the past, I felt it was the song that was doing it for me. Now I really believe it's *me*.

As I move forward, I want to improve as an artist as much as I can. I just want to do things better and better and be able to explore all the options out there. For me, music is 99 percent unexplored, and I plan to enjoy every minute of my exploration.

Why do you think dance music affects people so strongly and so positively?

When you speak about dance music, you're speaking about something very simple. It makes you dance and forget your problems. It's a form of physical entertainment. Dance music is experienced by listening and using your body. It is a feeling that is—complete. The first music that man ever created at the beginning of his existence—I'm guessing wasn't a melody, but rather a rhythm. They danced around a fire to beats. I think the reason dance music affects us so much is because it is actually primal.

Lightning Round with Sak Noel

The dance track that you never tire of hearing?
Oh, yeah. It's called "Sky and Sand" by Paul and Fritz Kalkbrenner.

Three artists you love listening to today?
Diplo and Skrillex—they are doing music in a way that's never been done before. And the other would be Reid Stefan, a friend of mine who isn't that well known yet. He should be!

Best social media outlet—Facebook, Twitter, Instagram or Snapchat?

Instagram. You have to pick one picture and explain it in the single best sentence you can come up with. Facebook, you can say anything—too much—which is not good. Twitter is not visual enough. Instagram has text and visuals, but requires you to be skilled to capture people's attention. I love social media—it keeps me connected to my fans. I'd almost say it's my hobby because I'm on it so much.

Best time of the day or night to post on social media?

For me, the best time is Wednesday around 8 PM Barcelona time. It's a good time to reach people in Asia, America and here in Spain.

If you weren't in entertainment, what do you think you'd be doing?

I'm pretty sure I'd be a journalist or in something where I could write and give my opinions and share my own message.

Sak Noel handled the remix of Inna's 2017 hit single "Gimme Gimme."

Paul Oakenfold
(DJ, producer, remixer)
"Starry Eyed Surprise" (2002)

"I've always worked tirelessly to improve myself, and that improvement doesn't come from following, but rather innovating."—Paul Oakenfold

It's extremely difficult to summarize the magnitude of Paul Oakenfold's career and influence upon dance music in a paragraph or two. He is considered a true icon and pioneer of DJ culture. Following early work as a promoter in the '80s for the Beastie Boys and Salt-N-Pepa, the three-time Grammy nominee and former DJ Mag World #1 DJ has been leaving an indelible mark on dancefloors since the '90s. The Brit is credited with being one of the leading ambassadors of international dance music trends, and his work has earned him residencies at trendsetting clubs such as Ibiza's Amnesia, Liverpool's Cream and London's Ministry of Sound.

Paul has produced widely lauded albums, such as A Lively Mind *(2006)—a portrait of his own artistry—and singles like "Starry Eyed Surprise" and "Southern Sun," both huge club hits in 2002. He's also produced remixes for U2 ("Even Better than the Real Thing," 1992),*

For more than three decades, three-time Grammy nominee and DJ/producer Paul Oakenfold has elevated and shaped the dance genre and remains one of the leading forces in the global music scene today.

Madonna ("What It Feels Like for a Girl," 2001), Justin Timberlake ("Rock Your Body," 2003), Michael Jackson ("One More Chance," 2003) and Bruno Mars ("Locked Out of Heaven," 2013). Oakenfold has branched out into composing scores and cues as well, contributing music to The Bourne Identity, Matrix Reloaded, Shrek 2 *and other films. His personal recording label, Perfecto Records (established back in the late '80s), played an important role in the growth of trance and progressive house music and continues to be among the most high profile in the industry. His successful and inventive 2016 singles "U Are" (featuring BRKLYN and Amba Shepherd), "Shanghai Baby" and "Bla Bla Bla" continue to solidify Paul's standing as one of this century's most innovative and important artists.*

Oakenfold granted a brief interview between gigs, offering some insights into his world.

Paul, do you remember a moment in your past—the spark that really launched your career in electronic music?

For me, the real birth of electronic music was in '87, when I went to Ibiza with three of my friends (a very famous story by now). We came back and all started our own clubs. The story has been documented many times—there is even talk of a movie being made about it. That trip had a big impact on our lives and also kicked off club culture like we'd never seen before.

Would you share one or two developments or extraordinary moments in your dance music history that you feel have also been key to the genre's evolution over the past few decades?

Within my own career, I recall two events, or series of events, that I participated in (and feel helped contribute towards taking dance music in new directions)—when I played the main stage at Glastonbury and the few times that I played Wembley stadium. The first time was for NetAid in between Bowie and Peter Gabriel, then when I played with U2 and Madonna on tour. Many of these moments were a first for dance music. It was a big moment to be a part of these events and to help carry dance music into other territories and music scenes.

What elements must be present in an artist's original track for it to move and inspire you to create a great remix?

A strong song and a wonderful melody. It's simple but effective.

How do you approach re-imagining an artist's latest work (someone like Madonna, Rihanna, Lady Gaga), when that artist has a long history and solid legacy in dance music? Is there a feeling or sense of pressure that you must live up to his or her past works and successes?

There is no real pressure in that respect, to be honest with you. They are coming to you to produce their music because they like what you do.

Do you feel more comfortable or creative working with established stars or exploring new territory with lesser known or unknown artists?

I really enjoy finding new acts and artists/talent. For example, I just came across a wonderful artist, Nikki Amber, who I am currently producing.

Can you recall a remix or production from your history that has challenged you the most? Why it was a challenge?

I think U2's "Even Better than the Real Thing." They are a rock band, and the brief was to make it work for the dancefloor. There was little of the original on the remix; I even added a female vocal. I was concerned the band wouldn't like it, but after speaking with Bono, they let me get on with it.

Are you ever completely satisfied with your work?

When it leaves the studio, it's the best mix I could've done. It's all based on that.

What percentage of your job as a producer, remixer and creator of dance music is to be an innovator vs. a follower (giving people what they expect and want to hear in current trends)? How challenging is it to maintain this balance?

I would say it's all about being an innovator. Why would I want to be a follower? You have to have confidence and belief in your music, otherwise you are wasting your time. I've always worked tirelessly to improve myself, and that improvement doesn't come from following, but rather innovating.

My label, Perfecto Recordings, is an established brand that is well-respected in the dance community, and people know exactly what they are buying into. We've worked very hard to grow the identity of Perfecto and establish something—sounds that music fans can identify, connect with and understand.

Are you equally comfortable in the very different roles of record label owner and creative artist?

No, I don't think so. I enjoy [and prefer] being on the artist side. It's where my true passion lies and where I feel most comfortable.

Do the changes in how dance music is monetized (away from selling the recorded music itself to event-oriented/performance revenue streams) inhibit the genre from birthing new artists and new sounds?

I *absolutely* agree—it inhibits it!

You have worked so closely and so well with Madonna—what's the basis of your chemistry?

I think Madonna is an innovator and is always pushing the barrier, and I have a similar outlook. As an artist you want to work with the best in the business, and Madonna is certainly one of the best artists this business has ever seen!

In the '80s and '90s, the DJ/remixer really began to take the spotlight. In the 2000s, they became the stars. What factors do you believe gave rise to this?

I think this occurred because the DJ is on the front line every weekend, and he is the one making [and serving] the music that works in the club. It's been a very natural progression. People generally come to the club for the DJ and the sound now.

You've had residencies at some of the greatest clubs in the world, and your tours attract enormous crowds. What do you believe it is about you that your audiences connect with most—what is at the core of your universal appeal?

I think it's the sound of the music I play. The connection with the audience I make [comes from] my desire to always try to take the experience one step further. With both

Ibiza and Las Vegas, for example, I set up residencies there before residencies became a thing. It was a fresh concept in terms of DJing and opened a door to an entirely new world.

Do you expect to see dance music contract in popularity now that it is so pop-mainstream? (I am reminded of the disco crash of '79, after over-saturation.)

I don't because it's been here for 40 years—so why would it contract now? If anything, I think it will continue to get more and more popular on a global level.

Has the influence of the gay community on dance music diminished over the last few years?

The gay community is still a very important part of the scene. Always has been and always will be, in my opinion.

Is there an element missing from modern dance music that was more prevalent in the past?

More originality.

Does the shorter attention span of younger fans affect your ability to create a track today in the way you might have created and explored a seven or eight minute sonic journey in the past?

Yes, it does, and a two to three hour set as well. But this is just the evolution of the scene. We have to embrace it and move forward. Dance music isn't about looking backwards but instead looking forward.

Though DJ and production work remain primarily a male game in dance music (with women representing a very small number of key players), do you see that changing?

Yeah I do—big time! There are a lot of very talented female artists coming through, which is good to see.

Your personal history and experience in dance music is quite extraordinary. How would you describe your relationship with dance music today after so many decades in the business and so many achievements?

I'll keep it simple—one word—*enjoyable*!

Is there a work (or body of work) or event in your life that you are most proud of to date?

I'm proud of writing music for film and [video] games. Performing for Nelson Mandela, playing at the Great Wall of China.

If you could identify the single most powerful way in which dance music has impacted the human race, what would it be?

It inspires unity.

Lightning Round with Paul

Favorite time in your career to date?

There is no one year. It's about the journey.

The one dance song you never tire of hearing?

Massive Attack—"Unfinished Symphony" (my remix).

Paul Oakenfold performs for a crowd of 40,000 fans during Madonna's 2012 MDNA Tour. This concert was held August 1, 2012, at the National Stadium in Warsaw, Poland.

Genre of music you enjoy privately that probably would surprise people?
Rock.

Least favorite aspect of fame?
Harassment.

If you hadn't been in entertainment, what would you be doing today?
I'd be a *chef*.

Suzanne Palmer
(vocalist)
"Hide U" (2001)

"I found dance music gave me freedom to be more original and have that energy—almost to a campy level. I only know it worked."—Suzanne Palmer

Suzanne Palmer, a Chicago native, has been delivering soulful and dynamic vocals to house music since her debut on the club scene in 1995. As the featured singer on The Absolute's anthemic club hit "There Will Come a Day" that year, Suzanne's powerful voice did not go unnoticed. She formed a long-standing creative alliance with Grammy-winning DJ Peter Rauhofer that produced a string of dance-floor classics on the now legendary Star 69 label, each helping to further define the big club sound of the early 2000s. She's also worked with a slew of the era's top cutting edge producers and remixers, including Tiësto, Offer Nissim, David Morales and Beat Hustlerz. While energizing worldwide audiences with her signature hits, such as "Home," "Luv 2 Luv" and "Show Me," Palmer's repertoire continues to expand. Most recently she released the hit single "Surrender."

Your roots in dance music extend back to the '90s. I'd love to know how you got your start in entertainment and what led up to your most welcome debut in the genre.

I actually am kind of shy, and find it a little hard to talk about myself. But you know us performers—once we get started, you can't shut us up!

I wanted to be an actress when I first started to think about being in the business. I was about 16 or 17 when I got into a comedy improv group, hanging around places like Second City in Chicago, where I still live. I actually quit high school to do that. My father, who was a jazz musician, understood that desire and said that if that's what I wanted to do—go on the road and perform—I should. I would never tell my daughter that, but that's another story. I joined a group called Chicago City Limits, and we performed in Las Vegas, Los Angeles and New York, where [the troupe] actually opened a theater. It may still be there. We'd do what we'd call a "Make-a-Blues" routine. I'd take a suggestion from the audience, and, along with a piano player, I'd make up a blues song. That's really how I started my singing career.

I was about 17 and working at Catch A Rising Star, and Pat Benatar was singing there—before she was even known as a rock star. I mention that because I was hanging out with all these entertainers and comedians, and she was one of the people that said to me, "You know you should sing!" I dismissed the idea at the time—it's kind of funny how life happened. I did end up getting out of that group and went to college to study theater. I just kept singing

Suzanne Palmer's long-running creative collaborations with producer/DJ Peter Rauhofer were essential dance recordings in the late '90s, paving the way for hits like "Hide U" in 2001.

and doing some acting. I was always attracted to the idea of telling a story, whether through music or acting. Life kind of came to me.

As I did more performing, I began to sing commercials for radio and TV, and I came to the attention of Mark Picchiotti, a house music producer from Chicago and his music collaborator, Craig Snider, a jingle writer and producer. In 1994, they asked me to do a demo for a song they were doing, "There Will Come A Day" (later released as The Absolute Introducing Suzanne Palmer). It was followed by a second single for The Absolute, this time "*featuring* Suzanne Palmer," called "I Believe." That's how I got my break in dance music. They did very well in England on the Tribal label.

I know you made an early connection in your music career with Maurice White, lead singer of Earth, Wind & Fire, who we just lost not long ago. Would you tell me about that?

Back in the day, I did a TV show called *Star Search*, maybe toward the end of the '80s or early in the '90s. I wish I could find a video of it. I had these hair extensions at the time—my hair was bigger than my body. The styles back then—*aaackk*! There was a female comedian also competing, Kim Coles (who later appeared on *In Living Color* and *Living Single*). She and I won and lost on the same show, which made us fast friends. She took a cassette of some songs I'd sung to an agency she was working with and told them they should book me. They called and booked me on the *Showtime at the Apollo* program. I was the first white girl to win the show! It's a tough crowd—you have to really bring it—and I was very nervous. I ended up getting this great vibe from the crowd, and it went really well.

It turns out Maurice White was watching it on TV. I had signed a deal with Epic Records that had just fallen through and came home one day feeling really bad. On my answering machine was a message from Maurice White. I couldn't believe it! My mood did a 360. He signed me to a production deal, and we worked together for a while. He produced some things for me, and it was incredible working with him—he actually sang back-up on some of the material. Unfortunately—again, it's such a crazy business. The album never saw the light of day. But I have the memories of a great experience with him.

When you began moving into dance music, what were your feelings about the genre?

I started off singing jazz, and it's my first love. But I was drawn to the dance genre early on. I think my favorite singer in my youth was Chaka Khan, upbeat R&B. Also, one of my favorite songs from back in the day was Thelma Houston's "Don't Leave Me This Way." I remember being under age and going to clubs and hearing that song play.

But as an artist myself, I was originally pursuing a rock-pop thing, and I didn't quite fit in with that genre. Different producers and record companies—they didn't know where to put me. When I did The Absolute record, it was a fluke. The producers just wanted me to sing it, but there wasn't really a plan behind it. I found that my voice really fit the genre though, and others agreed. I found dance music gave me freedom to be more original and have that *energy*—almost to a campy level. I only know it worked.

It *really* worked well, and you hit your stride when you began collaborating with Star 69 Records and Grammy-winning producer and DJ Peter Rauhofer in the late '90s and well into the 2000s. We have a sad anniversary taking place, as, quite unintentionally, it turns out he passed away from a brain tumor exactly three years ago today. Would you share with me how your partnership with him began and what it was like working with this iconic dance music innovator?

It's really good we are talking about this today. I'm so glad you appreciate that time period and what was going on. As I mentioned earlier, the records I recorded for The Absolute were both released on the Tribal label. When Tribal Records became part of Twisted/MCA Records, I signed a solo deal with them intending to do dance pop records. Again, I was still trying to find the right niche. The A&R person at Twisted introduced me to Peter. Peter was already signed to Twisted Records and was in the middle of recording his second album, *Style*. The first time we met was at a studio in Vienna. In 1997, Peter needed a voice for a record he was working on called "Much Better." Because Peter and I were both signed to Twisted Records, the A&R person asked if I wanted to try it. I had listened to some of Peter's work, and he had listened to some of mine, and we both agreed we liked each other's sound and style. I was flown to Vienna.

Peter and I worked great in the studio together. We had an extraordinary chemistry. A lot of people thought he was harsh. But we communicated really well. He liked to work hard, and I did as well. When I'm in the studio, I don't like to sit around and come into a session to eat pizza. I'm there to work, and he was of the same mindset. A lot of times in this business, people party and such. But when I'm working—I know it sounds corny—I'm on enough of a high singing and creating something. He was the same way.

I remember being in the studio with him, and he said [*Suzanne uses a German accent for her impersonation*], "Yes, Suzanne, you did that exactly wrong." The engineer tried to console me by saying I shouldn't take it personally. But no—I understood if we were working on this together, there has to be that honest feedback and give and take. We had that. I've referred to that feeling of not knowing where my voice fit. *He knew where I fit.*

I know around that time there were problems with Twisted Records.

Yes. Peter introduced me to two producers in Vienna, Werner Stranka and Martin Gellner. We wrote and recorded together for seven weeks in Vienna for an album, which was to be my solo debut. There were some great songs on that record; I'm still really proud of that work. Twisted was going to release it when they suddenly dissolved. We worked on it for so long, and it was a big setback to see it disappear. At that same time, I had lost some family members and had a miscarriage—I just decided to disappear for a while.

Some time later, around 2000, Peter called me and told me he was starting a label called Star 69 Entertainment. He wanted to know if I'd be interested in working together again. He wanted to rework the original version of "Hide U" and release it as a house record. When I heard the song, it was so simple and yet right on the mark. We recorded in New

York, and it went just perfectly. We did another song together called "Show Me," and it was kind of like he discovered me again. He had a keen understanding of where the clubs were at, at the time, and I was able to freely sing from my heart.

He seemed to be a very aloof person, one of the more mysterious DJs of the period. In terms of his personality, the things people may not know, how would you describe him?

Well, one of the biggest things to know was that he was very funny—a really great, dry sense of humor. Like myself, he was also a very shy man in many ways. [*Suzanne imitates his voice again.*] "If I could just be in another room spinning and look out at the crowd and not have them see me, that would be so great," he said. I felt the same kind of anxiety before doing shows. I think we both felt like hiding up in our hotel rooms before we'd do our set.

Did you know he had a condition that was affecting his health so severely?

No, I did not. I knew something was happening, but I wasn't quite sure. His death came as a big shock. I hadn't talked to him for about a year, several moths maybe—there was no problem between us. We just weren't working on anything at the time. I just wished maybe I could have talked to him a little sooner. But he was a man who had always seemed very fulfilled and excited about life and music. (He just wished nobody could see him living that life.)

I know there were times he could appear erratic and, depending on who you talk to, I'm sure you can find people who experienced some temper issues with him. He could talk himself up into something, and I remember trying to calm him down a few times. It would usually be because of promotion things or business that was getting him agitated. I wondered if his health might have contributed to some of that, too.

But I can tell you, when we were working on the music together, there was never anything like that going on.

Peter was a hugely popular DJ at clubs like the Roxy in New York, and you both forged a powerful connection with gay audiences. Your connection remains very strong today. How important was the gay community to your success?

Oh wow! They were absolutely important. *They got me!* My voice fits this audience. When I was working on the album for Twisted, they were planning on marketing it primarily to a straight audience. I often had to promote the project at straight clubs, and I have to say I didn't enjoy that nearly as much as being in the gay clubs. In a straight club, they watch you perform as if you are video or something. They don't care about you that much as a performer—who you actually are. But when I did promo gigs at gay clubs on my journey with Peter, it was a different story. I remember doing a club in Atlanta (my husband was with me—he was the only one I trusted to manage me), and the whole energy changed. With the gay culture, there's just a whole different level of respect for you as a performer—and it makes you sound different, better. I think the gay community brought out these great female voices in past decades as well. I'm so happy about the connection to this community I've enjoyed.

Are you observing that the gay community's influence on dance music may be waning?

I am. It used to be that music coming from gay clubs was trendsetting. How can I say this? It's almost like dance music isn't as affected by the gay community anymore—like it's been Disney-fied. It's almost like dance music became too broadly popular. It's gentrified.

It's like developers came in and took out the dangerousness of dance music (which is what made it so interesting), cleaned it up and sold it to the mainstream. Where it was once an influential sound coming from the gay clubs and the underground scene, it's now something much different.

I can tell you—I don't know any singer in dance music who works quite as much as we did before. There's no longer the number of venues out there, and their budgets are getting slashed all the time. There are still big events, but that club scene (like in the days of Sound Factory and places like that) is gone. I would see a beautiful drag queen running towards the stage I was on, and know I was gonna have a great show!

I think I saw a change, too, maybe starting 10 years ago, where they weren't playing a lot of vocals in the clubs anymore. That changed the energy, too. Then it became increasingly easy for everyone to create their own dance music on their Mac—everyone became an expert at making it.

I guess I feel that dance music, the scene and the sounds, have become diluted. That's the word I think I want to use. Look—everything changes, including music and nightlife.

You enjoyed a very prosperous connection with Mr. Rauhofer, and it seemed like your persona and talents were often promoted on the same level as his. Would you describe the shift in attention from the vocalist to the DJ in more recent years has been problematic?

I could see where it might be frustrating for many vocalists. I think it has contributed to less work for singers at events—I've heard that from many artists I've spoken with, quite honestly. But there again, if you have a voice and a following, you have to work at maintaining it.

I plan to be singing forever, no matter what. I will always keep striving to deliver fresh and new material. But we are definitely in a time where the work is not as plentiful. I don't know if I've resisted this current trend about DJs or adapted to it. It's like Peter—whatever anyone may say about him—he really respected singers. He didn't take all the credit—he gave it where it was due.

Suzanne, you worked with one of today's most popular DJs, Tiësto, just ahead of this DJ trend in 2002, on the track "643 (Love's on Fire)." Do you recall that experience?

I was signed to Star69 Records when I was asked if I wanted to work with DJ Tiësto. I didn't know who he was at the time. I asked Peter his opinion, and he suggested I do it, saying that it would be great for my career exposure. Some producers make your deal an exclusive thing, and they don't want you to sing with anyone else. But Peter wasn't like that.

I never actually met Tiësto, to be truthful. We spoke over the phone, we sent each other tracks and our managers worked with each other—ours was a distant love affair. [*Suzanne laughs.*] But it was monetarily a very good experience, I can definitely confirm that.

Ah, money. You stated earlier that you trusted only your husband in terms of management. Have there been many challenges to stay above the surface in the financial waters of the music industry?

Well, I think you can probably add my name to all the others you've interviewed who have experienced bad deals, being ripped off, etc. Yeah. Anybody who's worked in the business has to have signed or worked through a crappy deal where they got screwed out of money or rights. Not only were you younger, but you're tremendously excited to be involved in music. Many people will take advantage of that. But that was one of the reasons why I had my husband take over that side of things for me.

All that said, I don't think I have experienced anything worse than some of the others you have spoken with. It goes with the territory; you live through it and you learn. A simple thing like paying attention to those little clauses in your contract—gotta read 'em. And that's what lawyers are for.

How has it been for you maintaining a family life alongside a career in dance music?

It's always hard to do, but nothing that pays off—and by "pays off" I mean emotionally and that which builds you up as a person—isn't challenging. You'll remember I mentioned I had all those losses a few years back. I had pursued my career and waited a long time to have a family. My husband and I ended up adopting a beautiful baby girl from China (her name is Nora), and she's a teenager now. I can't believe it!

The year before we adopted her, I was promoting the song "Show Me" at Mardi Gras in Australia. I remember that because the airport there was the same one I visited to board a plane to pick up my daughter in China the following year. I was able to travel with my child, and I was able to be with her during the week at home. I would be recording, and she could be with me in the studio. I was very lucky. I think I had it easier than someone who had a nine-to-five and wouldn't be able to spend as much time with their child. I was and am so happy she is in my life.

When you look at the music you've created in the twenty-first century, and the works of others from this era, how do you think the music compares to the dance classics of previous decades? Do you think the music of today will be remembered as fondly as the classics?

I sure hope so. I think that every age, decade, has its world events and atmosphere—and the music represents that. Music has so many different roles. There's music to sit, listen to and think, music to make you laugh or cry, and music that you dance to in every era. I will say that I feel like a lot of the music from this century has been influenced by what came before. The rehashing of ideas, if you will. But I don't want to sound jaded. There is great new music out there today and many great artists. I think, yes, music of this generation will be remembered. I'm not sure what songs they will be or if I've heard them yet, but I'm hoping this era's dance music will be remembered as fondly.

What's the single best quality of dance music that makes it so special?

It makes you live at that particular moment in time. On the dancefloor, you are absolutely in the moment. I mentioned Thelma Houston's "Don't Leave Me This Way" at the beginning of our interview. I remember the awesome build-up that song has. I can hear it now, and it takes me back to the time when I felt so positive—free from worry and my soul alive. I think that's important to experience.

I'm very proud that for a few minutes in some people's lives I took them on such a journey. And you don't need to be on drugs or alcohol to feel that way—totally uninhibited. And that connects to your previous question. Dance music is timeless and always growing and evolving. But it will always be something that can make you feel free.

Lightning Round with Suzanne

Preferred drink to enjoy in a nightclub?

A vodka cranberry.

Have you ever forgotten the lyrics to one of your songs while performing?

[*Suzanne laughs vigorously.*] Yes; in fact I'm quite famous for that! I've had people say to me, "Oh wow, you really performed that song so differently!" It was because I forgot the lyrics or verse and invented something on the spot—some of my best creative moments.

The secret to surviving a Chicago winter?

Netflix!

Saver or spender?

I'm a bit of both, but I really like getting a good deal. So I'm not sure what that makes me.

Single biggest world problem that scares you the most.

People resorting to violence so quickly.

If you weren't an entertainer, what would you be doing today?

I might have been a teacher. I actually do music therapy with autistic children now. I have been volunteering at my daughter's school, and there are special needs kids there. In a way, teaching *is* performing. I think a teacher has to be a performer. Or a gardener. Maybe that's what I'd be.

Suzanne Palmer is an in-demand performer across the world, performing at major venues and festivals, including key Gay Pride events in Sao Paulo, Manchester, Sydney, Montreal and New York City, and at major clubs in Los Angeles, Paris, Rome, Tel Aviv and San Juan.

Ralphi Rosario
(DJ, producer, remixer)
"Cha Cha Heels"—Rosabel
(featuring Jeanie Tracy) (2004)

"I personally think, with my roots in disco and house and songs that had melodies, hooks and choruses, I have to continue to believe in those things."—Ralphi Rosario

Chicago native Ralphi Rosario is synonymous with clubland. After rising through the ranks in the '80s, where he is often credited with fostering the house music movement, Rosario's skills as a remixing and production virtuoso saw him become one of the most in-demand DJs and remixers of the '90s club scene. By the 2000s, he was re-envisioning tracks for such A-list artists as Pussycat Dolls ("Dontcha," 2008), Kelly Rowland ("Feedback," 2008) and Beyoncé ("Grown Woman," 2014).

As one half the duo Rosabel (formed in the early '90s), Ralphi's partnership with Miami's Abel Aguilera to produce and remix a series of ultra-stimulating club hits proved unstoppable. Their sound continues to advance the timeless appeal of energized, electronics-infused house music, and, to date, five of their productions have reached the top of the Billboard club chart. They include a 2000 update of "Don't You Want My Love" (featuring Debbie Jacobs-Rock), "That Sound" in 2002, "Cha Cha Heels" (featuring Jeanie Tracy) in 2004 and "Rhythm Intoxication" in 2006. The pair earned a Grammy nomination in 2012 for their remix of Rihanna's "Only Girl (In the World)," and during the summer of 2016, Rosabel once again reigned supreme at the top of the Billboard club chart with "Livin' for Your Love (Your Love)." Rosario also teamed up with Frankie Catalano for the Top Five dance hit "F$ck Your Boyfriend (F.U.B.F.)" (off his current LP, 2 Sides to the Story, released in the summer of 2016).

DJ/producer Ralphi Rosario has reached the summit of the *Billboard* Dance Club chart with several stompers, including "Everybody Shake It" with Shawn Christopher in 2010 and "La Jungla" with Julissa Veloz in 2015 (photograph by Annette Nieves).

Ralphi, I'd like to know a little about your early family life and how you first came into music.

There are seven siblings in my family, and I'm the youngest one. Family life was a bit of an uphill battle as a kid. We had a lot of ups and downs with a father who was an abusive alcoholic. Dealing with that was difficult. He really got down on my brothers' and sisters' dreams, but fortunately he never got to me like that. Music was a big time escape for me from all of this.

Actually, music really took off in my life during the disco era—I should clarify that—it really started for me in the mid-'70s with a lot of soul music. I graduated to disco, which really caught my ear. I was in awe of the famous disco DJs of the time, and when I was able to go to clubs, I'd watch them, sometimes hang out in the booth and observe. I'd buy some records, go home and practice—it became an everyday thing for me.

As a teenager, I didn't have any money, so I took a job washing dishes across the street from where I lived. I begged my mom to let me take the job because I needed money to buy the vinyl—I wasn't going to ask my parents for it, and they weren't keen on buying stuff like that back in the day.

Music was a hobby for me—I never thought of it as a possible career move. It was something I loved to enjoy at home. Eventually, I started DJing sets with my brother's salsa band, and I'd play during intermissions.

When did your hobby morph into a professional pursuit?

It was really by accident—luck of the draw you might say. I was a member of a record pool in Chicago for a number of years. I had a partner who helped me with mobile DJ set-ups and such. He'd get the gigs, and I'd spin—weddings, sweet sixteen parties, all that kind of stuff. My partner Julio, who was kind of guarding me, submitted some of my mix tapes to the record pool, who supplied them to a radio station (WBMX). This had been going on for a while, and one night they finally played one of my tapes on the air. I was about 16, jumping up and down that my mix was actually on the radio. Nobody wanted to believe that it was me! That was the start of my professional life.

I thought of these tapes and playing for the radio station as an art—it was very big thing for me outside of high school. I wasn't yearning to be so involved in it or pushing for it to happen; I just thought of it as something I loved and wanted to do. Before you knew it, a lot of radio listeners were gravitating to what I was doing, and I began to create my own identity, my personality, through the music I was playing.

After high school, I still enjoyed DJing, but I began to think I really would love to learn the art of actually making records. I was part of a group of Chicago DJs called Hot Mix 5 in the mid-to-late '80s, and a lot of us were into that mindset. It wasn't long before singers started coming out of the woodwork and pressing plants started working with us to make these records. It was a great marketing situation for us because we started creating these records and playing them on the air. It became a huge thing—even overseas.

The breakout record that is most often cited as your career launcher is a project with Xaviera Gold called "You Used to Hold Me" from 1987. Tell me about that track.

It is the record that broke me, I'd agree. There was a place in Chicago called the Riviera Nightclub—an old theater that was a club on the weekends. Jeff Davis, an old friend who used to work at the Century disco, was the resident DJ there. He had a friend named Cynthia

Baker (aka Xaviera Gold). She knew other members of our Hot Mix 5 team, including Kenny Jason, and she said she wanted to become a DJ like us. One day, I was driving around with her, and she started crooning some lines over a track I was playing in my car. She sounded amazing! I said, "Forget this DJ thing; you're gonna sing!" She came over to my place and we got the words down, I went in the studio and laid down the tracks, and she sang it in one or two takes. I took the track and mixed it. Now, at that time, everybody was doing jack records—jack your body and things like that. It felt weird to be doing a *real* song like what we came up with. And I didn't have a lot of confidence in it.

I submitted it anyway, and decided to just let everybody else decide whether it was any good. When it came out, the response was overwhelming. At that point, I felt I was doing something right. From there I was intrigued to dig deeper and see what else I could do in the studio, and that eventually brought me to the attention of the big labels.

At what point did you form the Rosabel production partnership with DJ Abel Aguilera? Tell me about the dynamics of this unique collaboration?

Rosabel formed around 1992 or '93. I went to Miami for the Winter Music Conference, and a friend told me to hit the club called Paragon and check out this man named DJ Abel. I went to the club—the biggest gay club I had ever seen, and it was packed. It was a massive spectacle. I heard Abel play and thought he was totally on the money. I approached him and gave him my card, but he didn't believe I was *the* Ralphi Rosario. Some other guy had pretended to be me earlier in the night, so he was skeptical. So, I said, "Okay, believe what you want," and I walked away. He came up to me a short time later and said he *did* believe me. We talked on the phone afterward and found we were on the same wavelength, connected with the same type of music, and loved the same type of energy.

One day he called me for some reason and started reaming me out on the answering machine over something that pissed him off—using Spanish words. [*Ralphi laughs.*] So rather than call him back, I thought, "Listen to this bitch screaming at me on the phone!" He was calling me a "fucking puta" [prostitute or slut]. I recorded it, put it in a sampler, and in less than three hours I had a track already designed. I played it over the phone to him, and he fell out. He thought we should call ourselves "Rosabel," call the track "La Puta" and get it out there. I submitted the track to Groovilicious, a label connected to Strictly Rhythm in New York, and it did really well. It went to number one on the *Billboard* cub chart in 1995.

You became an extremely prolific producer/remixer/DJ throughout the '90s and into the 2000s, both on your own and as part of Rosabel, and the artists you worked with were extraordinary. They included Pet Shop Boys, Pussycat Dolls, Mariah Carey, INXS, Kelly Clarkson and many others. Would you share a standout experience with an artist that made a big impression upon you?

Donna Summer was certainly a standout. The first experience I had with her was a song called "I Will Go With You" for Sony for the 1999 *Live & More Encore!* album. A friend of mine at Sony approached me and DJ Abel about remixing the song. I was doing some other smaller projects at the time, but this was *Donna Summer*—she was a goddess to me. I felt like if you worked with Donna Summer, you could end your career right there—it couldn't get better!

We worked on the song, experimented and got some feedback—back in those days you had to play your stuff over the phone to the artist, A&R people or producers as you worked on it. When it was done, we submitted it and played the waiting game. Donna had to listen to it and approve it herself. My friend at Sony called me one day, and said he had someone who needed to speak with me. I was expecting to be reamed out or something, fearing they hated what I did with the song. A woman gets on the phone and says, "Hey Ralphi, it's Donna Summer. I just wanted to tell you I sat here listening to 16 different versions of my song, and yours was the *only* one that stuck out." I dropped the phone and ran to the other side of the room and fell to the floor. I couldn't believe she was calling me to tell me this—the person I adored for so many years approved of my work!

The last track I mixed for Donna was "Fame (The Game)" in 2008.

How starstruck were you by iconic artists like Donna, Janet Jackson or Madonna—did you ever find their legacies intimidating when approached to remix one of their songs?

Honestly, I'm really not one to get star-struck. Maybe early on, but after a while you realize we are all reaching for the same thing. Yes, I will always tell them how much I have loved their work, but moving forward it's never a situation where I might get intimidated or overwhelmed by whoever they may be. They are artists, very simply, and we're all trying to reach the same goal.

I really don't like talking with the artist one-on-one, to be frank with you. I prefer to deal with the people who are working with them. It's easier that way to get the work done and get the point across. I don't take rejection (of a mix) personally, provided I know I have done the best I can. I have the utmost respect for these artists. The fact that they reached out to me on projects, well, I view that as a complete honor. During the process, I'm trying to achieve the best sound I can for them, but at the end of it, I'm not really in awe of the experience. There are some days it can really be just a job, you know?

Describe the process of creating one of your remixes.

I'm a technical person in addition to being a musical person. The technicality of my remixing was largely self-taught. But the process itself begins with the song. There's got to be a good chorus and a good hook there, because if I'm not singing along with the track as I am working on it—I'm not able to do my job. It has to stick with me. I look for that first.

Then I look at those technical aspects I just described. Is the song going to require a lot of time-stretching, and will that make [the artist] sound horrible? I have to be very clear and honest about these things—if they give me a Britney Spears song and it's got a weird tempo and will require a lot of manipulation, I would turn it down in most cases.

It's not about money—it never has been. It's about the integrity of the artist, the integrity of the song, and it's also about my signature.

Does the process differ in a collaborative situation with Abel, when you're working as Rosabel?

It's nearly the same. We both listen to the song first. Do we like the song in its original form? That's the question we have to ask ourselves. Is it really good? Is the song gonna stick with you so much that you want to play it in the car or at the gym? If not, we have to wonder if we are the right people to handle it.

With how quickly styles and trends are emerging in dance music, especially compared to the past, is it challenging for you to be an innovator rather than a follower in your creative process?

Here's the thing a lot of people don't realize about myself and/or Abel—integrity in what we do is so important to us. We're very, very true to our craft. I, personally, don't like to follow trends. Sure, there's elements that might be hot in dance culture at any given moment in time that I may incorporate into my mix or remix. I have to decide how to bring those elements into what's mine. Following the trends is practically impossible—there are so many sounds and emerging styles out there, and it would be easy to get lost in the shuffle.

There are many terms used to describe your sound—how do you describe the music that you create or refashion?
Energetic. Melodic. What's another word I want use? Big! [*Ralphi laughs.*] When I say big, I don't mean I think my track is going to be massive. I mean that when I create a track and it's played in a room, I want it to grab your attention the minute it comes on. Whether it's the rhythm or percussion or bass line coming in first, it's gotta grab you!

What's your personal measure of success when it comes to your music?
I'd say I have to see a reaction on the dancefloor, and I have to feel it in myself.

EDM currently dominates the dance music scene, and some critics accuse this music of being cold, soulless and lacking in passion. Do you find yourself at odds with this type of music?
I call EDM "rough around the edges." I personally think, with my roots in disco and house and songs that had melodies, hooks and choruses, I have to continue to believe in those things. I think about the '90s when hard techno was big, a very loud, in your face and edgy style of music—and I appreciated that music sometimes. I could appreciate how producers of that sound put their thing together. But for me, these sounds are fads. They hang around for a while, and then things change. Dance music always evolves. It's fine to hear these new trends and see how these sounds are incorporated into new tracks. But at the same time, and I am speaking only for myself, it is very important not to forget where you came from.

Style shifts represent one way in which dance music has experienced dramatic change over the past 17 years. Another has been the diminished billing of the vocalist over time. You've worked with so many of these great vocalists, including such heritage stars as Jeanie Tracy and Linda Clifford. What's your take on this issue?
I think a lot of the newer DJ/producers aren't using vocalists to their fullest potential. I feel like their productions are growing stagnant—there's no experimentation, no testing the waters. That's one of the things lacking in dance music today.

When I'm working on a remix or production, I still love to hear the hook of a great vocal. It's still very important to me. The sampling of voices and lack of focus today—I feel like they've opened a box, are tinkering around on *GarageBand* or something and just put the track out. That's how it is. The singers, and for that matter the musicians and recording engineers, are becoming obsolete. Sure, you're getting the point of your song across in a shorter amount of time, but the musicality is missing.

In turn, do you think dance music fans are also becoming less discriminating?
That's a great point. I'll be honest—yes, I think so. I think it started when the drug haze of the '90s entered the nightclub scene—that's when the music listener grew colder.

Yet we had drug use prevalent in the clubs going back to the '70s.

Yes, definitely, but it hadn't affected the music at that time. Back then, you had arrangements, live singers and musicians. As it progressed throughout the years, [drug use] just got a lot more aggressive and a lot harder. And as the music changed, a lot of the integrity was lost.

I think it will swing back to that original musicianship one day—and you can hear a lot of artists trying to bring that back. I like the fact that it's being looked at again. History always repeats itself.

Does the gay community still hold power in moving dance music culture forward in this century, as it has in the past?

In some ways, I want to say yes. But there is a blurred line now. I do feel music that is targeted to a gay audience today tends to sound sing-song, and it's missing a lot of the elements that might make for better tracks. But aside from that, the gay community—we were the ones who knew what to catch onto and who appreciated what Louis Vega, Frankie Knuckles and David Morales were doing back in the day. We made it our own, then it crossed over and went everywhere. I just feel like the gay community isn't making those discoveries as often today. We used to be far ahead of the game, whether it was movies, TV shows, books, dance music—whatever the case. I feel like the community has gotten lazier and a little more lax—as if they aren't really paying attention anymore. I feel like we're following the trends more, just like we were speaking about earlier.

I'd like to look at one of the more recent highlights in your formidable career—your 2012 Grammy nomination for the Rosabel Club Mix of the Rihanna track "Only Girl (In the World)."

Remixing for as long as I have, and with the track record I've been able to amass and the belief people have in Rosabel—I was still impressed that someone was really paying attention when that song came along. They were paying attention not only to their artist but to our work when they approached us about Rihanna. The A&R director at Island/Def Jam working with Rihanna and her people asked me what I thought about doing the Rosabel thing for a new record by her. Abel was intrigued, and so was I. The minute we heard the track, we knew it would be massive. It was already in the dance realm, which meant I could spend less time on being technical and more time being creative. Abel came in, and we took it on. We began programming drums over it first, tight as possible with the vocal. We worked for a solid week straight on it, submitted it, and the A&R director loved what he heard.

Once again, I dismissed it after that—ready as I always am to move on to the next project. Come that November in 2011, a friend calls and offers his congratulations. He told me we got nominated for a Grammy for Rihanna. I never paid attention to the Grammys—they were so political, and I never really cared. But I checked it out and—bam—there it was! I called Abel and asked him if he was sitting down. He said, "Who died?" I told him, no, we got nominated—and he couldn't believe it either. What made it so great was that neither of us had been pushing for it—it was because somebody out there liked what they heard. That's how it always should be.

It's interesting. I believe Rihanna was number one on the *Billboard* dance chart with "Needed Me" [in 2016], and then we moved into the top spot with "Livin' for Your Love (Your Love)," and then she moved back to number one.

Well, let's discuss "Livin' for Your Love (Your Love)" by Rosabel. We were talking about the plight of vocalists, and here we have a song that reached number one on the *Billboard* club chart in July of 2016, featuring, quite prominently, the voice of a great singer, Jeanie Tracy.

I love Jeanie, Martha Wash—all the divas that came from the '70s and '80s who are responsible for some of the genre's greatest works. They still can be utilized if it's done correctly. What I mean by that is, with Jeanie we understood very well how we could work together. We had a great chemistry, she loves our energy, and we love the energy she gives back. It gets better and better each time. I think the reason why the track resonated with people so strongly was because it was so different—it didn't sound like everything else out there. It took people by surprise and felt good—automatically.

A number one club song on the *Billboard* chart is still an awesome accomplishment, but the challenge of making a track profitable is a daunting task today. How are you coping with this reality?

You have to do a little bit of everything. Let's use Madonna, for example. She has seniority, stature, a ton of feathers in her cap. But it's still difficult for her to sell music today. If you are not Taylor Swift or Beyoncé, you're not going to survive on digital sales. Everyone has to tour. That's why some of Madonna's VIP tickets sell for between $1,500 and $3,000. She then has the biggest grossing tour of the season. She *has* to perform.

Sure, you still have to put out fresh music. I have an 18-track album that came out in June of 2016 called *2 Sides to the Story*. I love it. You have to continue to get your music out there to support the tour. Unless you have a huge catalog of massive hits, you're dead in the water. You have to continue to be relevant with your music, so there's a reason to see and hear about you online. The albums and our number one Rosabel songs are tools—you leverage them. You use them to market yourself. I recently spoke with David Morales about this. We agreed that you have to be branding yourself today in order to survive.

Back in the day, our remix budgets were around $10,000 to $15,000. No more. The record companies know they will never make it back. The only way to make real money is to sell tickets and do shows. They're sure not selling enough albums and singles.

Have you observed any other major changes in the dance music industry over the past 17 years?

One of the biggest changes I've observed has been going on for quite a while. There's just *too much* dance music. The market is oversaturated to the point where really *anybody* can be a DJ and *anybody* can be a recording artist. A very good friend of mine, remixer and programmer Jody den Broeder, came up with the best quote—and I love it. He said, "Just because you can make music doesn't mean you *should*." Music is piling up today, and there's no personality behind it. More of the same, over and over. Everyone's on Soundcloud; here's my podcast; I'm a DJ! I'm praying to God that the soul in music we talked about earlier comes back.

You're traveling around the world with your music. Do you feel the rise of terrorism will impact your ability to do so as we move forward—or weaken the culture of nightlife?

I always thought club culture would become a target eventually. Every circuit party I've done, I've always been terrified on some level. I always thought these events and venues were places where it would be easy to get in and have at it—create havoc. My worst fears have come to light, you know? I don't even like to talk about it.

I think the terrible event in Orlando last year has opened the eyes of many club-goers, managers, and club owners. Now they realize they have to protect their patrons. It may now mean heightened security at these venues, just like at the airports.

I feel it may affect nightlife, but part of me thinks maybe it won't. I think we still need a release. We still need a way to erase all these bad vibes. Part of that is being with friends, going out dancing, hearing a cool song—socializing. I think ultimately we will have to push on. We can't let it stop us from living our lives.

Is maturing in this business an issue for you?

It hasn't affected me yet. Yes, there are some days you look at all these EDM festivals and wonder how anyone could be there for hours listening to it. Guys like Tony Moran, David Morales and myself—we've been at this work for a long time, and we remain very true to our craft. I think we all put the other worries to the side—I think we all have that in common. Yes, we're getting older. So what? What should we do? Sit here and rot? No, we are gonna keep moving it! I mentioned earlier that in my youth music was a release—it still is. It makes me feel good. I have no plans of letting that feeling get lost.

I mean that—even if I wasn't getting paid. I went through a period not long ago where there was just no money coming in at all, and I was thinking how the hell was I going to survive. I'm being dramatic, but it was an uncomfortable dry spell. What was I going to do? Stop doing what I love? I got through it—and I won't stop!

Is there a moment in your career that really stands out as extraordinary?

Any time I got to work on a project by a major artist who was doing some great work. I think, for me, that singular moment was with the Rihanna project. There was a silent validation that came with that project, and that made me feel like I was really good at what I was doing. (I can tell you that 90 percent of the time, I doubt everything I'm touching!)

Though Ralphi Rosario's list of accomplishments, both solo and as part of Rosabel, are stunningly vast, *AllMusic* says the artist "will forever be known as the author of house's most infectious hit, 'You Used to Hold Me'..." (photograph by Kenny Yip).

What do you think has made dance music so appealing to the masses over the past few decades?

Rhythm. It's that simple. As raw as that word is, I think that's the key. The music feels good!

Lightning Round with Ralphi

A dance song you never get tired of hearing?

[*There's a long pause.*] That's a tough one. If I had to pick one, I'd say Donna Summer's "I Feel Love."

Best decade of dance music prior to the twenty-first century?

The '70s.

Craziest thing you ever saw take place on a dancefloor?

[*Ralphi laughs.*] Oh my God—Rosabel was playing "Cha Cha Heels" and we were going through this tremendous build-up (which would lead to this explosive kick-in of the song). The crowd was going crazy, and their hands were waving wildly in the air. The kick drum finally hits—and the dancefloor completely clears out because somebody *fell out*! He must have taken too much G and collapsed on the floor. It totally killed the moment and emptied the dancefloor! Abel looked at me and said, "See what you did?"

What aspect of your personality has helped you the most in your career?

Charisma.

What pisses you off the most?

Jealousy or any kind of vindictiveness.

Key necessity for surviving a Chicago winter?

Cocktails!

If you weren't in entertainment, what would you be doing today?

Training dogs.

Richard Vission
(DJ, producer, remixer)
"Music"—Madonna (2000)

"If you have a great vocal and you put it over a hot beat, it becomes something else entirely."—Richard Vission

Richard Gonzalez (once taking the moniker Richard "Humpty" Vission and now best known simply as Richard Vission) has a long and enviable history in dance music. He is a producer, remixer and DJ whose name has become synonymous with club-banging dance-floor shaking energy. His high profile credentials go back to the mid-'90s, when he teamed with Pete Lorimer to form the extremely popular remix duo known as Vission & Lorimer. Together, they turned both clubs and radio onto their pop-friendly reinventions of hits by artists such as The Shamen ("Destination Eschaton"), Ace of Base ("Beautiful Life") and Taylor Dayne ("Say a Prayer").

Working solo upon the commencement of the new millennium, Vission's Grammy-nominated remix and production work entered a phase of renewed popularity. His distinctive house flavor and flair for excitement have made him a sought-after remixer by the hottest stars in the industry today, including Lady Gaga ("Just Dance"), Usher ("Caught Up"), Justin Timberlake ("Sexyback"), Enrique Iglesias ("Tonight [I'm F**kin' You]"), and her majesty, Madonna ("Die Another Day"). His mix compilations (which have reportedly sold in the millions) and original productions, many produced on his own label, Solmatic Records—and often laced with infectious beats and street-credible lyrics—

Grammy-nominated DJ/producer Richard Vission once belonged to a group known as The Movement. The techno band was based in Los Angeles and included AJ Mora and DJ Hazze. The group enjoyed a *Billboard* Hot 100 hit with "Jump!" in 1992.

have been quick to rank high on the club charts. Among many other successful releases, his recent hits "I Like That, Hold Up!" and "Dirty Fingers," featuring vocalist Luciana, and "Walking on Sunshine," a collaboration with Nghtmre featuring Jackie Boyz on Ultra Records, have been near instant successes.

Please tell me a little about your youth and how you first connected to dance music.

A lot of people think I grew up in Canada, but I actually grew up in LA. I was born in Canada, but my mom and I moved to the Los Angeles/Hollywood when I was one year old. Then we moved to East LA when I was five. I remember my mom gave me my first record when I was like five years old. It was James Brown's "Mother Popcorn." I remember listening to it on the turntable in my room and thinking this was the greatest thing in the world. A short time later, we went to a Kmart, or a store like that, and she said I could buy any two records that I wanted. I was a little kid, and I didn't know who the artists were, so I was just looking at the covers. I gravitated to the *Saturday Night Fever* soundtrack and the Kiss *Alive!* album. So clearly I was into rock and dance music without even really knowing it. The next record I bought was by KC & The Sunshine Band, and that really instilled dance music in my head from that point on. The Bee Gees were cool, but—I don't know—KC had that funk and dance sensibility. His group was like Kiss, James Brown and everything else all rolled up into one band for me. To this day, I still listen to KC and The Sunshine Band.

It was interesting growing up in East LA. In high school there was a DJ explosion that happened. To give you an idea, in my high school alone there must have been about 50 DJs. Everybody was a DJ, and this was in the late '80s, when you probably wouldn't even think of DJs yet. I don't think it was that way in other parts of the country, but in my area there were these massive buckets of DJ crews throwing house parties and such—it was almost all Latinos playing dance music. That's how I kind of came up. There were kids on my block that had equipment, and that's how I started learning. Everybody did it.

Do you remember your first professional experience in music?

It's a pretty funny story actually. In high school, you know how they had a class president and things like that? They had a student position called "dance commissioner," which was in charge of the school dances. I ran for it, won—and I don't know how this happened—I convinced the high school [supervisors] that if they gave me a budget of $3,000, I could make them $10,000. I wanted to get a performing artist to come to the high school for one of these dances. So they agreed—I still don't know to this day why they gave a student a $3,000 budget. I must have made a good presentation. I got out my vinyl, picked an artist and started calling the number of the record company. I knew nothing about how to book an artist. I reached a secretary at the label and said, "Yeah, I wanna book The Cover Girls." She'd hang up on me, but I kept on calling. Finally, she tells me I needed to call the booking agent—I guess she was tired of me bothering her, so she gave me the number. I called the agent and told them I wanted to book The Cover Girls at my high school. Skeptically, the agent informed me it would be $1,700 and that I needed to deliver a deposit. I said, "no problem." Long story short—The Cover Girls' first LA performance was at my high school (Franklin High School), the dance sold out in under 30 minutes, and the school made $10,000!

I went on from there to book World Class Wreckin' Cru (which was Dr. Dre's group at the time), J.J. Fad and a bunch of other artists. From there, the first hip-hop station in the country, KDAY, gave me an internship, and I started mixing on *The High Energy Show*. I went from there to (KPWR) Power 106 as an intern and kind of worked my way up. A year later I began my professional career.

You formed a mixing partnership with Brit Pete Lorimer called Vission & Lorimer in the mid-'90s that was very successful, especially in the pop-crossover market. Was this move a game changer in your career?

It was a turning point—I can say that. I was in a group called The Movement, and we had some techno records out. Techno started dying, and I really wanted to get into house music. I can't remember who, but someone (I think perhaps my manager) suggested, along with Pete Lorimer's manager, that he and I get together for a session. The very first time we connected, we created a record called "The Feeling." It was just magic, and we went on from there. He was from London, so he didn't really understand American dance music, and I didn't have an understanding of British dance music. It was kind of unique at the time that we were able to put our vibes together. Today, with the Internet, it's all one big scene, but back then there were different techniques in each region. We had a lot of number one *Billboard* records and a great run. Our logo was the American flag and British flag together, and that was what our music was all about.

I can't exactly say my life changed dramatically from it, though. It was a gradual thing. My personal success came from putting out mix CDs on a national level and doing the remix work as Vission & Lorimer, and also being on the radio in LA. They all ran together and pushed my career forward. But there wasn't an overnight change. Pete and I put out "The Feeling" (which went to number two on the *Billboard* dance chart), but it took about six or seven records in before we were considered hot remixers.

The one thing I can say *was* life-changing was the fact that we did a publishing deal early on in our careers. For us, we weren't really writing music as songwriters, but we got a substantial publishing deal from EMI—and that kind of changed things. I went from renting to buying a house. But I never had that overnight moment where, say, I couldn't go to a club anymore because I was gonna get mobbed. I came up through the ranks.

What ended that partnership?

There were a couple of things that happened. We tried to become pop artists. We did this album [for a group called] Pure Sugar for Geffen Records, and it was the—let's just say my least favorite piece of music that I ever put out. I felt that we were—I won't say selling out—but we were no longer doing cool music. We were trying to do music for radio. I think that's always the kiss of death in dance music. I think we were kind of losing credibility with other DJs, and then right after that we remixed some kind of Cinderella record for Disney. I think we both realized Vission & Lorimer weren't cool anymore. We kind of jumped the shark to become pop artists and just decided we needed to take a break.

Moving onto your solo career in the 2000s, you've done remixes for a staggering list of top-tier artists: Madonna, Enrique, Lady Gaga, etc. Has it ever been intimidating to work with artists of this caliber in terms of providing them with a mix that will live up to their dance-floor history and club reputations?

I only felt that way once I would say. Normally, if someone is coming to you, they are doing so because they want you to do your thing. I rarely see it as pressure because at the end of the day I will work on something until I feel it's hot. Period. But there was one time when I *did* feel the pressure—my first remix for Madonna. At the time, Madonna was M-A-D-O-N-N-A, and she was, of course, on my bucket list of artists I was dying to remix. I got a phone call from her manager out of the blue. I thought it was bullshit at first—a joke. When I realized it wasn't I was really into the idea. They sent over the song, and guess what? It's fucking "American Pie." I thought the song was terrible—not Madonna's performance, but just the song in general. I was thinking, "How am I gonna remix 'American Pie'?" Now I'm really anxious because I can't make this sound cool. There was no way to make that vocal sound cool. It had *nothing* to do with Madonna; it was just an impossible song to remix.

I contemplated whether I should call Madonna's manager and tell her I can't do it—crushing any hope of doing another Madonna mix ever in my life. How do I work this out? I called her manager and told her I could do a full vocal mix in a safe radio style (because that's all I really *could* do), but I'm also gonna do a dub version with one little vocal snippet in it—but they *had* to put that version out. It was the only way this record was going to be cool. They agreed to it. They ended up re-cutting the video to my radio mix in some countries, and the dub became a really big deal. She was happy, and from there I was able to do something like three or four other singles for her.

What's generally the single most important element in your remix? Does the vocalist's general genre or style matter to you?

It's all in the vocal. Some of my biggest remixes weren't even originally in the dance category, like acid jazz. If you have a great vocal and you put it over a hot beat, it becomes something else entirely. If the song doesn't lend itself to a dance mix, I've simply turned it down. If I hear a song and there's nothing in the vocals that I feel that I can do justice with, I turn it down. I won't take on a remix unless I feel I can deliver something hot.

Has an artist ever come back to you and said, "No, this won't do"?

Madonna, again. I did "What It Feels Like for a Girl," and the first mix I sent in didn't work for her. She had liked something else I had done and asked if I could do it more in that style—of course I did. Artists normally leave a song in your hands, but it's not uncommon for them to point out two or three tracks you've done before that they liked. They have an idea of what they are looking for. I would say 90 percent of the time it's up to me.

What's your measure for determining whether one of your original songs or remixes is a success? When do you feel a sense of pure satisfaction?

The number one thing that's important to me is the audience reaction in a club. If I drop it in my DJ set and it goes off, then I've reached my ultimate goal. Does it work for the dancefloor? That's always been my goal when I remix something. Now, if it gets on the charts, number one on *Billboard*, that's great. But I still don't think anything is more powerful or gratifying than seeing the audience respond to the track.

As a DJ, you can just see when a record works and when it doesn't. It's just something I know when I see it. There's not just one thing that happens with the crowd. When I'm remixing a song and I haven't turned it in, I test it. I can quickly see when it's not working the way my other hot records have, and I'll go back in and make adjustments. You just feel the vibe.

How quickly do styles and trends generally emerge today in dance music? Is it challenging to be an innovator of these styles as opposed to a follower?

[*Richard pauses a moment.*] Yeah, it's challenging. You're always trying to create something new and different. If I'm doing a remix for a major artist and they have a record that needs to go up the pop chart, I don't take my mix that far underground—if that makes sense. Not as far as I would for an original song of mine. For a new and rising artist, I think you can be a little more daring. I did Alessia Cara's "Here" in 2015—I wanted to do something that would make some news for her because she was brand new on the scene. So we did a disco bass line remix that hasn't been done in years. People just kind of snapped on it. But on an established artist, it's a different approach. I just did some mixes for Pitbull's recent single called "Messin' Around." I made it a little more in-the-pocket because there's such a plethora of fans and DJs surrounding this artist that I want to make sure they can also play it.

Currently, we are seeing the DJ in the so-called "star" position, whereas in the past the music was largely identified with the vocalist. How do you view this shift?

You know, I think things really did start changing in the 2000s, when things became a little more about the track—having a hot track with the vocal. Even in the late '90s, with Armand Van Helden and the tracks he made—that started the trend. I don't think too much has changed since then. The DJ (now that dance music is today's pop music) is on a higher pedestal. But I don't think the process of the artist or remixer, their relationship, has changed. The artist needs a hot remix, and the remixer wants to deliver that (that's what we get paid for). The artist is asking the remixer to bring his fan base to their fan base and vice versa.

The DJ has become the star—right now. I think, however, you're going to see a shift back to the vocalist. What we will probably see is that the DJ isn't going to have the same longevity on radio as a singer or rapper. Guetta, who is an amazing producer/artist, has songs that are only going to be as good as the different artists he puts on them. A DJ/producer's fans aren't necessarily going to be as connected as a singer who is writing his or her own lyrics from their heart. The DJ is creating a hot song, and that's awesome, but they aren't singing it with passion. You know? So I think you're going to see the spotlight fall back on the artist a little more.

Which is more powerful in the marketing of a dance music track these days—social media exposure or word-of-mouth via the clubs?

Today, I think social media is the most important factor of the two, but they really go hand-in-hand. The people who hear the song in the clubs are going to go on social media and talk about it. From social media we get the links where to find the songs.

How difficult is it to achieve a profitable dance song today?

Thanks to streaming services, it's getting better. There's more of an opportunity to make money. To give you an example, a number one record on Beatport (nobody really sees the numbers, though) could have been a record that sold 600 copies. That's not a lot. But that same song can stream a million times. So I think from streaming, long-term financial prospects will be better. I've put out some underground records that weren't supposed to make money. I just wanted to put out a cool record. Because of streaming services, I actually saw digital income. I think that's the future of the monetization of dance music.

Do you think the dance music songs produced over the past 17 years will be considered as memorable as the classics of the '70s, '80 and '90s? Has the loss of physical product affected our ability to appreciate songs in any way over the long haul?

At the end of the day, people remember the song. I know we've lost physical product and people will say they remember sitting with a big piece of vinyl in their hands, but they are essentially still remembering the song itself—the great songs of those decades. Every generation is going to have its music. And technology is always going to change how we listen to it. For one generation, CDs were the thing—for another it was 8-track tapes. But ultimately, it's still the song. I still remember KC's "Shake Your Booty" and "That's the Way (I Like It)" and how great I felt hearing them. The song is what makes you happy. Radio or Spotify—it's the song that's gonna live 30 years from now.

And I do think the songs produced today are just as memorable as those produced by previous generations, and they will be remembered. Without a doubt. I've had this conversation with friends. In the '80s or '90s, people would say that nobody was gonna remember the stuff that was coming out then. That's what some say now. Everybody puts it down as it's happening. Twenty years later, it finally hits them that it *was* a really good song. It happens with every generation.

As a DJ, how do you prepare for a club event?

My process involves spending six to eight hours weekly creating special edits, special versions of songs that only I have. In a digital age where everyone has access to every song, you have to really work to set yourself apart. You have to really spend the time to find new tracks and to make sure you don't sound like everybody else. I'll practice a few mixes, and I just play the music I like.

You mentioned new tracks. How do you manage the saturation of music available—the literally hundreds of tracks that come out each day?

That's the part of the process that's tough—the part you really have to stay on top of. I probably get 200 promos emailed to me a week. I don't use Beatport or things like that because I really am not interested in playing a song that's Top 10 there. Everybody else is playing it. So that's part of my six- to eight-hour prep work. You can't listen to everything—so you look for good labels and producers you've played in the past. Sometimes a friend will turn you on to something new, too. But it's a big task to find those hot records.

In the '70s, '80s and '90s, drugs often played a huge part determining in the mood of the room and how a DJ picked material for his or her set. Is that still the case in the twenty-first century club scene?

I'm sure drugs still influence the scene. But for me, personally, I've never done any. I think I had one hit of weed once and all I did was cough. So I just pick and play music that excites me. I've played the underground where I know some people are on B [heroin] or whatever, but I'm just playing the records that I think will make for a hot night. I never let the room dictate what I'm playing in that way. I figure if I love this song without being on any kind of drug, it's gotta be hot.

There is, however, a relationship, a give and take, you have with the audience. Let's say I have 200 songs to choose from, and I'm gonna play 60. Depending on how the crowd is reacting (for whatever reason), I may go in one direction or another. There is always that give and take. You also want to see how they are responding to the music style itself, because EDM is kind of peaking and other styles are gaining momentum, like, say, deep house. I wanna see if the crowd will go with me there.

In 2006, *BPM* named you America's second favorite house DJ—what's the pressure like to stay on any list of "best DJs," and how much are you required to focus on your overall ranking? Is there stiff competition between today's top DJs?

Personally, I never concentrate on that. Honestly, yes, it's very competitive because some DJs utilize those rankings for bookings. They will do marketing campaigns to get higher on those lists. So even though it's important to a lot of DJs, I just don't focus on it. For instance, Kaskade is selling out the LA Convention Center (and had one of the biggest crowds at Cochella) in something like two or three weeks, but he is ranked 84 in the 2015 DJ Top 100 list. So there you go—sometimes that ranking doesn't even correlate to your actual popularity. At the end of the day, I make music, I put it out, and some will like it, some won't. You just have to be happy with yourself and not use a ranking to determine your worth.

Don't get me wrong, if I have a record and it hits the pop charts, I want to see it go up. But it's going up because people are streaming it, buying it and radio is playing it.

I've spoken with many other DJs and artists for this and previous books about the issue of aging in the music and entertainment business. Is it an issue at all for you?

It's not an issue, as long as you feel young and are happy with what you're doing—regardless of what business or industry you are in. There's always going to be someone younger, the next generation coming up. They add a certain amount of energy and flavor to whatever they are coming into—and that's what keeps thing exciting, I think. They're going to do their twist on things, and that's what keeps music moving forward. I'm still extremely happy to be doing what I'm doing, and I understand that I sort of have a veteran status in the scene. But I still love what I'm doing. I'm still doing things that shake the scene up. My record "I Like That" (and I realize it won't be documented as this) with Static Revenger and Luciana was one of the first EDM records to go into radio rotation straight from the streets in 2010. I think that record really kicked things off for the Guetta's and everyone else. So it's still exciting to be part of that equation.

Something I'm doing now that everybody's flipping out on is a tour I'm on with Bad Boy Bill called *Back to Vinyl*. I think we're the first EDM artists to do an all-vinyl tour; it hasn't been done before. Everybody seems to be flipping the fuck out about it. What's cool is that we are pressing new music on vinyl, not just rehashing stuff that's been out there. The reason we're doing that is because I'm realizing so many people have never seen a DJ play on vinyl. Being able to do things like this that are different in your career—that's what keeps life exciting. I appreciate the youth coming in, and I appreciate that I continue to contribute right alongside them.

Is there a personal accomplishment you've achieved so far that really stands out for you?

You know, I'm just so blessed that I've been in this business as long as I have and still have the same amount of excitement I did at the beginning. I go into the studio every day with the same enthusiasm that I went in there with five, 10, 15 years ago. The fact that I still wake up excited to be involved in music is really my greatest accomplishment at this point.

Would you give me your take on the dance music that's comprised the past four decades—what do you think has made it so great and so valuable?

It's been a release. There are two things that I believe occur in dance music. And Kanye [West] actually said this on a Daft Punk documentary a while back. He said something to the effect of, "If you make them dance, the song has a chance." He analyzed it in such a simple way that I thought he was absolutely right. If you can make people move their body and sing the lyrics to a song, that becomes something really special. That becomes a spiritual moment for a person. Even if it's in your home and you're just shaking your ass. That becomes an emotion and action that really affects you—and people from every decade have felt it. People will never stop dancing. Today, pop music *is* dance music, and people are embracing it like never before. And it's not like 2060 will come along and people will be saying, "Dancing isn't cool." It will never ever die.

Lightning Round with Richard

What is one track that never gets old for you no matter how many times you play or hear it?

"I'll House You" by the Jungle Brothers.

Diana Ross or Beyoncé?

Ooh, tough one. Damn. I'll have to go with Beyoncé.

Sports car or SUV?

SUV.

Best decade in dance music prior to the twenty-first century—'70s, '80s or 90s?

I'm gonna say the '90s.

Craziest thing you ever saw take place on a dancefloor?

People having sex.

What do you have no patience for?

Bad movies. I have

The deep, driving sound of Richard Vission carries on, evidenced by his popular remix of the 2017 dance hit by Austin Mahone, "Lady" featuring Pitbull.

no patience to waste two hours on a bad movie. I research the hell out of movies before I go to the theater and watch one.

Best thing to eat after a night of clubbing?

Egg whites and wheat toast. Then I don't feel bad. If I go out and have pancakes, I feel all *aaaarrggh*.

Favorite activity outside of music to unwind?

Definitely hiking.

If you weren't in entertainment, what do you think you'd be doing?

I'm pretty sure I'd be a teacher. Not sure if it would be music, but I like being around people. Some of the best teachers I've had, I can't remember what subject they taught. But they taught me about *life* (which I don't think school does enough of today). I would definitely be teaching about the real sides of life.

Afterword
by Martha Wash

Two-time Grammy nominee Martha Wash is truly one of the most remarkable talents in all of dance music, and she has a long-standing relationship with the genre. Since she first came into the spotlight as a back-up singer for the iconic Sylvester during the swinging '70s disco era, through the '80s and '90s, when she belted some of the biggest dance anthems of all time (think The Weather Girls' "It's Raining Men" and C+C Music Factory's "Gonna Make You Sweat (Everybody Dance Now)"), Martha Wash has become synonymous with high-energy, floor-filling, life-affirming music. It's no wonder she's been deemed by many as "The Queen of Clubland."

In the twenty-first century, Martha hasn't lost a beat, and she continues to hit the upper echelons of Billboard's *dance chart on a regular basis. Ms. Wash reached the number one position on the survey as lead vocalist on Tony Moran's 2015 smash, "Free People" and achieved a number two solo hit the same year with "I'm Not Coming Down." Martha's indie recording label, Purple Rose Records, recently produced a hit track for the First Ladies of Disco group called "Show Some Love," which featured vocals by the soprano herself and divas Evelyn "Champagne" King and Linda Clifford. The label also released "Ice," the 2016 comeback single of the disco era girl group The Ritchie Family. Ms. Wash has interviewed for chapters in two previous books from this series,* First Ladies of Disco *and* Stars of '90s Dance Pop.

A consummate professional, Martha Wash is undeniably one of dance music's most singular, enduring and mesmerizing performers.

Dance music is, quite simply, a celebration of life. From the disco era of the '70s through today, people have let dance music into their lives and allowed it to set them free. It releases people from their cares—a rare gift, indeed. Over the decades, that's the one thing about it that hasn't changed. The music has evolved, but the message has remained the same—*celebration!*

Having been a very active performer in all of contemporary dance music's many phases, I have, I suppose, a somewhat unique perspective of this genre. My professional singing career in dance music goes back to the late '70s with the legendary Sylvester, when Izora Armstead and I sang back-up as Two Tons o' Fun on such disco era classics as "You Make Me Feel (Mighty Real)" and "Dance (Disco Heat)." From there, we embarked on a career of our own (and had hits with "Earth Can Be Just Like Heaven" and "Just Us") and later morphed into The Weather Girls, singing the hit tongue-in-cheek anthem "It's Raining Men" in 1982. I can remember Izora and I sitting in the audience at the Grammys when we were nominated for that timeless track. (Okay, Chaka Khan won for "I Feel for You," but it was still a huge thrill!)

Afterword by Martha Wash

I launched my solo career in 1993, following my performances on C+C Music Factory's hit single "Gonna Make You Sweat (Everybody Dance Now)" and Black Box's "Everybody Everybody"—and a well-publicized litigation with the record labels over proper crediting for vocalists in the recording industry. I was pleased to see my solo tracks "Carry On" and "Give It to You" reach number one on the *Billboard* dance chart following that media frenzy.

As a new century was born, I started my own label, Purple Rose Records, while continuing to record and perform. Over the past 17 years, it's been a good feeling to see some of the tracks I have sung continue to reach the top spot on *Billboard*'s dance survey. It was a joy to work with my fellow heritage artists Evelyn "Champagne" King and Linda Clifford on the *First Ladies of Disco* project in 2015. I even sang at the White House for President William J. Clinton—an unforgettable highlight in my career. Yes, I guess this timeline does give me a unique point of view to reflect upon the history and scope of dance music.

One of the biggest changes I've observed in dance music over the past few decades is that the structure of the music itself has undergone so many alterations. I'll be honest with you—as a vocalist who has experienced all of these eras, I believe the orchestration of music from the classic disco era was the richest. There was a greater appreciation for the value of live instrumentation, live musicians and the depth a singer could contribute to those produc-

Martha Wash (photograph by Luke Jones).

tions. To me, it felt like we had more complete songs back in those days—a chorus, a verse, maybe a bridge, and then another chorus. There was fullness to the music that I think gradually ebbed as we moved into more electronic productions. This method of production (which really kicked in during the mid-to late '80s) attempted to replace live instruments, and the sound, to me, just didn't seem as lush. And as we traveled through the '90s and into the twenty-first century, electronics evolved, improved and became the standard. And here we are today. One of the most popular forms of contemporary music currently is, in fact, now an actual genre—*EDM* (electronic dance music).

It really works my brain to think about this evolution that dance music has undergone. While I admire the endurance of dance music in popular culture, fully accepting that music (like technology) develops and changes, I'll admit to you the dance music from the '70s and early '80s still feels more *real* to me. As a vocalist, I could feel it deeper in my soul in its more organic state back then. When I think about it today, I realize how much I appreciated and enjoyed hearing a band perform those classic tracks in the studio—the whole song, as opposed to the way music is produced digitally today. And here's something else about yesterday's dance music—for whatever reason, you might detect a slight kink in it from time to time. The casual listener might not notice a note played slightly off or a lyrical mistake sung by a vocalist (although we artists at the time usually did). But that just added to the realness, the "humanity" if you will, of this music. There was a genuine quality those classic dance songs had that, in retrospect, is truly unique to that time period.

Dance music of the twenty-first century entertains a very different audience, but I love that the people who enjoy it are still rallied to the dancefloor by the same type of power and draw it had in decades past. That positive, energizing feeling created by the music still affects people the way it did in the days of *Saturday Night Fever*, just without the polyester suits. Young people today, generally speaking, have been raised with a different kind of sound, and its electronic origins form the basis of their connection to it. They are much less aware of what sounds came before (unless they grew up listening to the music their parents played and enjoyed). I admit, it's a bit frustrating that the Generation Z is only exposed to the great music of the past, for the most part, when it's sampled in music that's coming out now. I wish they had more opportunities to hear the full, original versions, the real performances and recordings—I think it would add a whole new dimension and balance to their dance music experience. Well, maybe I am able to bring some of that authenticity and soulfulness to the songs I record today, many of which still reach the top of the dance charts. I'd like to think maybe my current recordings will inspire young people to explore the music of the past, which paved the way for so much of what they enjoy today.

James Arena, the author of this book, asked me how I felt about being such an important part (his words) of so many dance music eras. I laughed and jokingly said, old. Truthfully, it feels very strange to me. I think I may have said this previously in my interviews for James' other books—if people don't remind me about my history, I just don't trip on it. I just keep making music. It's what I do. I recognize that perhaps it's a testament to my longevity in the business that many DJ/producers today want to work with me. I appreciate that. I'll confess that I do turn down some requests, because, for me, not all the songs for which I am asked to lend my vocals are all that wonderful. But to be asked to work with such young, enthusiastic, creative people tells me that they did some investigating, and they know my background. That's a very good feeling, and it's very encouraging.

There's another side of today's music that bears mentioning, too. I really want to give today's artists a lot of credit for moving forward in a terrifically challenging monetary environment. As I oversee my own label, Purple Rose Records, and after being signed with major record companies for much of my career, I know in today's music industry you definitely have more freedom if you work independently. Thanks to technological advancements, anyone can try to be an artist. But in addition to talent, if you aren't a very wealthy or a phenomenally lucky singer or DJ/producer who can effectively run all aspects of his or her label and productions, from top to bottom, you will quickly discover how very hard it is to succeed. Aside from the daunting financial challenges of making a living from one's art, today's dance music artists are faced with a tidal wave of competition—thousands of new releases every week, all vying for the public's attention. (Many say the disco era was the victim of such overkill—that was nothing compared to the way it is today.) And, yes, I experienced my share of challenges working with big music companies, but without them behind you, getting that "push" into the spotlight could be brutally difficult. That's still true today. Likewise, today's artists must be willing to hustle like never before—getting out on the road and performing 364 days out of the year (one day off for Christmas, or whatever holiday one celebrates). Yes, I give this rising generation of dance stars a lot of credit for having the perseverance and determination needed to make it.

Personally, as I look towards my own future, I am excited to see what happens next in my life. I sort of fell into dance music and never climbed out. But I have never considered myself exclusively a dance artist. And I'll gamble most artists associated with the genre from the past and the present feel the same way. That's not to suggest there is anything to be ashamed of for being known as a dance music artist. (Haven't we had enough of that prejudice in the past?) Quite the opposite—it's an honor a performer or artist can accept with great pride. But my goal is always to keep making music—*of all types.* (However, as everyone knows today, no matter what type of song you sing, you've got to have a dance remix!) I still have a dream of doing a gospel project. I began one a few years ago, but put it on the back burner. It's definitely on my bucket list, and I look forward to checking that one off in the not too distant future.

As for the dance music community that supports the genre, I hope they will increasingly come to respect the contributions of heritage artists and realize that, in many cases, these singers, songwriters and producers can continue to contribute given the chance. This applies to all genres of music. Unfortunately, our culture has put so many artists out to pasture far too soon. It's been like this for decades. Europeans welcome great artists from the past far more readily than we here in America. They seem to have a greater passion for ensuring the longevity of these performers, and it's a feeling I hope will spread more to the shores of the U.S.

In that regard, I truly appreciate the books of interviews James Arena has sought to compile over the past few years—*First Ladies of Disco, Legends of Disco, Stars of '80s Dance Pop, Stars of '90s Dance Pop* and this volume, *Stars of 21st Century Dance Music & EDM.* To date, they are the only books that cover nearly five decades in dance music and that celebrate the careers of nearly 200 singers, songwriters, producers, DJs and industry professionals from nearly a dozen countries. These books let the artists speak about their lives and work in their own words and to express their viewpoints, positive and negative—a rare opportunity for some. I think it was tremendously important to capture this history and these perspectives, and I am so happy James was able to accomplish this.

Afterword by Martha Wash

Lastly, Mr. Arena asked me to offer my forecast for the future of dance music. In this genre, I've discovered that everything is cyclical. So maybe one day soon we'll go back to the orchestrated music of which I am so fond. I know that's a long shot because even as I write this I'm thinking, okay, that's going to cost *a lot* more money than just turning on a Mac! But a girl can dream, can't she? Hey, vinyl and cassettes came back, and they are making some money—who would have ever thought that was possible?

As far as any other hopes or predictions I can offer—I simply don't know. That's the truly great thing about dance music. As we revel in its beats and celebrate life through the swirling adventures it takes us on, we never know in which direction it will take us next.

So, here's my advice—just get on your feet and dance!

The Digital Dancefloor: Other Noteworthy Artists and Tracks

With advancements in technology and the rise of indie DJs and artists, many millions of dance, dance pop and EDM tracks have been released over the past 17 years, perhaps more than in the previous three decades combined. It certainly seems that way. The following is just a small sampling of some noteworthy hits by international artists who have found success in the twenty-first century and are not profiled elsewhere in this book. (In some cases, listings may refer to various remixes—take your pick—of a song's original pop version.) Some are well-known tracks, and others are a bit more obscure. A few may have been completely missed by aficionados when these recordings were first released. All are significant products of dance music's modern era by important artists who contributed great energy, excitement, and—most importantly—a lot of fun to the period. However, it is by no means intended to be a definitive representation of the vast range of sounds that make up the world of twenty-first century dance music.

Ann Lee: "So Deep," "No No No," "2 Times (2007 Version)"
Ace of Base: "Beautiful Morning"
Afrojack: "Take Over Control" (ft. Eva Simons), "No Beef" (Afrojack & Steve Aoki ft. Miss Palmer), "Ten Feet Tall" (ft. Wrabel)
A-Funk Allstars & Deni Hines: "Finger on the Trigger"
Agnes: "I Need You Now," "Release Me"
Ago: "Put on Your Red Shoes"
Alan Walker: "Faded," "Sing Me to Sleep"
Alessia Cara: "Wild Things"
Alesso: "Dynamite," "Heroes (We Could Be)" (ft. Tove Lo), "Take My Breath Away"
Alexandra Burke: "All Night Long" (ft. Pitbull), "Bad Boys" (ft. Flo Rida), "The Silence"
Alexandra Stan: "Mr. Saxobeat," "Lemonade," "Get Back (Asap)"
Alizée: "Moi.... Lolita," "J'en Ai Marre," "L'alizé," "Je Veux Bien," "Blonde"
Amanda Lear: "I Just Wanna Dance Again," "Copacabana," "Paris by Night," "I Am What I Am (From *La Cage aux Folles* Musical)," "Always on My Mind," "Sorrow," "La Bête et la

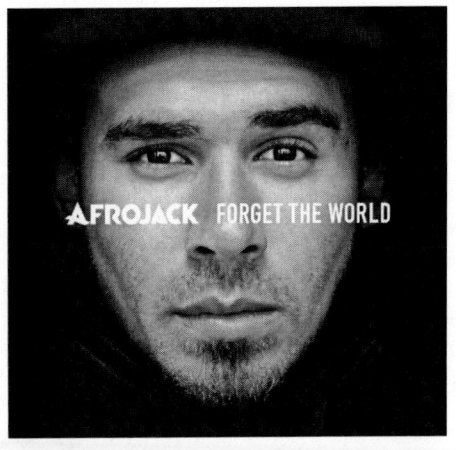

Afrojack (aka Nick van de Wall) is a Dutch DJ and producer who released his debut album, *Forget the World* (through his Van de Wall International, Ltd., label), in 2014—seven years after unveiling his breakthrough single, "Take Over Control." He has consistently ranked among the world's top paid DJs and has worked with major artists in the dance genre, including Pitbull, David Guetta, Mike Brown and Madonna.

Belle," "Chinese Walk," "I Don't Like Disco," "Money Money," "I Need Silence"

Amii Stewart: "Sunshine Girl" (ft. Gabry Ponte)

Anastacia: "Not That Kind," "One Day in Your Life," "Love Is a Crime," "Left Outside Alone"

Anders Neilsen: "Salsa Tequila"

Aquagen: "Girl (Uhh Uhh Yeah Yeah)," "Hard to Say I'm Sorry"

Ariana Grande: "Problem" (ft. Iggy Azalea), "Into You," "Bang Bang" (Jessie J, Ariana Grande, Nicki Minaj)

Armin van Buuren: "Shivers," "Forever Is Ours," "This Is What It Feels Like" (ft. Trevor Guthrie), "In and Out of Love" (ft. Sharon Den Adel), "We Are Here to Make Some Noise," "Another You" (ft. Mr. Probz), "Beautiful Life" (ft. Cindy Alma)

Avicii: *In December of 2016, Swedish musician Avicii, aka Tim Bergling, was ranked 51 among the 100 Greatest of All Time Top Dance Club Artists by* Billboard *magazine. Earlier that same year, the Grammy-nominated artist announced on his webpage that he would no longer be touring, although he still intended to create new music.* "Street Dancer," "Broken Arrows," "Hey Brother," "Addicted to You," "Fade into Darkness," "Levels," "I Could Be the One" (ft. Nicky Romero), "Wake Me Up," "The Nights," "Lay Me Down"

Axwell Λ Ingrosso: "Something New," "On My Way," "Sun Is Shining," "This Time," "Thinking About You"

Baauer: "Harlem Shake"

Bananarama: "Look on the Floor (Hypnotic Tango)," "Move in My Direction," "Love Comes," "Now or Never"

Barbara Tucker: "Love Vibrations," "Feelin' Like a Superstar"

Basshunter: "Boten Anna–Now You're Gone," "All I Ever Wanted," "Every Morning," "Saturday"

Benny Benassi: "Satisfaction" (Benny Benassi Presents "The Biz"), "Pulsedriver," "Close to Me" (ft. Gary Go), "Cinema" (ft. Gary Go), "Paradise" (Benny Benassi & Chris Brown)

Beyoncé: "Crazy in Love," "Baby Boy" (ft. Sean Paul), "Single Ladies (Put a Ring on It)," "Diva," "Beautiful Liar" (Beyoncé & Shakira), "If I Were a Boy," "Pretty Hurts"

Black Eyed Peas: "Boom Boom Pow," "The Time (Dirty Bit)"

Blank & Jones: "Beyond Time," "The Nightfly," "A Forest" (ft. Robert Smith), "Mind of the Wonderful" (ft. Elles), "Captain of Her Heart," "Still the Same" (ft. Mike Francis), "Summergroove"

B:Linda Project: "I Get Weak," "In Too Deep"

Bob Sinclar: "World, Hold on (Children of the Sky)," "Love Generation" (Bob Sinclar presents Goleo VI ft. Gary 'Nesta' Pine), "Rock This Party," "Sound of Freedom" (ft. Cutee B, Dollarman, Gary Pine), "Together" (Bob Sinclar & Steve Edwards), "Feel the Vibe" (ft. Dawn Tallman), "Someone Who Needs Me"

BodyRockers: "I Like the Way"

Britney Spears: "Oops! … I Did It Again," "I'm a Slave 4 U," "Boys," "Me Against the Music" (ft. Madonna), "My Prerogative," "Womanizer," "Break the Ice," "Gimme More," "Piece of Me," "Hold It Against Me," "I Wanna Go," "Slumber Party" (ft. Tinashe), "Make Me" (ft. G-Eazy)

Bruno Mars: "Treasure"

A native of Milan, Italy, Marco "Benny" Benassi began his career DJing in the late '80s. His 2002 electro-dance hit "Satisfaction" made him a world star (Energy Productions, SRL).

Beyoncé Giselle Knowles-Carter, seen here in a 2003 record label publicity shot, first gained fame as the lead singer of Destiny's Child. Reportedly, the artist has sold over 100 million records throughout her solo career (Columbia Records/Markus Kinko & Indrani).

Buster Inc.: "Summertime"
Calvin Harris: "Awooga, Let's Go" (ft. Ne-Yo), "Feel So Close," "Bounce" (ft. Kelis), "I'm Not Alone," "We Found Love" (ft. Rihanna), "Feel So Close," This Is What You Came For" (ft. Rihanna), "How Deep Is Your Love" (Calvin Harris & Disciples), "My Way," "Summer"
Carly Rae Jepsen: "Call Me Maybe," "This Kiss"
Cascada: "How Do You Do," "Truly, Madly, Deeply," "Perfect Day," "Faded," "Evacuate the Dancefloor" (ft. Carlprit), "Everytime We Touch," "What Hurts the Most"
The Chainsmokers: "Closer" (ft. Halsey), "Don't Let Me Down" (ft. Daya), "Roses" (ft. Rozes)
Cher: "Song for the Lonely," "A Different Kind of Love Song," "When the Money's Gone," "You Haven't Seen the Last of Me," "Woman's World," "I Walk Alone"
Chris Brown: "Beautiful People" (Chris Brown & Benny Benassi), "Yeah 3x"
Christina Aguilera: "Beautiful," "Dirrty" (ft. Redman), "Hurt," "Keeps Gettin' Better"
Coldplay: "Hymn for the Weekend" (Coldplay & Seeb)
Conways: "A Walk in the Park" (ft. Nick Straker), "Here I Am" (Conways Vs. Dominoe).
Crazy Frog: "Axel F"
Daft Punk: "Digital Love," "Around the World," "Harder," "Better, Faster, Stronger," "Technologic," "One More Time," "Get Lucky" (ft. Pharrell), "Lose Yourself to Dance" (ft. Pharrell Williams)
Dan Thompson & Solis & Sean Truby: "Aero"
Dancefloor Saints: "Ten O'clock Postman," "Mashup," "Mr. Tambourine Man"
Danzel: "Put Your Hands in the Air"
David Guetta: "Memories" (ft. Kid Cudi), "Sunshine" (David Guetta & Avicii), "Sexy Bitch" (ft. Akon), "One Love" (ft. Estelle), "Titanium" (ft. Sia), "When Love Takes Over" (ft. Kelly Rowland), "This One's for You" (ft. Zara Larsson), "Where Them Girls At," "Turn Me On" (ft. Nicki Minaj, Flo Rida), "Dangerous" (ft. Sam Martin)
Daya: "Sit Still, Look Pretty"

David Guetta's high-energy "Titanium" single, lifted from the French DJ and music producer's LP *Nothing but the Beat* (2011), his fifth studio set, was written and produced by Guetta, Giorgio Tuinfort and Afrojack, with vocals by Sia. The song was remixed by numerous DJ/producers, including Cazzette, Alesso, Nicky Romero, We Are Stardust and other notables. "Titanium" reached number one on the UK charts and was a top 10 hit on *Billboard*'s Hot 100 chart.

Deadmau5: "Strobe," "Ghosts 'n' Stuff," "Slip," "I Remember" (Deadmau5 & Kaskade), "Some Chords," "Raise Your Weapon"
Deborah Cox: "I Never Knew," "Absolutely Not," "Up & Down (In & Out)," "Play Your Part," "House Is Not a Home," "Higher" (ft. Paige)
Demi Lovato: "Neon Nights"
Despina Vandi: "Gia," "Opa Opa"
Dionne Bromfield: "Yeah Right"
Dirty Vegas: "Days Go By," "Walk into the Sun," "Changes," "Let the Night"
DJ Bobo: "Colors of Life," "Hard to Say I'm Sorry," "What a Feeling" (DJ Bobo & Irene Cara), "Chihuahua," "Secrets of Love" (J Bobo & Sandra), "Everybody's Gotta Dance"
DJ Ostkurve: "The Wanderer," "Do the Limbo Dance" (ft. David Hasselhoff)
DJ Ötzi: "Hey Baby," "Einen Stern (Der Deinen Namen Trägt)" (ft. Nik P.)
DJ Snake: "Talk" (ft. George Maple), "Ocho Cinco" (DJ Snake & Yellow Claw), "Get Low" (DJ Snake & Dillon Francis)
DNCE: "Cake by the Ocean," "Body Moves"
Donna Summer: "I Got Your Love," "Power of Love," "Fame (The Game)," "I'm a Fire," "Stamp Your Feet," "Power of Love," "To Paris with Love"
Duck Sauce: "Barbra Streisand"
Ed Sheeran: "I See Fire," "I'm in Love with the Coco," "Drunk," "Shape of You"
Ellie Goulding: "Guns and Horses," "Starry Eyed," "Anything Could Happen," "On My Mind"
Elvis vs. JXL: "A Little Less Conversation"
Empire of the Sun: "Walking on a Dream," "Alive," "High and Low," "DNA"
Enigma: "Seven Lies," "Boum-Boum," "Eppur Si Muove," "Sadeness Pt. II"
Enrique Iglesias: "Hero," "Escape," "Away" (ft. Sean Garrett), "I Like It" (ft. Pitbull), "Dirty Dancer" (ft. Usher, Lil Wayne), "Finally Found You" (ft. Sammy Adams)
Eric Prydz: "Call on Me," "Opus," "Pjanoo," "Liberate," "Niton (The Reason)"
Erica Jayne: "One Hot Pleasure," "Party People (Ignite the World)," "Painkillr," "Crazy" (ft. Maino)
Faithless: "Insomnia 2.0"
Ferry Tale: "Memory of Me" (ft. Hannah Ray)
Fifth Harmony: "Worth It" (ft. Kid Ink)
First Ladies of Disco: "Show Some Love"
Flo Rida: "My House," "I Cry"

Fragma: "Toca's Miracle," "Memory"
French Affair: "Poison," "Sexy," "I Want Your Love," "Do What You Like," "I Like That," "Comme Ci Comme Ça," "Symphonie D'amour"
Funky Green Dogs: "You Got Me (Burnin' Up)," "Rise Up"
Galantis: "You," "Smile," "Runaway (U & I)," "No Money"
Gazebo: "Ladies," "Queen of Burlesque," "Blindness"
Gigi D'Agostino: "La Passion" (E.P.), "Super" (Gigi D'Agostino & Albertino), "L'Amour Toujours (I'll Fly with You)," "The Riddle," "Bla Bla Bla," "Silence," "Soleado" (Gigi & Molly), "Con Il Nastro Rosa" (Gigi & Molly), "Welfare," "I Wonder Why"
Giorgio Moroder: "Right Here, Right Now" (ft. Kylie Minogue), "Tom's Diner" (ft. Britney Spears)
Gloria Gaynor: "I Never Knew," "Just Keep Thinking About You"
Guru Josh Project: "Infinity 2008"
Hannah: "I Believe in You"
Happy Weekend: "Solo Por Ti"
Helene Fischer: "Atemlos durch die nacht," "Mitten im Paradise," "Everything I Need," "Phänomen," "Fehlerfrei," "Marathon"
Hermes House Band: "Que Sera Sera," "(Is This the Way) To Amarillo" (ft. Tony Christie)
Ice Fran vs. Fun Fun: "Colour My Love 2005"
Ida Corr & Fedde Le Grand: "Let Me Think About It"
Ilan Tenenbaum ft. Shena: "Don't Stop Me Now"
Infernal "From Paris to Berlin," "The Cult of Noise" (Infernal vs. Snap!), "Self Control," "Love Is All"
Janet Jackson: "All for You," "Just a Little While," "Someone to Call My Lover," "All Nite (Don't Stop)," "Feedback," "Make Me," "Dammn Baby"
Jason Derulo: "Want to Want Me"
Jennifer Lopez: "Let's Get Loud," "I'm Glad," "On the Floor" (ft. Pitbull), "Do It Well," "Papi," "Dance Again," "Booty" (ft. Iggy Azalea), "Ain't Your Mama"
Jennifer Rush: "Echoes Love"
John Otti Band: "Bette Davis Eyes"
Justin Timberlake: "Rock Your Body," "Cry Me a River," "Like I Love You," "Sexyback," "What Goes Around…. Comes Around," "Can't Stop the Feeling!"

When this publicity photo was released by Epic Records in 2001, Latina Jennifer Lopez was actively using the "J.Lo" nickname so popular with her fans. The actress and singer would go on to score a number of dance chart hits in the years to come, including the 2011 smash "On the Floor" (ft. Pitbull). Ms. Lopez ranked number nine on *Billboard* magazine's Greatest of All Time Top Dance Club Artists chart, published in 2016 (Epic Records/Michael Thompson).

Kaci Battaglia: "Paradise," "Crazy Possessive," "Body Shots"
Kamaliya: "Crazy in My Heart," "No Ordinary Love" (Kamaliya and Thomas Anders)
Kaskade: "It's You It's Me," "Steppin' Out," "Atmosphere," "Move for Me" (Kaskade & Deadmau5), "Angel on My Shoulder" (ft. Tamra)
Kate Ryan: "Scream for More," "U R (My Love)," "Only If I," "Désenchantée," "Libertine," "Mon Coeur Resiste Encore," "Je T'adore," "Alive," "Voyage Voyage," "Ella Elle L'a," "Babacar," "Evidemment," "Comment Te Dire Adieu"
Katy B: "On a Mission"
Katy Perry: "Hot 'N Cold," "California Gurls," "Firework," "Rise," "Wide Awake," "Roar"
Kelis: "Milkshake," "Trick Me," "Acapella"
Kelly Clarkson: "Stronger (What Doesn't Kill You)," "Dark Side," "Catch My Breath," "Heartbeat Song"
Kevin Aviance: "Alive," "Give It Up," "Strut"
Ke$ha: "We R Who We R," "Your Love Is My Drug," "Tik Tok"
The Killers: "Human," "Spaceman," "Runaways," "Miss Atomic Bomb"
Kungs: "This Girl" (Kungs vs. Cookin' on 3 Burners), "Don't You Know" (ft. Jamie N Commons)
Kygo: "Firestone" (ft. Conrad), "Stay" (ft. Maty Noyes)
Kylie Minogue: "Can't Get You Out of My Head," "Love at First Sight," "All the Lovers," "Put Your Hands Up (If You Feel the Love)," "Timebomb," "Better than Today"
La Roux: "Bulletproof"
Lady Gaga: "Just Dance," "Born This Way," "Poker Face," "Alejandro," "Bad Romance," "Just Dance," "Paparazzi," "Lovegame," "Applause," "Till It Happens to You"
Lana Del Ray: "Summertime Sadness" (Lana Del Ray vs. Cedric Gervais), "Young & Beautiful," "West Coast"
Laura Branigan: "Gloria 2004," "The Challenge," "Winner Takes It All"
Laura Tesoro: "What's the Pressure"
Lazard: "Your Heart Keeps Burning," "Living on Video," "I Am Alive"
Lily Allen: "The Fear"
Linda Jo Rizzo: "Day of the Light"
LMFAO: "Party Rock Anthem," "Sexy and I Know It"
LTN: "Hold on to Your Heart" (ft. Christine Novelli)
Lucamino: "More than This"
Madison Avenue: "Everything You Need," "Who the Hell Are You?"
Madonna: "Don't Tell Me," "Music," "American Pie," "Sorry," "What It Feels Like for a Girl," "Turn Up the Radio," "Give It to Me," "Celebration," "Hung Up," "4 Minutes" (ft. Justin Timberlake), "Give Me All Your Luvin'" (ft. Nicki Minaj & M.I.A.), "Girl Gone Wild," "Bitch I'm Madonna" (ft. Nicki Minaj), "Living for Love"
Mai-Tai: "Baby I Want You Back," "One Nite Man"
Major Lazer: "Light It Up" (ft. Fuse ODG)
Maroon 5: "Misery," "Sugar"
Martin Garrix: "Animals," "Now That I've Found You" (ft. John & Michel), "Don't Look Down" (ft. Usher), "In the Name of Love" (Martin Garrix & Bebe Rexha), "Scared to be Lonely" (ft. Dua Lipa)

Martin Solveig: "The Night Out"
Master Blaster: "Hypnotic Tango," "How Old R U," "Can Delight," "Walking in Memphis," "Back to the Sunshine"
Michael Mind: "Ride Like the Wind," "Blinded by the Light" (Michael Mind ft. Manfred Mann's Earth Band)
Mika: "Big Girl (You Are Beautiful)," "Emily," "Rain," "Blame It on the Girls"
Mike Perry: "The Ocean" (ft. Shy Martin), "Inside the Lines" (ft. Casso)
Mike Posner: "I Took a Pill in Ibiza," "Be as You Are," "Cooler than Me"
Milk Inc.: "Breathe Without You," "Whisper"
Moby: "We Are All Made of Stars," "Lift Me Up," "Slipping Away," "Last Night," "New York, New York" (ft. Debbie Harry), "Disco Lies," "One Time We Lived," "After"
Modern Talking: "China in Her Eyes," "Win the Race," "Ready for the Victory," "Tv Makes the Superstar"
Modjo: "Lady (Hear Me Tonight)," "What I Mean," "Chillin'"
MS Project: "Won't Let the Sun Go Down on Me," "In the Sky 2k16"
Mylène Farmer: "C'est Un Belle Journée," "Q.I.," "Dégénération," "Lonely Lisa," "Monkey Me," "Stolen Car" (ft. Sting), "City of Love" (ft. Shaggy), "Slipping Away" (Mylène Farmer & Moby)
Natalie Cole: "Livin' for Love"
NERVO: "We're All No One" (ft. Afrojack, & Steve Aoki), "Reason" (ft. Hook N Sling), "The Other Boys" (ft. Jake Shears, Kylie Minogue & Nile Rodgers), "Forever or Nothing" (NERVO & Savi ft. Lauren Bennett)
Nicki Minaj: "Pound the Alarm"
Nicole Scherzinger: "Right There" (ft. 50 Cent)
Oceana: "Endless Summer," "Losing Control," "Body Rock"
OneRepublic: "Wherever I Go"
Oscar G & Ralph Falcon: "Dark Beat (Addicted 2 Drums)"
Paps N Skar: "Turn Around," "Mirage (La Luna)," "Balla," "La Dance"
Paris Hilton: *The great granddaughter of Conrad Hilton, founder of the luxury Hilton hotel chain, socialite Paris Hilton was initially known for her modeling career and as a television personality featured in the series* The Simple Life *(2003–2007). Her debut single from the summer of 2006, "Stars Are Blind," merged reggae with dance and reached the number one spot on* Billboard's Hot Dance Club Songs *chart.* "Stars Are Blind," "Nothing in This World," "Screwed," "Turn It Up," "High Off My Love"
Parov Stellar: "Booty Swing," "Jimmy's Gang"
Passion Fruit: "Wonderland," "Sun Fun Baby (Looky Looky)," "Bongo Man"
Pet Shop Boys: "I'm with Stupid," "Love, Etc.," "Did You See Me Coming?," "Love Is a Bourgeois Construct," "The Pop Kids"
Pharrell Williams: "Happy"
P!nk: "Get the Party Started," "God Is a Dj," "U + Ur Hand," "Funhouse"
Pitbull: "I Know You Want Me (Calle Ocho)," "International Love" (ft. Chris Brown), "Timber" (ft. Ke$ha), "Nayer Give Me Everything," "Feel This Moment" (ft. Christina Aguilera)
Pixie Lott: "Boys & Girls," "Gravity," "All About Tonight," "Cry Me Out"
Planet Funk: "These Boots Are Made for Walking"
PSY: "Gangnam Style"
Pussycat Dolls: "Don't Cha" (ft. Busta Rhymes), "When I Grow Up," "I Hate This Part," "Hush Hush; Hush Hush"
Rebel: "Kiss Me"
Ricky Martin: "La Mordidita," "I Don't Care"
Rihanna: "Umbrella" (ft. Jay-Z), "Don't Stop the Music," "Shut Up and Drive," "We Ride," "Disturbia," "Diamonds," "Bitch Better Have My Money," "Love on the Brain"
Rimini Project: "I Remember You Like Yesterday," "A Day in the Sun"
R.I.O.: "Shine On," "Like I Love You," "When the Sun Comes Down," "Turn This Club Around" (ft. U-Jean)
Rob Cole: "Dancing on the Beach" (ft. Spagna)
Robin Schulz: "Prayer in C Minor" (Robin Schulz, Lilly Wood & The Prick), "To You," "Tutti"
Robin Thicke: "Blurred Lines" (ft. T.I. & Pharrell)
Robyn: "Dancing on My Own," "Indestructible," "Hang With Me"
Rozalla: "If You Say It Again"
S Club 7: "Don't Stop Movin'," "You"
Sabrina Salerno: "Erase-Rewind," "Colour Me"
Sandra: "Forever," "Such a Shame," "In a Heartbeat," "The Night Is Still Young" (with Thomas Anders), "Maybe Tonight"
Sarah Brightman: "Running," "Harem"
The Saturdays: "What About Us" (ft. Sean Paul)
Scissor Sisters: "I Don't Feel Like Dancing,"

"Filthy Gorgeous," "Fire with Fire," "Let's Have a Kiki"

Scooter: "The Night," "Shake That!," "Suavemente," "The Logical Song," "Posse (I Need You on the Floor)," "Ramp! (The Logical Song)," "Nessaja," "Maria (I Like It Loud)" (Scooter vs. Marc Acardipane & Dick Rules), "Ti Sento," "C'est Bleu" (ft. Vicky Leandros), "Can't Stop the Hardcore"

September: "Satellites," "Cry for You," "Can't Get Over," "Me & My Microphone"

Shakira: "Hips Don't Lie" (ft. Wyclef Jean), "She Wolf," "Can't Remember to Forget You" (ft. Rihanna)

Sia: "The Greatest" (ft. Kendrick Lamar), "Cheap Thrills" (ft. Sean Paul)

SNBRN: Beat The Sunrise (ft. Andrew Watt)

Sonique: "It Feels So Good"

Sono: "Keep Control," "Blame," "2000 Guns," "Flames Get Higher"

SPC & Gloria Estefan: "Santo Santo"

Spiller: "Groovejet" (ft. Sophie Ellis Bextor)

StoneBridge: "Put 'Em High," "Take Me Away" (ft. Therese), "Believe It" (ft. Luv Gunz & Koko LaRoo), "If You Like It" (ft. Elsa Li Jones)

Sun: "Without Love," "Gone," "Fancy Free"

Superman Lovers: "Starlight"

Swedish House Mafia: "Save the World," "Greyhound"

Taio Cruz: "Dynamite," "Higher" (ft. Kylie Minogue), "There She Goes" (ft. Pitbull)

Thomas Anders: "Lunatic"

Tiësto: "Flight 643," "Love Comes Again" (ft. BT), "In the Dark," (ft. Christian Burns), "Adagio for Strings," "Red Lights," "C'mon" (Tiësto vs. Diplo), "Wasted" (ft. Matthew Koma), "Summer Nights" (ft. John Legend)

Tomcraft: "Prosac," "Overdose," "Into the Light"

Tom Novy: "Your Body" (ft. Michael Marshall), "Pumpin' 2008" (Tom Novy & Eniac)

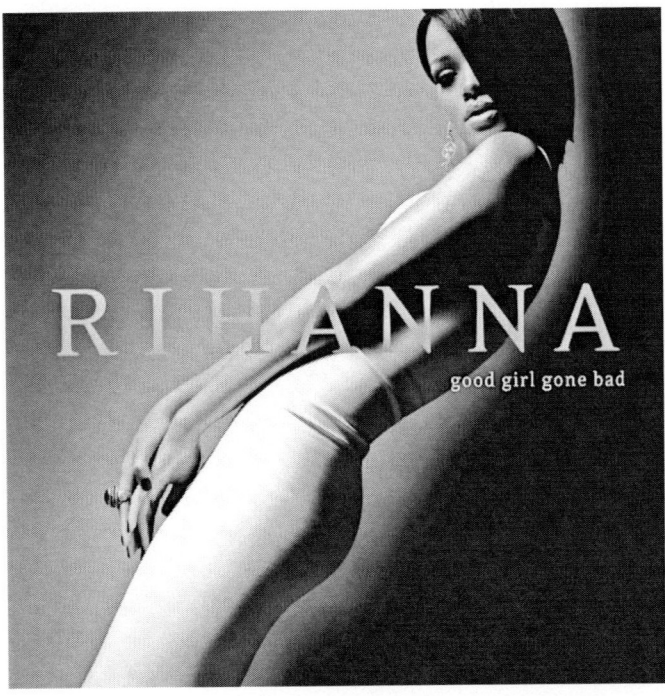

Barbadian singer Rihanna (Robyn Rihanna Fenty) scored an international breakthrough with her 2007 set *Good Girls Gone Bad*, which merged pop, R&B, reggae, hip-hop, funk and dance sounds. *Billboard* magazine ranked Rihanna number three among the 100 Greatest of All Time Top Dance Club Artists in 2016.

Tragma: "Things Can Only Get Better"

Twenty 4 Seven: "Like Flames"

Usher: "Scream," "U–Turn," "More"

The Wanted: "Lightning," "Chasing the Sun," "I Found You," "All Time Low," "We Own the Night"

Westbam: "Recognize," "It's Not Easy," "Right On," "Like Ice in the Sunshine," "Highway to Love" (Westbam And The Love Committee)

Wisin: "Adrenalina" (ft. Jennifer Lopez & Ricky Martin)

Wolfgang Gartner: "Wolfgang's 5th Symphony," "Illmerica," "Flexx"

Wynonna: "Sing"

Young Cardamom & HAB: "#1 Spice"

Zedd: "Stay the Night" (ft. Hayley Williams of Paramore), "Clarity" (ft. Foxes), "Beautiful Now" (ft. Jon Bellion), "Spectrum" (ft. Matthew Koma)

Index

Abba 13, 15, 110
Abdul, Paula 69, 176
Adele 2, 22, 24, 37, 71
Afrojack (Nick van de Wall) 160, 233, 235, 238
"The Age of Love" 58
Aguilera, Abel 209, 211
Aguilera, Christina 67, 69, 235, 238
Alberini, Ingrid (In-Grid) 165–172
Alcazar 13–21
Aly-us 94
Amber, Nikki 198
American Idol 3, 81, 173 - 177
Amstead, Izora 227
Aquagen 109, 113, 234
Army of Lovers 13, 15
Audé, Dave 22–30
Avicii 33, 35, 51, 83, 116, 154, 157, 234, 235
Ayak 181, 184–185

Baccara 15
Bad Boy Bill 224
Baker, Jo (Bart & Baker) 39–47
Bard, Alexander 13, 15
Barenaked Ladies 23
Bart & Baker 39–47
Beck, Robin 56
Benassi, Benny 234, 235
Benatar, Pat 202
Beyoncé 22, 27, 29, 37, 108, 117, 119, 123, 172, 209, 215, 225, 234, 235
Bimbo Jones 49–59
Bjerre, Terri (Terri B!) 31–38, 110, 113, 114
Björklund, Mats 186
Blige, Mary J. 2, 3
Body & Soul 42
Bohlen, Dieter 32
Boney M. 51, 186
Brown, Angie 10, 186
Brown, Chris 133, 177, 234, 235, 238
Brown, James 4, 8, 110, 219
Brown, Jocelyn 93, 113, 114

C+C Music Factory 68, 227, 228
Cahill 178
Carlsson, Magnus 13
Cazzette 31, 35, 235
The Chainsmokers 25, 235
Chicane 85
Claussell, Joaquin 42

Cohen, Jon 1, 2
Coldplay 22, 56, 82, 235
Conte, Paolo 46
Cooper, Alice 141, 142
Corsten, Ferry 60–65
The Cover Girls 219
Cowell, Simon 3, 176
Cox, Chris 57, 67–76
Cox, Deborah 236
The Cube Guys 44

D-Magnify 1
Daft Punk 45, 75, 125, 132, 152, 155, 225, 235
Dagger, Lee (Bimbo Jones) 49–59
Darude 77–86
Dash Berlin 148
Day, Inaya 57, 87–94
Deadmau5 54, 123, 124, 236, 237
Deepend 95–103
den Broeder, Jody 215
Dimitri from Paris 40, 43
Dirtydisco 105–108
Di Stefano, Alex 65
DJ Chuckie 159, 160
DJ Novus 137–149
Dlugosch, Boris 88
Dohr, Jürgen 109, 112
D.O.N.S. 31–33, 109–118

Edwards, Bernard 116
Ellis-Bextor, Sophie 120, 123, 239
Erasure 23

Fatboy Slim 23, 45, 123, 152
First Ladies of Disco 7, 10, 227, 228, 230, 236
A Flock of Seagulls 81
Frankie Goes To Hollywood 172
Freemasons 119–127

Gaillard, Slim 43
Gaynor, Gloria 8, 102, 114, 125, 162, 178, 236
Ghali, Xenia 128–135
Goedicke, Oliver 33, 109–118
Gold, Xaviera 210, 211
Grandmaster Flash 55
Grimmie, Christina 179
Groove Coverage 137–149
Gryffin (Dan Griffith) 150–156
Guetta, David 27, 31, 33, 36, 55, 75, 83, 99, 101, 114, 116, 123, 126, 154, 157, 159, 160, 222, 224, 233, 235

Harding, Steven (Milk & Sugar) 181–189
Harris, Barry 69
Harris, Calvin 27, 35, 36, 116, 123, 124, 235
Harrison (Harrison Shaw) 157–164
Harrison, Danny 2–5
Hilton, Paris 238
Hot Mix 5 210
Houston, Thelma 21, 203, 207
Houston, Whitney 32, 67, 69, 74, 112
Hurley, Steve "Silk" 68

In-Grid (Ingrid Alberini) 165–172
Inner City 31, 75, 109, 113, 237

Jack, Junior 58
Jackson, Michael 36, 67, 88, 89, 129, 198
Jackson, Randy 174, 176, 177
JB, Marc (Bimbo Jones) 49–59
Jean, Wyclef 128, 131, 133, 239
The Jungle Brothers 57–225

K, Michael (Milk & Sugar) 181–189
Kalkbrenner, Fritz 195
Kalkbrenner, Paul 195
Kaskade 224, 236, 237
KC and the Sunshine Band 8, 51, 219
Kjaergaard, Annikafiore 13, 15
Knuckles, Frankie 68, 92, 113, 214
Konrad, Axel 139, 140
Krivit, Danny 42
Kygo 99, 103, 237

Lady Gaga 1, 22, 24, 49, 54, 56, 59, 75, 198, 218, 220, 237
Lauper, Cyndi 54, 55
Lee, Toney 121
Lewis, Blake 81
Lewis, Leona 3
Limerick, Alison 126
Locke, Kimberley 173–180
Lopez, Jennifer 23, 67, 236, 237, 239
Lorimer, Pete 218, 220
Lundstedt, Andreas 13–21

Madonna 22, 24, 27, 54, 62, 67, 68–70, 129, 198, 199, 201, 212, 215, 218, 220, 221, 233, 234, 237
Marc JB 49–59

Mars, Bruno 22, 26, 37, 198, 234
Massive Attack 200
Mendes, Sergio 58
Merkel, Tess 13, 15, 20
Miles, Robert 115
Milk, Mike 181–189
Milk & Sugar 181–189
Miranda, Nina 44
Moonman 60, 61
Moore, Jackie 122
Morales, David 68, 93, 183, 202, 214–216
Moto Blanco 2–5
Mousse T. 87–90
Münch, Melanie (Groove Coverage) 137–149

Naté, Ultra 10, 25, 92–94
New Order 32, 112, 113, 126
Noel, Isaac (Sak Noel) 190–196

Oakenfold, Paul 23, 197–201
Ofoedu, Ben 120
Oldfield, Mike 137, 141, 149
Orbit, William 60, 63, 65
Osbourne, Kelly 67, 73

Palmer, Suzanne 202–208
Paul, Sean 190, 193, 234, 238, 239
Perry, Katy 23, 28, 49, 67, 69, 160, 237
Pet Shop Boys 40, 41, 211, 238
Pettibone, Shep 68
Phats & Small 119–121
Picchiotti, Mark 203
Pignagnoli, Larry 10, 165, 166
P!nk 49, 56, 238
Pitbull 128, 131–133, 190, 193, 222, 233, 236–239
Polgar, Lajos (Louis) (Dirtydisco) 104–108
Prince 5, 31, 32, 90, 142
Prydz, Eric 102, 236

Rauhofer, Peter 202–206
Rihanna 23, 49, 54, 59, 67, 69, 71, 73, 198, 209, 214, 216, 235, 238, 239
Robin S 10, 87, 188
Rodgers, Nile 13, 16, 102, 125, 162, 238
Rodriguez, Luis 32, 35
Rokelle 24, 25, 125
Ronson, Mark 22, 26
Rosabel 209–217
Rosario, Ralphi 209–217
Ross, Diana 13, 31, 108, 117, 172, 225

Sak Noel 190–196
Salovaara, Jaakko (JS16) 79
Salvat, Josef 150, 153
Sampson, Bart (Bart & Baker) 39–47
Santini, Pierre 39, 46
Saturday Night Fever 219, 229
Sayer, Leo 50, 57, 58
Schaffarzyk, Markus (Groove Coverage) 137–149
Schulz, Markus 60, 64
Schulz, Robin 101, 238
Shaw, Harrison (Harrison) 157–164
Sheeran, Ed 81, 159, 236
Sheila and B. Devotion 13, 16
Simons, Matt 95–98
Skyy 87
Small, Russell (Freemasons) 119–127
Smith, Arthur 1–2
Smooth, Joe 47
Soncini, Marco 166, 167
Stardust 117, 121, 125
Stevens, Rachel 52, 56
Stewart, Bryan 176
Sugarm Steven 181–189
Summer, Donna 8, 29, 37, 38, 67, 68, 74, 102, 125, 135, 162, 186, 211, 212, 217, 236
Swift, Taylor 26, 165, 167, 215
Sylvester 8, 227
System F 60–62
Systematik 56

Terri B! 31–38, 110, 113, 114
Tiësto 31, 55, 60, 100, 142, 202, 206, 239
Toy Armada & DJ Grind 191
Tracy, Jeanie 8, 209, 213
Turner, Tina 122
2 Eivissa 31, 32

Underworld 148
U2 60, 63, 197–199

van Buuren, Armin 63, 77, 85, 95, 97, 100, 114, 146, 234
van de Wald, Nick (Afrojack) 160, 233, 235, 238
van den Aker, Falco (Deepend) 95–103
van Ratingen, Bob (Deepend) 95–103
Village People 8, 14
Virtanen, Ville (Darude) 77–86
Vission, Richard 218–226

Warp Bros. 109–118
Wash, Martha 8, 102, 215, 227–231
West, Kanye 225
White, Maurice 203
Wierk, Ole 140
Wiltshire, James (Freemasons) 119–127

Young, John Paul 186